LANGUAGE & LITERATURE

AN EMC COURSEBOOK

OCR AS/A Level
English Language
& Literature (EMC)

Oxford Cambridge and RSA

This is an OCR endorsed resource

English
&Media
centre

ACKNOWLEDGEMENTS

Written and edited by Barbara Bleiman and Lucy Webster

Design: Sam Sullivan

Cover: © Elena Ray/Alamy

Cartoons on page 172: Neil Paddison

Published by the English and Media Centre, 18 Compton Terrace, London N1 2UN © 2015

ISBN: 978-1-906101-35-0

Printed by Stephens & George

Thanks to the following teachers for comments on the text:

George Norton, Mitch Larney, Carolyn Field and to teachers attending EMC courses on close reading and Language & Literature during 2014.

Thanks to the following publishers, agents, estates and writers for permission to reproduce copyright texts

Carcanet for Eavan Boland: New Collected Poems (2005); Pan Macmillan, Picador for Carol Ann Duffy: Rapture (2006); Faber & Faber for Seamus Heaney: Opened Ground – Poems 1966-1996 (© 1998), Brian Friel: Translations (© 1981, this edition 2000); Bloodaxe Books for Jacob Sam-la Rose: Breaking Silence (© 2011); Bloomsbury Methuen for Timberlake Wertenbaker: Our Country's Good (1995, 2013); Bloomsbury Paperbacks for Madeline Miller: The Song of Achilles; Nick Hern Books for Jez Butterworth: Jerusalem (2009, 2011); Penguin Classics for Tennessee Williams: A Streetcar Named Desire (© 1947, renewed 1975 The University of the South, Reprinted in Penguin Classics, 2000), Chinua Achebe: Things Fall Apart (William Heinemann 1958 © 1958 Published in Penguin Classics 2001); George Orwell: Down and Out in Paris and London (Penguin Classics; New Ed edition (27 Sep 2001)); Truman Capote: In Cold Blood (Penguin Classics; New Ed edition (3 Feb 2000) (1st pub by Random House US, 1966); Harper Collins/Fourth Estate Harper Perennial 2004 Arundhati Roy: The God of Small Things (©1997 Published in paperback by Harper Perennial 2004 Harper Collins/Fourth Estate); Jhumpa Lahiri: The Namesake (©2003 First published in GB in 2003 by Flamingo Harper Collins/Harper Perennial, 2004); Alexander Masters: Stuart – a Life Backwards (© 2005 HarperCollins/Harper Perennial, 2006); Random House/Vintage Ian McEwan: Atonement; (©2001 First published in GB in 2001 by Jonathan Cape This edition Random House/Vintage 2014); Xinran: What the Chinese Don't Eat © 2006 Random House/Vintage, 2006; Jeanette Winterson: Why be Happy When you Could be Normal © 2011, Corgi Children's; New Ed edition (3 Aug 2006), Random House/Vintage, 2012; Stephen Grosz: The Examined Life Vintage (2 Jan 2014); Caitlin Moran: Moranthology (© 2013, Ebury Press, Random House), Allie Brosh: Hyperbole and a Half Published by Square Peg, 2013; Black Swan, Random House for Bill Bryson: The Lost Continent – Travels in Small Town America (1989, this edition Black Swan 1999); Corgi Children's, Random House for Adele Geras: Ithaka (Corgi Children's; New Ed edition 3 Aug 2006); Canongate Books for Margaret Atwood: The Penelopiad Canongate Books New cover edition (7 Feb 2008); Granta for Jenny Diski: Skating to Antarctica © 1997 This edition Granta, 1998; Anna Funder: Stasiland © 2003 First published by Granta Books, 2003 This edition published by Granta Books, 2011; Guardian Books for I am the Secret Footballer Guardian Books, 2012; Guardian for TV review by Sam Wollaston, published in the Guardian on 2nd September 2013. The article is now available online at http://www.theguardian.com/tv-and-radio/2013/sep/02/jamie-oliver-money-saving-meals-peston; Gillard, J. (9 October 2012). 'Speech on misogyny'. Transcript available on Parliament of Australia website. This content is available under Creative Commons Attribution-NonCommercial-NoDerivs; The Estate of Alistair Cooke, 2008 for Cooke, A. (2008). Reporting America: The Life of the Nation 1946-2004. London: Allen Lane. 105-106. Introduction and all 'Letters from America' copyright © The Estate of Alistair Cooke, 2008; Transcript of a lecture by Grayson Perry from: I Found Myself in the Art World. 2013. Reith Lectures 2013. BBC Radio 4. London. Air Date: 5 November 2013. Sam Leith, emagazine in April 2013; Ben Goldacre: 'Blue Monday' is churnalism. Beware any journalist who puffs it. January 24th, 2009; Hodder Paperbacks Russell Brand: My Booky Wook: Hodder Paperbacks (10 July 2008)

Every effort has been made to trace and acknowledge copyright, but if accidental infringement has been made, we would welcome information to redress the situation.

Contents

CONTENTS

CONTENTS

Introduction and Teachers' Notes

THE APPROACH

Language and Literature: an EMC Coursebook has been written to provide classroom resources for students sitting the OCR AS/A Level English Language and Literature (EMC).

The approaches taken in the book reflect the spirit and principles underlying the specification: that this is a course about texts, spoken and written, to be explored in a range of ways, drawing on, for example, linguistics, stylistics, narratology and rhetoric. It reflects the specification's emphasis on creative writing as well as analysis, in other words 'reading as a writer' and 'writing as a reader'. Activities encourage students to engage with both their own texts and others, developing the skills and confidence to read incisively and freshly.

Throughout the book we have provided explanations, exemplification and discussion points, with commentaries, as well as activities. These offer a clear sense of concepts, approaches and the requirements of the examination.

THE ORGANISATION OF THE COURSEBOOK

Divided into six main chapters, the coursebook introduces students to the study of language and literature and tackles each of the examined and non-examined elements at both AS and A Level.

- Chapter 1: Introducing Language and Literature

- Chapter 2: The OCR/EMC Anthology of Non-fiction Texts
  (Component 1 AS and A Level)

- Chapter 3: Studying Poetry (Component 2 AS and A Level)

- Chapter 4: Studying Dramatic Texts (Component 2 A Level)

- Chapter 5: Studying Narrative Texts (Component 2 AS and
  Component 3 A Level)

- Chapter 6: The Non-examined Component (Component 4 A Level)

There is also an index of key terms used in the coursebook and a short list of suggested reading.

The material is intended to develop the skills students need to succeed at both AS and A Level. Where an activity within these chapters focuses specifically on the requirements for the AS or A Level exam, these are clearly signalled. Chapter 4: Drama and Chapter 6: The Non-examined Component are only relevant to students preparing for the A Level exam.

NOTES ON SPECIFIC ACTIVITIES

Text extracts used in the activity 'Grouping and categorising' (pages 10-13)

TEXT	
1. Caitlin Moran's Twitter feed	6. Jeanette Winterson's *Why Be Happy When You Could Be Normal?*
2. Alan Bennet's diary	7. Jacob Sam-La Rose's 'After Lazerdrome, McDonalds, Peckham Rye'
3. Emily Poste's *Etiquette Guide*	8. Captain Scott's diary
4. Julia Gilliard's speech to the Australian parliament	9. Tennessee Williams' *A Streetcar Named Desire*
5. Charlotte Brontë's *Jane Eyre*	10. Jamie Oliver

Text extracts used in the activity 'Spoken and written – key differences' (p.27)

TEXT	
1. Alistair Cooke's obituary of Marilyn Monroe	5. Alan Bennett's diary
2. Grayson Perry's Reith Lecture	6. A speech by Chief Joseph
3. Jonathan Swift's *A Modest Proposal*	7. Russell Brand's evidence to a House of Commons Select Committee
4. Caitlin Moran's Twitter feed	8. A *Horrible Histories* script for CBCC

Text extracts used in the activity 'Texts over time' (p.46)

TEXT	IN DATE ORDER
1. Alan Bennett's diary	4
2. Jonathan Swift's *A Modest Proposal*	2
3. Edward Thomas's letter to his wife	3
4. Libby Page: 'Graduating is scary, but you've got to take control.' 10 June 2013, 'Comment is Free', *Guardian* website	5
5. Gwynyth Paltrow and Chris Martin on Paltrow's Goop website, March 2014	7
6. Samuel Pepys' diary	1
7. Caitlin Moran's Twitter feed	6

Choosing a foil (p.53)

The clip of Mary Berry making holly leaves is available at http://www.bbc.co.uk/programmes/p02dd1h3 (checked March 2015).

1.
INTRODUCING LANGUAGE & LITERATURE

1.

INTRODUCING LANGUAGE & LITERATURE

What Does a Language and Literature Student Study?

The simple answer is texts. All kinds of texts, spoken, written, literary, non-literary, formal, informal.

Whereas Literature students study only literary texts – poetry, drama, fiction, literary non-fiction – a Language and Literature student is interested in any kind of text, including literary texts but a lot more besides. It makes you a student of anything that's spoken or written – an amazingly rich field of study.

GROUPING AND CATEGORISING TEXTS

Here are some extracts from some of the texts that appear on the OCR (EMC) Language and Literature specification.

1. Try grouping and categorising them in as many different ways as you can. For instance, one very obvious way of grouping them would be as literary texts versus non-literary texts. Look for less obvious categories as well.

2. Share the categories you came up with, across the class.

3. Did any of your categories cause you difficulties in deciding where to place texts? If so, what do you think that reveals about texts and the boundaries between types of texts?

A list of the texts these extracts were taken from is included in the Teachers' Notes on page 7.

Do you have any new thoughts now that you know what the texts are?

EXTRACT 1

Caitlin Moran @caitlinmoran

WELL DONE LADIES. First ever BBC prime-time show hosted by two women. *Looks at watch. Notes it's 201 Sighs*

Marianka Swain @mkmswain 3h

@caitlinmoran Also...Bake-off moving to BBC1 with its two female presenters

Ceri Fowler @cerifowler 3h

@caitlinmoran Is it happening? Ohmigosh it will be amazing.

EXTRACT 2

2nd (Lord's Day) Some of our maids sitting up late last night to get things ready against our feast to-day, Jane called us up about three in the morning, to tell us of a great fire they saw in the city. So I rose, and slipped on my night-gown, and went to her window; and thought it to be on the back side of Marke-Lane at the farthest; but being unused to such fires as followed, I thought it far enough off; and so went to bed again, and to sleep. About seven rose again to dress myself, and there looked out at the window, and saw the fire not so much as it was, and further off. So to my closet to set things to rights, after yesterday's cleaning. By and by Jane comes and tells me that she hears that above 300 houses have been burned down to-night by the fire we saw, and that it is now burning down all Fish-Street by London Bridge.

EXTRACT 3

Nearly all the faults or mistakes in conversation are caused by not thinking. For instance, a first rule for behavior in society is: 'Try to do and say those things only which will be agreeable to others.' Yet how many people, who really know better, people who are perfectly capable of intelligent understanding if they didn't let their brains remain asleep or locked tight, go night after night to dinner parties, day after day to other social gatherings, and absent-mindedly prate about this or that without ever taking the trouble to *think* what they are saying and to whom they are saying it! Would a young mother describe twenty or thirty cunning tricks and sayings of the baby to a bachelor who has been helplessly put beside her at dinner if she *thought*? She would know very well, alas! that not even a very dear friend would really care for more than a *hors d'oeuvre* of the subject, at the board of general conversation.

EXTRACT 4

Thank you very much Deputy Speaker and I rise to oppose the motion moved by the Leader of the Opposition. And in so doing I say to the Leader of the Opposition I will not be lectured about sexism and misogyny by this man. I will not. And the Government will not be lectured about sexism and misogyny by this man. Not now, not ever.

EXTRACT 5

I resisted all the way: a new thing for me, and a circumstance which greatly strengthened the bad opinion Bessie and Miss Abbot were disposed to entertain of me. The fact is, I was a trifle beside myself; or rather *out* of myself, as the French would say: I was conscious that a moment's mutiny had already rendered me liable to strange penalties, and, like any other rebel slave, I felt resolved, in my desperation, to go all lengths.

'Hold her arms, Miss Abbot: she's like a mad cat.'

'For shame! for shame!' cried the lady's-maid. 'What shocking conduct, Miss Eyre, to strike a young gentleman, your benefactress's son! Your young master.'

'Master! How is he my master? Am I a servant?'

'No; you are less than a servant, for you do nothing for your keep. There, sit down, and think over your wickedness.'

They had got me by this time into the apartment indicated by Mrs. Reed, and had thrust me upon a stool: my impulse was to rise from it like a spring; their two pair of hands arrested me instantly.

'If you don't sit still, you must be tied down,' said Bessie. 'Miss Abbot, lend me your garters; she would break mine directly.'

EXTRACT 6

I am short, so I like the little guy/underdog stories, but they are not straightforwardly about one size versus another. Think about, say, Jack and the Beanstalk, which is basically a big ugly stupid giant, and a smart little Jack who is fast on his feet. OK, but the unstable element is the beanstalk, which starts as a bean and grows into a huge tree-like thing that Jack climbs to reach the castle. This bridge between two worlds is unpredictable and very surprising. And later, when the giant tries to climb after Jack, the beanstalk has to be chopped down pronto. This suggests to me that the pursuit of happiness, which we may as well call life, is full of surprising temporary elements - we get somewhere we couldn't go otherwise and we profit from the trip, but we can't stay there, it isn't our world, and we shouldn't let that world come crashing down into the one we can inhabit.

EXTRACT 7

After Lazerdrome, McDonalds, Peckham Rye

where I say goodbye to south-east London for the next 3 years

a gaggle of us   still damp   spilling in from the night before

early flock for a Sunday   six or seven A.M.   sleepless

drowning in light and all this quiet   after all that sweat

and darkness   all that flighty noise

EXTRACT 8

The seductive folds of the sleeping-bag.

The hiss of the primus and the fragrant steam of the cooker issuing
from the tent ventilator.

The small green tent and the great white road.

The whine of a dog and the neigh of our steeds.

The driving cloud of powdered snow.

The crunch of footsteps which break the surface crust.

The wind blown furrows.

The blue arch beneath the smoky cloud.

EXTRACT 9

(*Two men come around the corner, STANLEY KOWALSKI and MITCH. They are about twenty-eight or thirty years old, roughly dressed in blue denim work clothes. STANLEY carries his bowling jacket and a red-stained package from a butcher's.*)

STANLEY   (*to Mitch.*): Well, what did he say?

MITCH: He said he'd give us even money.

STANLEY: Naw! We gotta have odds. (*They stop at the foot of the steps.*)

STANLEY   (*bellowing.*): Hey there! Stella, Baby!

(*Stella comes out on the first-floor landing, a gentle young woman, about twenty-five, and of a background obviously quite different from her husband's.*)

STELLA   (*mildly.*): Don't holler at me like that. Hi, Mitch.

STANLEY: Catch!

STELLA: What?

STANLEY: Meat!

(*He heaves the package at her. She cries out in protest but manages to catch it: then she laughs breathlessly. Her husband and his companion have already started back around the corner.*)

EXTRACT 10

JAMIE: Oh God, this show it's – it's a bit mad really. It's the first time a show's ever been done like this, so it's kind of – it's a bit of stress on me – but basically it's kind of like a day in the life of Jamie Oliver – bit mad, bit spoofy, bit pantomimey, but at the end of the day there's loads of really nice recipes, loads of enthusiasm.

REFLECTIONS ON THE TASK

You have probably categorised these texts in many different ways. Here are some of the approaches you could have taken but you are likely to have thought of others yourselves.

Literary v. non-literary	Poetry v. prose v drama
Spoken v. written	Informal v. formal
Digital v. non-digital	Private v. public audience
Monologic v. dialogic (1 voice v. more than 1 voice)	Planned v. unplanned
Functional purpose v. artistic purpose	Modern v. old

In making these distinctions, you are beginning to think about texts as objects of linguistic and literary study. You are already thinking as a Language and Literature student.

In also recognising how blurred some of the boundaries are in texts, you are beginning to understand the complexity of this kind of study. Texts aren't always one thing or another: genres break rules or blend into each other; texts can have several different purposes or functions; there can be shifts and developments within them, that make them one thing at first, and something different later, for instance, a personal diary extract that is later published.

The A Level course will be all about helping you to analyse and make subtle and sophisticated comments on how and why texts work in the ways that they do.

What Do Language & Literature Students Do with (or to) Texts?

Literature students read literary texts using literary concepts (e.g. imagery, rhythm, rhyme) and methods of analysis (e.g. close reading, exploring alternative interpretations).

Language students apply linguistic ideas (e.g. pragmatics, discourse, phonology) and approaches to texts (e.g. conversation analysis, discourse analysis).

Language and Literature students use *both*, making *judgements* about which ideas and methods are most useful, given the text being studied and the nature of the question. During the course, you will develop your understanding of what these ideas and methods are and learn how to make decisions about using them appropriately.

Here's a first activity to get the ball rolling.

1. Look at the 10 text extracts you've already considered (pages 11-13). Decide which you think you would definitely want to analyse using literary techniques, which you would analyse using linguistic techniques and which might benefit from a mixture of the two. Justify your decisions to others in a small group, or as a whole class.

AN EXAMPLE TO GET YOU STARTED

Caitlin Moran Twitter feed – linguistic techniques. Not a literary text and doesn't use any obvious literary devices that could be explored using literary methods. But maybe a different kind of digital text might be interesting to look at using literary concepts, for instance a text message poem, or a text message that deliberately uses puns, or metaphorical language?

2. In pairs or threes, choose one text to explore in closer detail.

   • If you decided your extract needed a literary focus, what would that be? What are the interesting things worth commenting on? If you thought a language, or a mixed approach, was more fruitful, what would you want to say about it?

   • Share your analysis of your extract with the rest of the class. Talk about the different aspects of the texts that groups chose to focus on.

3. What follows on page 16 are commentaries on two of the extracts.

   • Talk about the kinds of things that are discussed and how far they match your own discussions. Discuss whether each commentary is using literary or linguistic methods and ideas, or a mixture of the two.

   • If there are differences between the approaches taken in the commentaries, what are they? Here are a few possible issues you might consider. Talk about which ones seem to apply more to one commentary than the other and which apply equally to both. Use them to explore any subtle differences.

     — More precise analysis of language effects.

     — More use of linguistic terms.

     — More use of literary terms.

     — Gives a sense of the immediate context of the text – its audience, purpose, genre or mode of delivery.

     — Shows how choices of language impact on meaning.

     — Explores non-verbal as well as verbal language (e.g. movement, facial expression, gesture, positioning and so on).

COMMENTARY ON THE TEXTS

TEXT 1

JAMIE: Oh God, this show it's – it's a bit mad really. It's the first time a show's ever been done like this, so it's kind of – it's a bit of stress on me – but basically it's kind of like a day in the life of Jamie Oliver – bit mad, bit spoofy, bit pantomimey, but at the end of the day there's loads of really nice recipes, loads of enthusiasm.

COMMENTARY

This extract from a 'to camera' behind the scenes video of a Jamie Oliver cookery programme has all the features of spontaneous speech – lots of unfinished or interrupted constructions (for instance, 'it's kind of – it's a bit of stress on me', repeated hedges (like 'kind of like') and a rambling structure as if it's entirely unrehearsed. The informality is part of Jamie Oliver's trademark style and it's what audiences have come to expect. So his use of informal, colloquial lexis, as in 'spoofy' or 'pantomimey', where he actually invents new adjectives from the original nouns, or uses informal, vague words like 'loads of', is seen as part of the charm of it, rather than a shambolic, ineffective use of language on screen. Had this been a newsreader speaking, there would have been hundreds of complaints! The informal address, to camera, has the effect of making the viewer Jamie's confidante, as if he's talking to a friend, right from the start pulling us in with his exclamation 'Oh God' and his fronting of 'this show it's –', signalling to us that he's just your average man, chatting away happily to us. The informality and 'cheeky chappie' style of Jamie, demonstrated here, has radically changed the genre of cookery programmes, from a very obviously rehearsed and choreographed kitchen set-up, to something that seems much more relaxed and informal.

TEXT 2

> **After Lazerdrome, McDonalds, Peckham Rye**
>
> where I say goodbye to south-east London for the next 3 years
>
> a gaggle of us   still damp spilling in from the night before
>
> early flock for a Sunday   six or seven A.M.   sleepless
>
> drowning in light and all this quiet   after all that sweat
>
> and darkness   all that flighty noise

COMMENTARY

The title of this poem places it very clearly in a particular moment in time and a precise situation, with the setting of 'McDonalds' instantly signalling its contemporary, urban context. The first line follows straight on from the title, with the reader having to make the connection that it's McDonalds 'where' the narrator bids farewell to his roots. While the first line is quite conversational in tone, from the second line on there are all kinds of linguistic devices and playful techniques that could be said to suggest the disorientation of the early hours after a night of clubbing. The long spaces between phrases 'still damp' or 'six or seven A.M.' are deviations from the written norm and maybe suggest that slow-thinking, vagueness of drifting around, tired from lack of sleep. The opening of the poem is structured around oppositions. Noise is contrasted with sound, light with darkness, morning with night. There is an understated use of figurative language, linking 'gaggle' and 'flock' – the crowd are like birds gathered together. This lexical group is sustained by the use of the word 'flighty' to describe the noise of the club. Though its meaning is silly and not very serious, it has echoes of 'flight' that subtly link with the idea of a gaggle of geese but also, perhaps more importantly, with the underlying idea of the poet's 'flight' or departure from his familiar world.

Ways of Analysing Texts – the Literary and the Linguistic

During your A Level course, you will be introduced to a number of broad ways of approaching texts, drawn from the disciplines of literary and linguistic study.

Here are some of the approaches you will be taught about.

WAYS OF ANALYSING TEXTS – LITERARY AND LINGUISTIC
Narratology – the study of narrative technique, such as narrative voice and point of view, the use of time, narrative structure, the use of dialogue, frame narratives and so on.
Rhetoric – the study of the art of discourse: how people use language most effectively to persuade and motivate others.
Dramatic technique and stagecraft – the study of drama texts as theatre, exploring the ways that plays are designed to be performed, for instance the use of stage directions, dialogue, action, climaxes, conflict and contrasts.
Conversation analysis – analysing the features of spoken conversation and the way it works, not just the words spoken but every aspect of how it works (power relationships in conversation, who speaks most, interruptions, the sub-text of what's actually said, politeness and impoliteness and so on).
Stylistics – applying systematic linguistic analysis to literary and other texts, by closely analysing the grammar, the lexical choices, the sound patterns, the structural organisation, the repetitions and deviations from expected linguistic choices in other contexts, and using these to analyse or interpret texts.   As you work through the chapters on poetry, drama and narrative you will learn more about the discipline of stylistics and the insights it can give you into literary texts.
Close reading – usually a phrase associated more with literary analysis, involving reading in a detailed and reflective way to develop an interpretation. In practice, close reading often brings in elements of many of the above approaches. Some literary critics, for instance, take a highly linguistic (or stylistic approach) in their close reading. Others are more focused on literary techniques.

- Look again at the short extracts you have already explored in this chapter. For each approach listed above, choose one text that you think would lend itself particularly well to that way of analysing texts.

A FIRST TASTE OF STYLISTICS

The following activity gives you just a taste of stylistics and what it can offer. It focuses on particular word classes in a short extract (163 words in total) from the opening of Arundhati Roy's *The God of Small Things*, a set text for **Component 2 of the AS specification** and **Component 3 of the A Level**.

1. Read the extract and look closely at the table of verbs and noun/noun phrases.

May in Ayemenem is a hot, brooding month. The days are long and humid. The river shrinks and black crows gorge on bright mangoes in still, dustgreen trees. Red bananas ripen. Jackfruits burst. Dissolute bluebottles hum vacuously in the fruity air. Then they stun themselves against clear windowpanes and die, fatly baffled in the sun.

The nights are clear but suffused with sloth and sullen expectation.

But by early June the south-west monsoon breaks and there are three months of wind and water with short spells of sharp, glittering sunshine that thrilled children snatch to play with. The countryside turns an immodest green. Boundaries blur as tapioca fences take root and bloom. Brick walls turn mossgreen. Pepper vines snake up electric poles. Wild creepers burst through laterite banks and spill across the flooded roads. Boats ply in the bazaars. And small fish appear in the puddles that fill the PWD potholes on the highways.

It was raining when Rahel came back to Ayemenem.

VERBS (31 WORDS)	NOUNS AND NOUN PHRASES (85 WORDS)
is	May
are	Ayemenem
shrinks	a hot, brooding month
gorge	The days
ripen	The river
hum	black crows
stun	bright mangoes
die	still dustgreen trees
(are) baffled	Red bananas
are	Jackfruits
(are) suffused	Dissolute bluebottles
breaks	clear window panes

VERBS (31 WORDS)	NOUNS AND NOUN PHRASES (85 WORDS)
are	the sun
snatch	The nights
play	sloth and sullen expectation
turns	the south-west monsoon
blur	three months of wind and water
take root	Short spells of sharp, glittering sunshine
bloom	thrilled children
snake up	The countryside
burst	an immodest green
spill	Boundaries
ply	tapioca fences
appear	Brick walls
fill	Pepper vines
was raining	electric poles
came back	Wild creepers
	laterite banks
	the flooded roads
	Boats
	the bazaars
	small fish
	the puddles
	the PWD potholes
	the highways
	Rahel
	Ayemenem

Here are eight factual observations about the data collected.

2. Which two or three do you think could be used to make the most interesting analysis or interpretation of the text?

3. What is the analysis or interpretation that you would make from the factual observations you've chosen? What does this information lead you to think about the text, or about the impact of the language choices on the reader?

1. Most of the verbs are in the present tense.
2. There is a shift from present tense verbs to past tense at the very end.
3. Most of the verbs are verbs of action, not stative verbs, such as 'is' or 'are'.
4. Many of the verbs express natural growth, fecundity, ripeness and are from the lexical field of plant growth.
5. There is a large number of noun phrases (phrases with nouns as the head word) rather than nouns.
6. Many of the noun phrases are pre-modified (rather than post-modified) by adjectives. (Pre-modified means the adjective or other modifying word comes before the noun.)
7. A large number of the nouns or noun phrases seem to start the sentence and this forms a repeated pattern.
8. There is a distinctive use of some sound groups in the noun phrases in particular – the use of plosives (specially 'b' and 'p') and the 's' and 'sh' sounds.

4. Now read this commentary on one of the factual observations above. If you focused on the same thing, does it coincide with your analysis, or is it different? If you focused on a different factual observation, think about your own analysis and whether seeing this one might make you develop your own more fully.

DEVELOPING POINT 6

The abundance of pre-modified noun phrases (sometimes modified by two adjectives, as in 'hot, brooding month', 'still dustgreen trees' or 'sharp, glittering sunshine'), creates a sense of lushness and over-abundance, with the writer piling on the detail of the landscape and weather. The modifiers, such as 'Brooding', 'dissolute' and 'sullen', 'immodest' and 'wild' could be seen to be giving the landscape human qualities. The contrast between May and June is signalled in shifts in the use of modifiers for colour, from 'dustgreen' to 'immodest green' and 'mossgreen', showing the dramatic effect of the rain on the landscape.

Reading as a Writer, Writing as a Reader

One key aspect of the OCR (EMC) specification is the idea that writing and reading inform each other. If you experiment with writing yourself, you can discover more about how writers make choices. Equally, if you read a lot, and think about how writers make choices, this will be enormously helpful in the development of your own writing.

In this specification, you are examined on both reading and writing, with a recognition of the relationship between the two. That's why, in the AS, the first component involves reading non-fiction and writing non-fiction. In the A Level, one whole component, on narrative, is called 'Reading as a Writer, Writing as a Reader'. And in the non-examined unit for A Level, you read a non-fiction text (alongside a text of your choice), and also write a piece of non-fiction yourself.

It's helpful to do little experiments in writing along the way as you're reading any of the texts you're studying, whether set texts or short text extracts to develop your analytical skills.

A WRITING EXPERIMENT

1. Re-read the opening of *The God of Small Things*.

2. Look back at the list of eight factual observations about the use of language in the opening, on page 20.

3. Drawing on as many of these as you can, try writing a short paragraph about your home town or village, in the style of this opening. See how much you can mimic the style of Arundhati Roy in your own writing. Don't worry about how 'good' your writing is! It's the process of thinking hard to try to capture the style that is important.

4. Share your experiments and talk about which aspects worked particularly well and which would need to be changed to make it more like her style. Discuss what you have discovered about Roy's writing by doing this writing exercise.

EMC

2.
THE OCR (EMC) ANTHOLOGY

2. THE OCR (EMC) ANTHOLOGY

An Introduction to Component 1 (AS and A Level)

INTRODUCING THE ANTHOLOGY

The anthology is a collection of varied non-fiction texts, from the 17th century up to the present day. It includes spoken and written texts, all of which have had a public audience either in print, online or as a public speech event (included as transcripts). The texts have been chosen because they show a wide range of different uses of language, that will allow you to find out about key aspects of how non-fiction texts work, with different:

- genres

- modes

- audiences

- purposes

- linguistic strategies and features (phonological, graphological, lexical, grammatical, pragmatic and discourse features)

- contexts of production and reception.

A note about transcripts in the anthology

The transcripts of spoken texts have been written without trying to capture in conventional transcription marking such sound elements as pauses, overlaps, pitch changes and non-fluency features such as 'ums' and 'ers'. The reason for this is that often these are difficult to do accurately and at A Level these can make the reading of the text a challenge and can encourage you to spend too much time focusing on features that are typical of *all* unscripted speech and not especially significant in relation to the texts under discussion.

WHAT WILL THE ASSESSMENT INVOLVE?

If you are doing AS you will be expected to compare two anthology texts, or extracts from texts, to show your ability to analyse and compare the texts on the basis of the knowledge you have developed about how non-fiction texts work linguistically.

If you are doing A Level, your understanding of how non-fiction and spoken texts work linguistically will be tested differently, with the expectation that you can compare a text, or extract from a text from the anthology with a short text that you've never seen before. The unseen text could be any non-fiction or spoken text, including transcripts of spontaneous speech for a public audience.

In both exams, key elements of assessment will be:

- how well you can select significant aspects of the texts to write about, rather than just writing down everything that you notice

- how well you use your observations to analyse the effects

- how well you can draw on the context of the text, its likely audience and purpose, in order to analyse it effectively

- how well you use comparison of two texts to highlight what is distinctive about each

- how good your judgements are about which bits of linguistic knowledge and which approaches are most appropriate for the texts you're writing about and the analysis you want to undertake.

Key words here are: **select, analyse, significant, comparison, judgement, appropriate, linguistic knowledge, context.**

1. Using all of the words in bold above, write your own sentence (or two), explaining to yourself, in your own way, the assessment for Component 1 and how it works.

Here's one version of this.

2. How far does it match your own?

COMMENTARY

The component is all about teaching you how to make use of linguistic knowledge effectively, by judging and selecting what is most appropriate and significant to help you do a comparative analysis of non-fiction and spoken texts, recognising the context in which the text was produced and received.

Texts – Audiences, Purposes and Contexts

When looking at any text, it's worth considering the wider context in which it was written, before focusing closely on the detail. You will be able to analyse the detail better, by understanding:

- what the text is

- what its purposes are

- what its intended audience is

- what genre or type of text it is

- where and when it might have been written.

This need not be a laborious process. Nor need you write about every single aspect of this in an essay, though some things might be important enough to talk about. But as a way into thinking about a text first of all, it's a good place to start.

QUICK 5 MINUTE OVERVIEWS

- Work in pairs or threes, with each group focusing on a different text from the anthology. For the text you have been given, spend no more than five minutes exploring the prompts above. Then give a one-minute overview to the whole class. In your overview, identify which you think are the one or two most interesting issues in relation to the text you've been allocated. For instance, you might feel that there are particularly interesting issues in the way it plays with genre and generic conventions. Or you might feel that the way it veers between a private or public audience is what makes it specially interesting.

Here's an example to give you a sense of what you might notice.

COMMENTARY

Alan Bennett

Diary entries but clearly not entirely private. Published in a book so seem to be intended for a public audience as well.

Records events in Bennett's life but also written entertainingly, to amuse, in a literary style, not in note form, so not just to record what happened.

Genre of the literary diary – in the tradition of other famous people who know their work is likely to be published.

Each entry interestingly different. Some short, some long. Some more interesting for an outside readership. So clearly some blend of the private and personal.

LANGUAGE AND LITERATURE

Spoken and Written – Key Differences

Speech and writing are very different – they have different rules and conventions, different modes of delivery, different genres, different audiences and sometimes different purposes. But sometimes these differences can be either overstated or over-simplified – there are more similarities than people often realise.

1. Read these statements about speech and writing and decide which you agree with, which you disagree with and which you're unsure about. Discuss these as a class.

• Speech and writing are equally valuable and important.

• Speech has its own rules and its own grammar – it's not just a complete free-for-all with no structure.

• You can judge the effectiveness of spoken texts, just as you can written texts.

• Speech and writing are two quite separate and distinct ways of communicating, with no connections or overlaps.

• Writing has changed much less over time than speech.

• One of the most important differences between speech and writing is that speech isn't planned in advance.

• One of the most important differences between speech and writing is that speech has an immediate audience whereas written texts are often read at a distance and after a period of time has elapsed.

• Speech is an interactive conversational medium, involving exchanges between people, whereas writing is a solitary act.

• The biggest differences between speech and writing are to do with the ums and ers, hesitations, backtracking and other non-fluency features in speech.

• Writing is highly crafted and can be artistically shaped, whereas speech is more ordinary and everyday.

---

2. Now look at the short extracts from texts in the anthology on pages 28-29.

    • First decide which are speech texts and which are written texts.

    • Look back at the statements above and see whether you want to modify your decisions in any way, or adapt any of the statements.

A list of the texts these extracts were taken from is included in the Teachers' Notes on page 7.

    • Talk about your decisions in the light of the knowledge of where they are from.

During the course

3. Come back to the statements on page 27 during your study of the anthology to see whether your views remain the same, or become more complicated or subtle. Think afresh about which statements are most significant. Reframe them, if you need to, or add any new ones of your own.

EXTRACT 1

Marilyn Monroe was found dead in bed this morning in her home in Hollywood, only a physical mile or two but a social universe distant from the place where she was born thirty-six years ago as Norma Jean Baker. She died with a row of medicines and an empty bottle of barbiturates at her elbow.

EXTRACT 2

But I think there's another aspect that is sort of part of becoming an artist, if you like. And I don't want to add to the cliché of the suffering artist in his garret, but I think there is a thing where the human being, the human mind, has this amazing capacity to transform traumatic events; and so artists who've had quite significant difficulties in their upbringing, often they're able to transform this by some sort of amazing process in their mind that turns kind of like terrible events into gold and into marvellous masterpieces that we can all appreciate.

EXTRACT 3

I think it is agreed by all parties, that this prodigious number of children in the arms, or on the backs, or at the heels of their mothers, and frequently of their fathers, is in the present deplorable state of the kingdom, a very great additional grievance; and therefore whoever could find out a fair, cheap and easy method of making these children sound and useful members of the common-wealth, would deserve so well of the publick, as to have his statue set up for a preserver of the nation.

EXTRACT 4

Colin Wright @ColinTheMathmo 2h

@caitlinmoran @pozorvlak What about Great British Bake-off? Does that not count? Didn't watch, so honestly don't know.

Moose Allain @MooseAllain 2h

@richardosman @caitlinmoran Ah – you're thinking of Hinge and Bracket?

LaurenG @geeoharee 2h

@ColinTheMathmo @caitlinmoran @pozorvlak good point. I'd argue it counts. Paul and Mary were 'judges, Mel and sue 'hosts.'

EXTRACT 5

By luck we manage to get into Trinity and Trinity Great Court, which R. has never seen and which still seems to me one of the sights of Europe. The chapel is notable chiefly for Roubiliac's statue of Newton 'voyaging through strange seas of thought, alone'; Newton a young man and unwigged so that his head seems quite small and (appropriately) apple-like.

EXTRACT 6

I only ask of the Government to be treated as all other men are treated. If I cannot go to my own home, let me have a home in a country where my people will not die so fast. I would like to go to Bitter Root Valley. There my people would be happy; where they are now they are dying. Three have died since I left my camp to come to Washington.

When I think of our condition, my heart is heavy. I see men of my own race treated as outlaws and driven from country to country, or shot down like animals.

EXTRACT 7

Q243 CHAIR: Thank you. Mr Somers, we will have specific questions for you, but if you want to chip in—if I may put it like that—at any stage, please feel free to do so. Is there anything you want to add to what you have heard so far?

CHIP SOMERS: I think he is doing splendidly.

RUSSELL BRAND: Thanks, Chip. Chip runs the treatment centre where I got clean so –

CHAIR: Yes, we are coming on to him in a minute, Mr Brand.

RUSSELL BRAND: He is already the puppeteer behind each and every articulation.

EXTRACT 8

NEWS ANCHOR: Hello and welcome to the news at when. When? Prehistoric time, when caveman slowly evolved into modern man, very slowly and in many different stages. Here to guide you through them is Bob Hale, with the Stone Age report. Bob.

BOB HALE: Thanks Anne. Well, as you can see it's about 750, 000 years ago. That, believe it or not, is Britain and here comes the Stone Age. And there go the stones.

Key Aspects of Language – Different Levels of Analysis

Whatever approaches you take to a text, there are five fundamental aspects of language that you will be expected to pay attention to. These are outlined below.

FIVE FUNDAMENTAL ASPECTS OF LANGUAGE
1. **Phonology** – the way sounds are used in words and longer stretches of language, both spoken and written.
2. **Lexis and semantics** – words, the fields they come from, the impact and reasons for their choice and the subtleties of their meanings and connotations.
3. **Grammar** – the structure of the language, including syntax (the way sentences or utterances are structured) and morphology (the way individual words are structured and undergo change, for instance by the addition of suffixes or prefixes, or according to alteration in their function in a sentence).
4. **Pragmatics** – the way language is understood in its context; how meaning relies on manner, time, place and other aspects of context rather than just residing in the words uttered or written.
5. **Discourse** – a unit of language longer than a single sentence, in other words stretches of text or whole texts. More broadly, discourse can also be used to mean the use of language in particular social contexts, e.g. the discourse of the law, academia or other communities who share language practices.

On page 31 is a short non-fiction text used by the train operating company First Capital Connect to promote good behaviour on their trains. It is followed on page 32 by a set of statements about aspects of the language of that text.

- Decide which of these five aspects of language each of the statements is about. They are repeated below the statements as a reminder.

LANGUAGE AND LITERATURE

Before embarking upon your journey

Some initial comments on procuring tickets
- and keeping things ticketyboo!

DO keep fit by running regularly, if you wish.

DON'T do your training at the station.

It always amazes me to observe, as I wait contentedly on the platform for my low-fat mochaccino to cool, how some of my fellow travellers attempt feats of multitasking and timekeeping that defy several laws of physics (including gravity), not to mention common sense!

All the more amazing, when one considers how many ways there are now to obtain train times, tickets and service updates in advance – using the telephone, the internet web (which is a sort of Bradshaw's Guide to the universe), or even – so I'm told – 'applicating' machines that can be 'loaded down' onto your intelligent mobile device or 'smart telephone'. Truly remarkable!

My advice to those who give every appearance of needing to risk life and limb in their haste? You can still make your meeting - without meeting your maker!

COMMENTING ON ASPECTS OF LANGUAGE

1. There is a juxtaposition between modern, colloquial, twenty-first century words and words and phrases from a very different era.

2. The use of complex, multi-clause sentences is unexpected in a contemporary instructional/promotional text, where readers' attention span is usually thought to be very limited and simple and minor sentences are more the norm.

3. People expect adverts asking them not to behave in anti-social ways to be dull. This text depends on the reader understanding that the voice of the text is a deliberately constructed, old-fashioned persona from times gone by. The message only works if one recognises the humour behind this — that the train company has deliberately created a fogeyish character struggling to get to grips with modern life.

4. The use of minor sentences (without a verb), such as in the penultimate paragraph, and in the sentence 'Truly remarkable!', gives a flavour of a spoken voice.

5. 'Ticketyboo' is a silly-sounding word, conjuring up a past era. Its use so early in the text signals very early on a humorous element to the text. There's also an obvious echo of the word 'ticket', a play on the idea that this is a text about rail travel.

6. This is a highly unusual example of its genre, using much more written text than is commonly the case in public service messages. Its use of a first-person narrator ('I') is equally unusual, where one would normally expect a much more neutral form of address, with a more corporate, anonymous voice.

7. The balancing of the clauses in the final sentence relies for its effect partly on the playfulness of the sound effects around the words 'meeting', 'make' and 'maker'.

8. The use of the terms 'applicating machine', 'intelligent mobile device' or 'smart telephone' requires the reader to recognise that there is a reversal of the modern trend of shortening words or coming up with snappy versions ('app' and 'smartphone'). The humour lies in the fact that these longer versions never existed. The reader can laugh because of this contextual knowledge. Without it, there is no joke.

Five Fundamental Aspects of Language

1. Phonology

2. Lexis and Semantics

3. Grammar

4. Pragmatics

5. Discourse

Key Aspects of Language – Deciding What Is Most Significant

Here is the opening of a speech made by the comedian, writer and musician Tim Minchin, addressing a graduation ceremony at the University of Western Australia in 2013.

1. Read the speech and talk about your first impressions. If possible, watch the speech opening online – find it by searching 'Tim Minchin graduation speech'.

TIM MINCHIN – OCCASIONAL ADDRESS TO A GRADUATION CEREMONY AT THE UNIVERSITY OF WESTERN AUSTRALIA 2013

In darker days, I did a corporate gig at a conference for this big company who made and sold accounting software. In a bid, I presume, to inspire their salespeople to greater heights, they'd forked out 12 grand for an Inspirational Speaker who was this extreme sports dude who had had a couple of his limbs frozen off when he got stuck on a ledge on some mountain. It was weird. Software salespeople need to hear from someone who has had a long, successful and happy career in software sales, not from an overly optimistic, ex-mountaineer. Some poor guy who arrived in the morning hoping to learn about better sales technique ended up going home worried about the blood flow to his extremities. It's not inspirational – it's confusing.

And if the mountain was meant to be a symbol of life's challenges, and the loss of limbs a metaphor for sacrifice, the software guy's not going to get it, is he? Cos he didn't do an arts degree, did he? He should have. Arts degrees are awesome. And they help you find meaning where there is none. And let me assure you, there is none. Don't go looking for it. Searching for meaning is like searching for a rhyme scheme in a cookbook: you won't find it and you'll bugger up your soufflé.

Point being, I'm not an inspirational speaker. I've never lost a limb on a mountainside, metaphorically or otherwise. And I'm certainly not here to give career advice, cos... well I've never really had what most would call a proper job.

However, I have had large groups of people listening to what I say for quite a few years now, and it's given me an inflated sense of self-importance. So I will now – at the ripe old age of 38 – bestow upon you nine life lessons. To echo, of course, the nine lessons and carols of the traditional Christmas service. Which are also a bit obscure.

You might find some of this stuff inspiring, you will find some of it boring, and you will definitely forget all of it within a week. And be warned, there will be lots of hokey similes, and obscure aphorisms which start well but end up not making sense.

So listen up, or you'll get lost, like a blind man clapping in a pharmacy trying to echo-locate the contact lens fluid.

2. Look at the list of linguistic features below. They draw on a range of key aspects of language. They are all found in the text but some could be seen as more significant than others. Which six or seven would you select as being the most significant and worthy of comment, and why?

3. Argue for your viewpoint as a class.

LINGUISTIC FEATURES
• Mix of formal and informal, colloquial lexis.
• Second-person address (addressing the reader or audience as 'you').
• Generalised rather than specific lexis (e.g. 'stuff', 'thingie') or placeholder names. Placeholder names are used in place of the more specific names of objects or people, where the name is either unknown, forgotten or irrelevant (e.g. 'whatshisname', 'hey mister').
• Use of figurative language (language not used in a literal way, for instance metaphor, simile, personification, symbolism, metonymy).
• Rhetorical questions.
• Ellipsis (missing out a word or part of a sentence).
• Use of coordinating conjunction 'and'.
• Speech-like use of demonstrative pronouns ('this', 'that', 'these', 'those').
• Reflecting on the nature of what he's chosen to say and how he says it.
• Paralinguistic features (non verbal clues such as voice, body language, gestures, facial expressions).
• Narrative structure to the introduction to the talk.
• Listing in threes.
• Imperatives (commands).
• Question tags (short questions at the end of statements).
• Simple sentences.

WRITING IN THE STYLE OF...

1. Do one of the following short writing experiments, trying to imitate the style of Tim Minchin to see if you can make your writing style as close to his as possible. Draw on the linguistic features you selected as most significant in the previous activity, to help you imitate his style. And remember that this is a written text intended to be delivered as a spoken one.

   - What Tim Minchin goes on to say next.

   - Another speech opening by Tim Minchin, to a convention of mountaineers.

   - A talk to a Year 11 assembly, in the style of Tim Minchin.

2. When you have had a go at it, share your writing with one or two other students and ask them to identify anything that worked well and anything that seemed a bit less convincingly 'Tim Minchinesque'.

These activities will help you to prepare for **AS Component 1 task B 'Writing non-fiction'** and **'Original non-fiction writing'** for the non-examined element of **A Level Component 4**.

THE OCR (EMC) ANTHOLOGY

Spoken Texts – Conversation and Dialogue

WHY IS IT WORTH STUDYING CONVERSATION FOR THIS COMPONENT?

The anthology for this component contains a few texts that are varieties of spoken conversation, for public, and (for three of the four texts) broadcast, audiences:

- Jeremy Paxman: Interview with Dizzee Rascal and Valerie Amos, *Newsnight*.

- Grayson Perry: extract from his 2013 Reith Lecture, including the introductory interview with Sue Lawley.

- Russell Brand: Evidence to a Parliamentary Select Committee.

- Ed Leigh and Tim Warwood: The Snowboarding Final, Sochi.

There are also some written texts in the anthology that draw on conversational styles. Understanding how these texts work requires an understanding of how they are similar to, or different from everyday conversation. In the A Level examination, the unseen text chosen for comparison could be a piece of spontaneous conversation for a public audience, such as an interview or chat show conversation, to provide an interesting contrast with the anthology text.

If you are studying Language and Literature for A Level, conversation analysis also provides a really good set of tools for exploring drama texts in Component 2.

So it is important to understand everyday conversation, to be able to use this knowledge and apply it to whatever texts you encounter.

CONVERSATION ANALYSIS

Conversation, in whatever contexts, has its own unique rules and conventions.

Conversational texts can be analysed to look for the way these rules and unique features work, in order to look at such issues as:

- the power relationships between speakers

- what speakers want to achieve, what they want from each other and how they go about getting that

- the ways in which politeness and impoliteness are conveyed in conversation

- the implied meanings as opposed to what's actually said and the way speakers assume knowledge from wider contextual information (pragmatics)

- the way conversation can play a wide range of different functions, from performative functions (to get things done), to playful functions (having fun), to interpersonal talk (chatting, gossiping) and so on.

Conversation analysis provides a set of tools for analysing the way a conversation works, including aspects such as power relationships and pragmatics.

Some of the things that conversation analysis considers are listed in the table below.

CONVERSATION ANALYSIS
• Who holds the floor (i.e. who talks most).
• Who sets or changes the agenda (i.e. decides what the subject of discussion is, or changes it).
• Who interrupts or overlaps with the other speaker(s) (i.e. speaks over them).
• Who hesitates.
• How much backchannelling there is and by whom (i.e. commenting on what's being said and the way it's being said).
• How participants address each other.
• How they show politeness or impoliteness towards each other.
• How body language, gestures and facial expression contribute to the interaction in the exchange between people.
• What's stated and what's implied, and how that is received.
• Use of declaratives (statements), interrogatives (questions), exclamatives (exclamations), imperatives (commands) and what that reveals.
• Use of, or failure to use, expected conversational patterns (such as adjacency pairs of question/answer or greeting/greeting).

USING CONVERSATION ANALYSIS TO EXPLORE SPOKEN CONVERSATION

Here is a short extract from a conversation between a manager and a trainee at Sainsbury's, recorded for the documentary *I'm Running Sainsbury's* about life in Sainsbury's stores. It was clearly recorded with TV cameras and a film crew watching, so may not be as 'spontaneous' as everyday conversations but nevertheless it is a stretch of conversation in an everyday context.

I'M RUNNING SAINSBURY'S: 'STORE STANDARDS' (TRANSCRIPT)

T has been told that he's been put on a fast track course to train him to manage a store. It was a surprise to him. M is the manager of the new store where he'll be training.

M: You're playing at the top of the Premiership I suppose if you want to make a football analogy and that's what we are y'know we are. The Manchester United. Even though I support Liverpool we are the Manchester United (*laughs*)

There's 98 thousand square feet. 65 thousand customers a week. It's a bit like emptying a football ground at the weekend straight into the store. 800 colleagues.

T: I've only got 16 so it's gonna be a bit different and obviously.

M: On top of that you've obviously got a great sales number. Fantastic looking store. I mean who wouldn't wanna work here.

M: What's your thoughts compared to where where you come from?

T: The first thing that hits me is how big it is. It's not just a step up. I feel like Dorothy. I've just landed in Oz (*laughs*).

M: (*laughs*)

T: There's no grasping how big this place is and how small my place is. It's a big big difference big big change but ... I'm sure it'll be fine. I'm sure we'll handle it (*laughs*). Got no choice now (*laughs*).

M: What I'm probably gonna be looking for I suppose in the next couple of weeks is gonna be things like passion, commitment, self drive and self motivation is is very very key and if you get all of that right then really what you become is a bit of a role model. So you're a role model for the colleagues and you're a role model for the managers really and and that's what we're looking for.

1. Use the conversation analysis list on page 37 to explore the following issues:

    • Who is more in control and how can you tell?

    • What's going on in terms of the relationship — how formal or informal is it — and how can you tell?

    • What is the purpose of the conversation? Is it simply friendly chat, or are there other underlying purposes and intentions? How can you tell?

    • What are the pragmatics of the conversation — is there anything that's implied and understood in context, that isn't explicitly stated?

2. Look at any of these texts involving conversation in the anthology:

    — Jeremy Paxman: Interview with Dizzee Rascal and Valerie Amos, *Newsnight.*

    — Grayson Perry: extract from his fourth Reith Lecture, including the introductory interview with Sue Lawley.

    — Russell Brand: Evidence to a Parliamentary Select Committee.

    — Ed Leigh and Tim Warwood: The Snowboarding Final, Sochi.

3. For the conversation you are looking at, skim through the list of conversation analysis suggestions and choose any that you think seem most interesting to comment on in relation to the conversation you are discussing. Share your choices and your analysis with others in your class.

4. Compare what you observe about the conversation in the anthology text you looked at, with what you observed in the Sainsbury's 'fly-on-the-wall documentary' conversation.

    • What's different about the context for the conversation?

    • What can you tell about the power relationships?

    • What difference does it make to have an explicit audience for the conversation, rather than it just being a private conversation?

A TEXT ABOUT CONVERSATION – EMILY POST'S ETIQUETTE

- Read Emily Post's guide to the art of conversation. Apply it to the following informal conversation, coming up with a decision on whether Emily Post would regard each of the speakers as good conversationalists or not, and giving reasons for your decision. (Note: this is for developing your understanding of the way conversation works. Spontaneous speech that is not for a public audience is not included in the anthology and will not appear in the exam.)

AT THE GARAGE

Kevin and Christine chat to a long-standing customer who is picking up her car from the small garage where she has taken it to be serviced. Kevin is the garage owner and mechanic. Christine is his business partner, who runs the reception and does administrative duties.

CHRISTINE: Mine just went as Batman because he didn't want to be scary.

KEVIN: Cos he didn't want to –

CHRISTINE: Cos he didn't want to scare

KEVIN: – scare, no.

CHRISTINE: But there was little children came to the door and we had all my little bits all ready for them, for whoever came to the door and 'oh my goodness, I'm so scared, I'm so scared oh my god', and 'who's the eldest, who the youngest here?', 'I'm the youngest da-da-da'. (*Laughs.*) And for some reason they wouldn't stop knocking on the door, cos first we have the children and then the grownups come and eeerr we'd throw [*inaudible*] at the door and *Casualty's* on at that time. (*Laughs.*) 'Do you want trick or treat? What you want?'

KEVIN: Yeah well you say to the kids not... don't get nothing from strangers you know? But... and then suddenly you're allowing them to knock on the door and get some sweets from strangers you know?

I... I... I mean no-one came round on Saturday, bit lucky there. Cos usually once you they start knocking on the door you're always getting up and down

CHRISTINE: 'Yeah go to number 11 they'll give you, they'll give you...'

KEVIN: Yeh yeh yeh. That's right he'll give you sweets...

CUSTOMER: It's terrible if you realise you've got nothing there though isn't it

CHRISTINE: If you haven't, you know –

CUSTOMER: – and suddenly realise

KEVIN: Yeh yeh yeh.

CHRISTINE: – and if you don't open the door they just throw flour at your door and in the morning 'Oh my god, where there's flour everywhere'.

IS CONVERSATION ANALYSIS USEFUL FOR OTHER TEXTS?

Conversation or not? Could you use conversation analysis to explore each of these other texts in the anthology, even though they are not, in themselves conversations?

— Marjane Satrapi: *Persepolis*

— Caitlin Moran: Twitter feed

— NSPCC: Can You Help Me?

1. Look at each of these texts and talk about whether conversational features are used in them and, if so, in what ways.

2. What's the effect of using conversational techniques in a written text?

3. Look back at the list of statements that opened this chapter, on page 27. Does reading these texts and exploring their conversational techniques make you want to re-think your views in any way?

As you go through the course, begin to collect short texts that might be interesting to analyse using conversation analysis.

The Art of Rhetoric: Speeches, Lectures and Persuasive Texts

Speeches, lectures and promotional texts, such as adverts or leaflets, can be analysed using the key aspects of language that are highlighted both in this book and in the AS and AL specifications:

- Phonology

- Lexis and semantics

- Grammar and morphology

- Pragmatics

- Discourse.

However, the academic study of **rhetoric** can also provide a valuable additional set of concepts and methods, if you are analysing texts that aim to persuade. This might be speeches or lectures but could also include written texts with a persuasive element to them.

The ancient Greeks studied rhetoric. They saw it as a way of training themselves in the art of persuasion. You might use rhetoric in your own writing, during the course, or use it to analyse the techniques of persuasion in texts in the anthology. In an article for *emagazine* in April 2013 Sam Leith describes rhetoric in these ways:

The study of rhetoric has never been so relevant: we have more of it about us than at any previous point in human history. And far from being a bad thing, it is what makes modern life possible. 'Rhetoric' isn't just fancy language, and it isn't just formal speech-making. It isn't lies – or it isn't necessarily lies. It's simply the word that describes any attempt to influence another human being in words. Rhetoric is the art of persuasion. As such, it's what underpins the whole of Western civilisation. What are the two biggest and fanciest public buildings in any capital city? The parliament and the law courts. Both are temples to rhetoric.

The rhetoric we find in politics and the law is still with us. But if those applications of rhetoric have been constant since ancient times, think about how many more we have now. The Greeks and Romans didn't have widely distributed codex books, or newspapers, or radio, or television, let alone the internet. More than half of the population – women – had no place in public life; which is to say, no voice.

Every day, every one of us is bombarded by advertisements and marketing. We are assailed constantly by political messages in the news. Every day, every single newspaper carries dozens of leading articles and comment columns, seeking to persuade us of a point of view.

We in turn use rhetoric ourselves. We make speeches at weddings and retirement parties, in pitches for business and in job interviews. We use rhetoric to manage our colleagues – be it appeasing the boss, negotiating with a colleague, or motivating a subordinate. Any parent trying to persuade his daughter to brush her teeth before bed is using rhetoric. And the vast explosion of social media means that anyone who wants to can post a blog or a tweet, deliver a polemic on YouTube, or even publish a book to a potential public of millions.

Here are nine key techniques identified as being part of the art of rhetoric.

NINE KEY RHETORICAL TECHNIQUES
Repetition – repetition of sounds, or words, or grammatical constructions (parallelism) for persuasive effect. One example is anaphora, where exactly the same phrase is repeated at the beginning of neighbouring clauses, for emphasis (e.g. 'This blessed plot, this earth, this realm, this England').
Hendiadys – two words linked by the conjunction 'and' rather than one modifying the other (e.g. 'sat and talked' rather than 'sat talking' or 'the sound and the fury' rather than 'furious sound').
The rule of three – three part sentences (tricolon), or other lists coming as a three (e.g. 'Life, liberty and the pursuit of happiness').
Contrastive pairs – two parts to a sentence, often one in contrast or antithesis to the other (e.g. 'I never promise what I can't deliver and I always deliver what I've promised').
Rhetorical questions – questions where no answer is expected, or even possible (e.g. in a political speech: 'Do you want more of the same? Wouldn't you rather have a new approach?').
Imagery (metaphors, similes, metonyms) – a comparison is made that illuminates something by reference to something else (e.g. 'He's as warm and generous as a big, fluffy duvet on a cold night').
Hyperbole – using exaggerated language to make a point (e.g. 'It lasted an eternity').
Understatement – the opposite of hyberbole (e.g. 'She's not happy' for a boss who is furious with an employee).
Bathos – anti-climax, i.e. starting with something serious or high-flown and ending in the silly or mundane (e.g. 'They came... they saw... they did a bit of shopping' – a bathetic version of Julius Caesar's reported words: 'They came, they saw, they conquered').

1. Look at the four short text extracts below and on page 45. Two are taken from the anthology, one from one of the set texts and one from elsewhere. See whether you can observe any of the rhetorical techniques listed on page 43 being used in the extracts. Talk about their impact.

2. Range across the other texts in the anthology. Choose one where you think that using the tools of rhetorical analysis might help you to explore how it works as a text. Whether it's a predominantly persuasive text or not, you might find that it uses rhetorical techniques to put across its messages.

3. Analyse its uses of rhetoric, then share your findings as a whole class, justifying why rhetorical analysis seemed useful in exploring that text.

EXTRACT 1

I have heard talk and talk but nothing is done. Good words do not last long unless they amount to something. Words do not pay for my dead people. They do not pay for my country now overrun by white men. They do not protect my father's grave. They do not pay for my horses and cattle. Good words do not give me back my children. Good words will not make good the promise of your war chief, General Miles. Good words will not give my people a home where they can live in peace and take care of themselves. I am tired of talk that comes to nothing. It makes my heart sick when I remember all the good words and all the broken promises.

EXTRACT 2

JOHNNY: (...) I've got rare blood. Rarest there is. Romany blood. All Byrons have got it. I've got it and you've got it too. Listen to me, now. This blood, it's valuable. To doctors. Hospitals. Every six weeks, I go up Swindon General, and I give 'em a pint of my blood. And they give me six hundred pound. They need it, see, and I'm the only one they know's got it. (*Pause.*) And when I sit in that waiting room, waiting to go in, they treat me like a king. I can sit there, with the other patients all around, and I can smoke, have a can, right there in front of the nurses. And they can't touch me. People complain. They can't touch me. They need me. See. They need me. So don't ever worry, because anywhere you go. If ever you're short. Back to the wall. Remember the blood. The blood.

He kneels in front of his boy. Clasps his shoulders. Holds his eye.

School is a lie. Prison's a waste of time. Girls are wondrous. Grab your fill. No man was ever lain in his barrow wishing he'd loved one less woman. Don't listen to no one and nothing but what your own heart bids. Lie. Cheat. Steal. Fight to the death. Don't give up. Show me your teeth.

MARKY does so.

    You'll be fine.

JOHNNY hugs MARKY to him.

EXTRACT 3

'Blue Monday' is churnalism. Beware any journalist who puffs it.

The Guardian, Saturday January 24th, 2009 by Ben Goldacre

And is there good evidence of season having an impact on our collective mood? Seasonal affective disorder is its own separate thing. If you look at the evidence on the population's mood, depression, and suicide changing over the seasons, you do, in fact, find a glorious mess. Come into my anal and obsessive universe.

Back in 1883 Esquirol commented on the higher incidence of suicide in spring and early summer. Swinscow showed the same thing with all UK suicides from 1921-1948. So that's not really winter blues. A study in 2000 looked at all UK suicide data from 1982-96 and found that even this seasonal pattern had pretty much disappeared.

What about elsewhere? A 1974 study on all suicides in North Carolina (3,672) and admissions to their Veterans Hospital Psychiatry Service (3,258) from 1965 to 1971 showed no seasonal variation. A 1976 Ontario study found peaks of suicide and admissions for depression in spring and autumn. Suicide is highest in Summer, says a paper from Australia in 2003. I'm really not getting this Blue January thing.

Maybe you want data from the general population on mood. A study in 1986 looked at 806 representative males from Finland and found low mood more common in the summer. Some studies do find higher rates of depressive symptoms in the winter (Nayyar and Cochrane, 1996; Murase et al., 1995), but then, some find the opposite results, like a peak in the spring (Nayham et al., 1994) or summer (Ozaki et al., 1995). One study from just last month proactively asked 360 patients to rate their mood regularly, rather than waiting for an event, and found no relationship, again, between mood and season.

EXTRACT 4

Thank you very much Deputy Speaker and I rise to oppose the motion moved by the Leader of the Opposition. And in so doing I say to the Leader of the Opposition I will not be lectured about sexism and misogyny by this man. I will not. And the Government will not be lectured about sexism and misogyny by this man. Not now, not ever.

The Leader of the Opposition says that people who hold sexist views and who are misogynists are not appropriate for high office. Well, I hope the Leader of the Opposition has got a piece of paper and he is writing out his resignation. Because if he wants to know what misogyny looks like in modern Australia, he doesn't need a motion in the House of Representatives, he needs a mirror. That's what he needs.

Let's go through the Opposition Leader's repulsive double standards, repulsive double standards when it comes to misogyny and sexism.

Texts over Time

One aspect of analysing any text and understanding its context is recognising when it was written and what difference this might make to the kinds of language used and the context for those choices. This understanding might include the following:

- Awareness of how modes of communication have changed over time.

- Awareness of how audiences' expectations have changed over time.

- Awareness of words or patterns of language use that have gone out of use, or come into use.

- Linguistic developments and shifts (for instance, in attitudes to formality and informality, in expectations around uses of grammar and punctuation and so on).

- Shifts in attitudes to language, for instance in ways of talking about race, or gender, or sexuality.

1. Look at this mix of extracts of written texts from the anthology and other sources (below and pages 47-48). Try to sequence them in terms of date, and note the reasons that led to your decisions.

For instance, you might notice aspects of lexis that make one text more obviously modern than another, such as 'coparent' in extract 6, or aspects of graphology like non-standard spelling of 'cloathing' in extract 2, or aspects of syntax, such as 'As to my own part' in extract 2, which is an archaic adverbial phrase no longer in common use.

2. Share your decisions across the class, before finding out what the sequence is (see Teachers' Notes on page 7).

EXTRACT 1

5 January. A lorry delivers some stone lintels at No. 6 The driver is a stocky, heavy-shouldered, neatly coiffed woman of around sixty. While she doesn't actually do the unloading, she humps pallets up and down the lorry and does everything a male (and younger) lorry driver would do, with only a certain doggedness to her actions an indication of her gender. One or two passers-by look twice and a neighbour posting a letter stops to talk – and what enables him to break the ice is that she is a woman doing a man's job.

EXTRACT 2

As to my own part, having turned my thoughts for many years, upon this important subject, and maturely weighed the several schemes of our projectors, I have always found them grossly mistaken in their computation. It is true, a child just dropt from its dam, may be supported by her milk, for a solar year, with little other nourishment: at most not above the value of two shillings, which the mother may certainly get, or the value in scraps, by her lawful occupation of begging; and it is exactly at one year old that I propose to provide for them in such a manner, as, instead of being a charge upon their parents, or the parish, or wanting food and raiment for the rest of their lives, they shall, on the contrary, contribute to the feeding, and partly to the cloathing of many thousands.

EXTRACT 3

We shall be enormously busy now. Rubin goes off tomorrow on a course of instruction – and may be a captain before long; our sergeant major has left with a commission. One officer has to be at the O.P. every other night. So it will be all work now till further notice – days of ten times the ordinary work too. So goodnight and I hope you sleep no worse than I do.

Sunday. I slept jolly well and now it is sunshine and wind and we are in for a long day and I must post this when I can.

All and always yours Edwy.

EXTRACT 4

I think the things that scare me and my friends most are the things about our careers that seem out of our control. In many industries jobs aren't even advertised, and you get ahead instead by making connections and 'being in the right place at the right time'. But what if you just aren't well connected, and if you happen to be in the wrong place at the wrong time instead?

Graduating in a recession is scary, but I am learning that the only way to progress is to try to take control. We may have been dealt a rough hand with the rocky jobscape we are setting out into, but there are plenty of worse hands to be dealt. And the important thing is to play your cards to the best of your ability.

There are also exciting parts to graduating in uncertain times. The number of business start-ups is on the rise and for many savvy graduates opportunities will be made, taken and demanded instead of given. Being young and free of commitments is as liberating as it is daunting.

EXTRACT 5

Conscious Uncoupling

It is with hearts full of sadness that we have decided to separate. We have been working hard for well over a year, some of it together, some of it separated, to see what might have been possible between us, and we have come to the conclusion that while we love each other very much we will remain separate. We are, however, and always will be a family, and in many ways we are closer than we have ever been. We are parents first and foremost, to two incredibly wonderful children and we ask for their and our space and privacy to be respected at this difficult time. We have always conducted our relationship privately, and we hope that as we consciously uncouple and coparent, we will be able to continue in the same manner.

Love Gwynyth & Chris

EXTRACT 6

This is very true: so as houses were burned by these drops and flakes of fire, three or four, nay, five or six houses, one from another. When we could endure no more upon the water, we to a little ale-house on the Bankside, over against The Three Cranes, and there staid till it was dark almost, and saw the fire grow, and, as it grew darker, appeared more and more, and in corners and upon steeples, and between churches and houses, as far as we could see up the hill of the city, in a most horrid malicious bloody flame, not like the fine flame of an ordinary fire.

EXTRACT 7

Caitlin Moran @caitlinmoran

WELL DONE LADIES. First ever BBC prime-time show hosted by two women. *Looks at watch. Notes it's 201 Sighs*

Marianka Swain @mkmswain 3h

@caitlinmoran Also... Bake-off moving to BBC1 with its two female presenters

Ceri Fowler @cerifowler 3h

@caitlinmoran Is it happening? Ohmigosh it will be amazing.

James Barker @JamesBarker82 3h

@caitlinmoran Hahahahaha what about Mel and Sue?? Does that count?

Kate Conway @C4NewsKate 3h

@caitlinmoran First TV news programme hosted by two women C4 News... 2013! Hurrah... Ish

Comparing Texts – Finding a Foil

Comparing texts is much more than just an exam task, a form of assessment of your knowledge. Putting a text alongside other linked ones is often a very valuable way of understanding it more fully. Seeing one text in the light of another can illuminate it, bringing out what is unique, or special about it, or alternatively highlighting what typical generic features or conventions it uses. Reading a transcript of someone talking in different contexts, for instance, or reading texts published for different audiences, can throw into relief the ways in which people adapt their language for different contexts, audiences and purposes.

The term **foil** is a helpful one for describing something that contrasts with something else, to highlight its particular characteristics in the way described above.

Using one text as a foil for another is a key element in several components of the Language and Literature course, not just Component 1. For instance, comparing poems is a key part of Component 2, as is comparison of your own choices of text for the non-examined component at A Level.

FOILS WITHIN THE ANTHOLOGY

Several of the texts in the anthology act as foils for each other, for instance, speeches, diaries or interviews, where looking at more than one example of the genre shows what's special about a given example. At AS, you will be expected to compare texts, or text extracts from the anthology, that allow you to use one to illuminate the other. The examiner will choose these pairings for you.

1. Working in pairs or threes, skim through the anthology and find two texts that seem to you to act as a foil for each other.

For example, Edward VIII's abdication speech and Chief Joseph's speech might be very good foils for each other because they are both 'performative' speeches by public figures at different periods. Both show speakers who represent their people (a Chief and a King) – one 'performing' an abdication, the other a surrender. By contrast, Emily Post's guide to conversation from *Etiquette* would not be a very good foil for Edward VIII's speech, as there are so few points of contact between the two texts.

2. Prepare to explain to the rest of the class what is illuminated in each of the texts you have chosen by seeing them in relation to each other. For instance, is it their different use of the same genre? Or is it their common use of conversational techniques? Or is it their different use of formal rules of politeness and etiquette? Or their similar use of incongruous juxtapositions of language to create humour? Or something else?

THE OCR (EMC) ANTHOLOGY

FOILS BEYOND THE ANTHOLOGY – FRESH TEXTS AND UNSEEN TEXTS

In the A Level, fresh, unseen texts will be given to you, to act as a foil for one of the anthology texts. A text might throw light on one of the anthology texts in one of the following ways:

- It deals with the same subject matter, in a different genre or text type.

- It is written or spoken by the same person, showing them using language in a different way within a fresh context.

- It is another example of the same genre, or text type, being used in a different way.

- It is a response to the original text.

A FOIL FOR JAMIE OLIVER'S TV PRESENTATION ON 'HAPPY DAYS TOUR LIVE!'

1. Look at the anthology text where Jamie Oliver talks to camera. Think about the kind of language he uses and the context in which he finds himself. You might like to consider:

- the nature of the communication, the purpose, audience and the context in which he speaks

- levels of formality or informality, in terms of address to the audience, lexical and syntactic choices and so on

- whether you think it's scripted, unscripted or semi-scripted.

2. Make a few initial notes for yourself about what you notice about Jamie Oliver's linguistic behaviour in this text.

A foil for the anthology text

3. Now read the extract on page 51 from a TED Talk by Jamie Oliver. TED describes itself as 'a nonprofit organisation' devoted to spreading ideas, usually in the form of short, powerful talks (18 minutes or less).' Many of its talks are up on the TED website and on YouTube. Jamie Oliver did a talk for an American audience in February 2010. It has had nearly 6 million views on the TED website.

4. Think about what's similar and what's different about these two examples of Jamie talking in public, the anthology text and the TED talk. Do you see common aspects to his uses of language? Are there features of his 'idiolect' (his own personal language style) that you can identify in both? Are there significant differences and, if so, can you speculate about the reasons behind these? Is it to do with the context, the kind of audience, whether it's fully scripted or not and so on? What is illuminated for you in seeing both of these examples of Jamie's public speech?

FOIL 1: JAMIE OLIVER – TED TALK

0:11   Sadly, in the next 18 minutes when I do our chat, four Americans that are alive will be dead from the food that they eat.

0:24   My name's Jamie Oliver. I'm 34 years old. I'm from Essex in England and for the last seven years I've worked fairly tirelessly to save lives in my own way. I'm not a doctor; I'm a chef, I don't have expensive equipment or medicine. I use information, education.

0:50   I profoundly believe that the power of food has a primal place in our homes that binds us to the best bits of life. We have an awful, awful reality right now. America, you're at the top of your game. This is one of the most unhealthy countries in the world.

1:16   Can I please just see a raise of hands for how many of you have children in this room today? Please put your hands up. Aunties, uncles, you can continue to put your hands up, aunties and uncles as well. Most of you. OK. We, the adults of the last four generations, have blessed our children with the destiny of a shorter lifespan than their own parents. Your child will live a life ten years younger than you because of the landscape of food that we've built around them. Two-thirds of this room, today, in America, are statistically overweight or obese. You lot, you're all right, but we'll get you eventually, don't worry.

1:57   (*Laughter.*)

1:58   Right? The statistics of bad health are clear, very clear. We spend our lives being paranoid about death, murder, homicide, you name it; it's on the front page of every paper, CNN. Look at homicide at the bottom, for God's sake. Right?

2:15   (*Laughter.*)

2:17   (*Applause.*)

2:22   Every single one of those in the red is a diet-related disease. Any doctor, any specialist will tell you that. Fact: Diet-related disease is the biggest killer in the United States, right now, here today. This is a global problem. It's a catastrophe. It's sweeping the world. England is right behind you, as usual.

2:46   (*Laughter.*)

2:50   I know they were close, but not that close. We need a revolution. Mexico, Australia, Germany, India, China, all have massive problems of obesity and bad health. Think about smoking. It costs way less than obesity now. Obesity costs you Americans 10 percent of your healthcare bills, 150 billion dollars a year. In 10 years, it's set to double: 300 billion dollars a year. And let's be honest, guys, you ain't got that cash.

3:24   (*Laughter.*)

3:27   I came here to start a food revolution that I so profoundly believe in. We need it. The time is now. We're in a tipping-point moment. I've been doing this for seven years. I've been trying in America for seven years. Now is the time when it's ripe – ripe for the picking. I went to the eye of the storm. I went to West Virginia, the most unhealthy state in America. Or it was last year. We've got a new one this year, but we'll work on that next season.

A second foil

Another text relating to Jamie is included on page 53. In this case, it is a review of a new TV series *Jamie's Money Saving Meals* by *Guardian* journalist, Sam Wollaston, who is well-known for his humorous approach to reviewing.

1. Does this text work as an interesting foil for the anthology text, showing Jamie speaking to camera? In what sense does Wollaston draw on Jamie's characteristic idiolect (an individual's distinctive way of speaking), his TV presence and the discourse of his TV programmes, to comment on them. Does that illuminate the anthology text in any way?

A third foil – Mary Berry and Paul Hollywood's Masterclasses

This time, the text isn't by Jamie but by another TV chef, Mary Berry.

2. Read the text and if possible watch it as a clip on BBC TV website (see notes on page 7).

3. Think about how differently Mary Berry (and Paul Hollywood) present a cookery item to camera. You might want to consider, among other things:

- the audience as compared with Jamie's

- the kind of clip and what it is intended to achieve

- what difference it makes to have a second chef there, so that the conversation is with someone else, as well as the TV audience

- levels of formality and informality in the uses of language and structure of the discourse

- what Mary Berry's idiolect is like and how it compares with Jamie's.

4. Share your findings as a class.

Evaluating what you've discovered

5. Now that you've read three different texts with points of connection to the anthology text, talk about which has been most illuminating. For instance, some people might feel that analysing Jamie in the anthology and in his TED talk is most illuminating because these two texts show his unique uses of language, even in adapting to quite different contexts. Others may feel that comparing two similar TV formats with different chefs is most illuminating because it highlights what's special about Jamie's style of communication in a specific context.

FOIL 2: SAM WOLLASTON'S TV REVIEW (GUARDIAN 2013)

Jamie Oliver is on a mission. I know! Again! (*Sighs*) What is it now? *Jamie's Money Saving Meals* (Channel 4)? Well, that's OK, I guess, given everything. I always find I can fill myself up nicely for not much money with a value meal at Maccy D's or KFC ... Only joking, Jamie, booooooo, I'll be making my own pizza too now of course, and freezing my own herbs and herby butter. Because, I know, *eating cheaply doesn't need to mean eating unhealthily*.

Did I say cheaply? And unhealthily? Booooooo, again. Because the first thing to go in this age of austerity is the old El Wye. Adverbs, unnecessary expenses – who needs 'em? It's all about shopping smart and cooking clever. Gotcha. But no adverbs doesn't mean talking uncolourful. So give this mothership money-saving brisket of beef a good rub up, then fire it up, get in my son, that's what we want. Do something with up, a phrasal verb, that's the general rule. Rub it up, fire it up; then wok up the leftovers with a chopped up onion for a dish cranked up to the max with poached eggs on top. Poached up eggs. Mmmm, it does look good. And it seems to serve up a whole roomful of attractive and fashionable young nutritionistas and price-checkers, and... and who knows who they all are; just part of the gang, I guess. All for about 7 pence a portion. Oh Jamie, you can be just a teeny bit twerpy and irritating, sometimes rub up the old brisket mothership *the wrong way* – literal the wrong way, if you know what I'm saying – but you are a little bit brilliant too.

FOIL 3: MARY BERRY'S PERFECTLY CURVED CHOCOLATE HOLLY LEAVES (TRANSCRIPT)

MARY B:	I thought I'd make some holly leaves. You can have these made on the computer. (*Looking at Paul.*) Please know, I didn't do them. The children'll do them in no time. And then, if you take some non-stick baking parchment and you put it on top...Then I'll do another one on top at that end. (*Pause.*) I've got some ordinary, plain melted chocolate. I have actually put a nozzle in the end. You could just snip the end of the nozzle if you wanted to. Using the template I'm going round to make these holly leaves. (*Music and pause.*) Like that...
PAUL H:	Hm – hh.
MARY B:	Then down the middle. If you do that line down the middle it strengthens the whole thing. (*Pause.*) Are you just going to serve Christmas pudding on Christmas Day or are you going to do an alternative pud?
PAUL H	(*Laughs.*) When I was growing up if you didn't like Christmas pud you got just custard 'cause we had custard with the pudding and my brother didn't like the pudding so he'd literally just have custard. But we'd have a sixpence piece in there for him. (*Pause.*) That's a nice squiggle.
MARY B:	You can squiggle. I'll time you – you'll do it much quicker than me.
PAUL H:	Oh thank you very much indeed. My hand's not very in tune at the moment.
MARY B:	I will then put them on the rolling pin, because holly leaves aren't flat – they have a slight curve. (*Pause while arranging on rolling pin.*) That's right. And you put half an egg box – pop it on the top there on the left – that's it and that stops it moving. Now these can be made a couple of days ahead and once they're set you can just keep them in the fridge.

FOILS FOR CAITLIN MORAN'S TWITTER FEED

Here are some foils for Caitlin Moran's Twitter feed, one of the anthology texts. They will give you an idea of the kind of unseen texts you might be given in the A Level exam. Each text might allow you to think about the Caitlin Moran Twitter feed in a different way.

1. First, in pairs or small groups use the list below to help you decide which way each one acts as a foil.

   - It deals with the same subject matter, in a different genre or text type.

   - It is written or spoken by the same person, showing them using language in a different way within a fresh context.

   - It is another example of the same genre, or text type, being used in a different way.

   - It is a response to the original text.

2. Next, choose the extract that you think allows you to make the most interesting comments about the original text alongside the new one. (There is no right answer – it is just a question of what interests you most and what you judge to be most fruitful for comparison.) Prepare to present your thinking to the rest of the class.

FOIL 1: CAITLIN MORAN – EXTRACT FROM MORANTHOLOGY

I Love the BBC

OK, I'm going to start with everything that's wrong about the BBC. It's over-staffed. Its management appears rudderless and timid. There are so many layers of bureaucracy and compliance that thousands of great ideas get slowly choked to death under piles of paperwork and fear. The amazing wardrobe department got sold off. They keep firing women over the age of fifty (Moira Stuart, Arlene Phillips, that bird off *Countryfile*). They've got far too many panel shows where a bunch of male comedians essentially shout 'YOUR AGENT IS INFERIOR TO MINE!' at each other. BBC3 is still embarrassing. The afternoon dramas on Radio 4 never fail to sink the spirits. But, none the less, the afternoon dramas on Radio 4 are works of genius compared to the comedy shows on Radio 4, which emit a palpable grey mist of dolorousness that can, over time, cause mildew in the houses of listeners.

So that's the bad stuff.

Pretty much all the other stuff about the BBC, though, is good stuff. Really. Even the things people currently think is bad stuff is actually good stuff.

Caitlin Moran: Moranthology

FOIL 2: BBC'S STRICTLY TWITTER FEED

BBC StrictlyVerified account @bbcstrictly
EXCLUSIVE We are pleased to confirm Tess and Claudia as our Strictly co-hosts when we return to @BBCOne in the autumn pic.twitter.com/RIOnoOCQ58 RETWEETS 1,612 FAVOURITES 1,680

Charlene @KnickyEganByrne May 9
@bbcstrictly @BBCOne YAY!!!! Fabulous!!!! X

Kirsty Boyle @kirsty_boyle May 9
'@bbcstrictly: EXCLUSIVE confirm Tess and Claudia as Strictly co-hosts when we return in the autumn pic.twitter.com/xgMCVuCKh5' Best Choice!

Sarah @SarahMay_ May 9
@bbcstrictly Great news!!!!! Doing it for the girls!!

Helena Todd @helenatodd May 9
@bbcstrictly @BBCOne hurrah

Jennie Talbot @jenAKtalbot May 9
@bbcstrictly @BBCOne Yay :D soooo excited

Heidi Stephens @heidistephens May 9
@bbcstrictly @BBCOne this is outstanding news.

Mighty Voice Show @Mighty_Voice May 9
@bbcstrictly @BBCOne well there's a surprise!

Harry Clayton-Wright @HClaytonWright May 9
@bbcstrictly @BBCOne YASSSSSSSSSSS #WinkleDalyFTW

kayliemansfield @kayliemansfield May 9
@bbcstrictly @BBCOne booooooooooooo Claudia is so annoying

Amy @scifisunsets May 9
@bbcstrictly @BBCOne @Zoetrope11 YAAAAAAAAAS. I mean, nicely done Claudia.

Dee's Brain Aches... @DeeClayton May 9
@bbcstrictly @BBCOne brilliant!!!!! So pleased you didn't feel a need to have a man and a woman. This is great!!!

Jean @notSupermum May 9
RT @bbcstrictly We are pleased to confirm Tess & Claudia as our Strictly co-hosts when we return in the autumn pic.twitter.com/s4zKxCgpXA > yes!

am narula @accessam May 9
@bbcstrictly @BBCOne the right choice to beat #xfactor @danwootton

Mandy H. @ImADerbyGirl May 9
@bbcstrictly @FurnessGirl @BBCOne Awful lot of Photoshop going on there.

Rebekah Wilson @RebekahWilson92 May 9
@bbcstrictly @BBCOne Hope you confiscate Claudia's eyeliner and cut her fringe beforehand!

FOIL 3: DAILY TELEGRAPH NEWSPAPER COLUMN

Claudia Winkleman is to join Tess Daly as the pair are confirmed as the new regular hosts of *Strictly Come Dancing,* following the departure of Sir Bruce Forsyth.

The announcement by the BBC ends weeks of speculation prompted by Sir Bruce's decision to step down from the show after a decade.

Daly and Winkleman were strongly fancied to land the permanent slot together after impressing viewers with their on-screen chemistry in the weekly results show and during Sir Bruce's occasional absences.

The pair will take over in the autumn when the series returns, with Daly switching to Sir Bruce's usual position introducing each of the dances and probing the judges for their reactions.

Winkleman, who will be upstairs hosting the post-dance interviews, said: 'I have loved *Strictly* since the second it appeared on our screens and I am honoured and thrilled to now be part of the Saturday night team.

'Working alongside Tess is always fantastic and I can't wait to spend the weekends with her, our amazing dancers and the greatest judging panel on the planet. Sir Bruce is a living legend and we'll all miss him very much.'

Daly said: 'I'm so pleased that I'll be working with Claudia – she's long been part of the *Strictly* family and I've loved doing the Sunday show with her.

'It's really exciting having two women host the show, and we are great mates so there'll be lots of fun to be had on and off the dance floor, and of course I'll look forward to being reunited with Brucie for the *Children In Need* and Christmas shows.'

Programme judge Bruno Tonioli recently declared he would love to see the duo given the role, when he said: 'I'll be delighted to have Tess and Claudia – they are fantastic, they work very well together.'

Show bosses are currently in talks to finalise the line-up for the professional dancers.

Charlotte Moore, the controller of BBC1 said: 'Tess and Claudia are a fantastic duo and natural successors to *Strictly's* presenting line up now that Sir Bruce has decided to step down.

'Their commitment and passion for the show make them the perfect pairing to take *Strictly* into a new era.'

The Daily Telegraph, 2014

EMC

FOIL 4: SPECTATOR NEWSPAPER COLUMN

I was pleased to see that June Sarpong had added her weight to Kathy Lette's petition to get a woman to present the BBC's remake of *Civilisation*. I've often wondered what became of her after *Five Go Dating*, a show I used to watch religiously, and one which – if you're listening, Channel 4 – equally deserves to be resurrected.

Lette's letter is in yesterday's *Times*. She complains that Kenneth Clark's original had little to say about women historian' should take the reins this time. 'A female presenter', argues the Australian novelist, 'would ensure that the series is not just about History but also Herstory. It's imperative that women also have a voice in the story of our world.'

As well as Sarpong, the motley crew of signatories includes Shami Chakrabarti, Caitlin Moran, Bianca Jagger, Sandi Toksvig, and ex-*Peak Practice* star, Haydn Gwynne. There are no men among the 50-odd names. Either no man agreed to sign a letter that included the word 'herstory', or none was asked.

The potential presenters Lette throws into the mix are: Mary Beard, Sue Perkins (only joking), Lisa Jardine, Amanda Vickery, Marina Warner, Bettany Hughes, Frances Stonor Saunders, AS Byatt and Hermione Lee. It's not a bad list, most of them are intellectual heavyweights. I'm unconvinced AS Byatt is a natural TV presenter, but then neither was Kenneth Clark.

What I find offensive is the idea that only a woman can ensure that women would be fairly represented. It's sexist and patronising, to women and to men. It also shows a fundamental ignorance of the original series, which focused on western art, architecture and philosophy – not the whole of history. And which was famously subtitled 'A Personal View'.

More problematically, it's all very well saying women's contribution to history and the arts should be reflected, but how's that going to work in practice, given that women were prevented from contributing much to civilisation?

Anna Baddley: The Spectator, 2014

Textual Webs

In exploring the texts in the anthology, whether for AS, where you compare two texts from the anthology, or in preparing for the A Level exam, where you also discuss an unseen text, it is worth finding your own texts that act as foils. This will give you both practice in thinking about what's worth comparing and experience of many different texts to sharpen your analytical skills.

Here's one example of a web (just showing text types rather than actual texts) to show you the kind of thing you might look for. It suggests how you can develop your experience of analysing a wide range of different texts and linguistic styles and choices, using an anthology text as a starting-point:

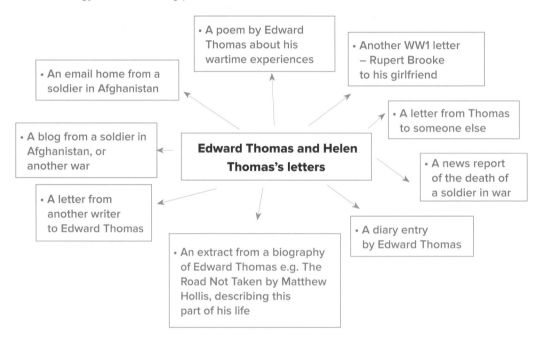

1. Work on a text in the anthology.

2. Find texts of your own that relate to the anthology text in some way.

3. Identify the reasons why you have made the connection.

4. Explore what the new text reveals to you about the anthology text, looking at aspects that are similar, and aspects that are different.

5. Create a physical web in the classroom, where linking texts are displayed, with arrows and Post-it notes identifying points of similarity and difference.

Unseen Texts – Mixing and Matching to Anthology Texts

In the A Level exam, you will be expected to comment on an anthology text or extract in relation to a text you have never seen before. Your work on foils and textual webs should help you to do this confidently, taking unseen texts in your stride.

Here's another activity that will help you see how to explore the relationships between anthology texts and other texts.

- Here are four extracts from unseen texts. For each one, decide which anthology texts they would make good foils for and be prepared to argue your reasons. (There may be one very obvious connection but think more imaginatively as well. For instance, you might think that the Innocent packaging text most obviously connects with the NSPCC advert. But might it also connect with one of the spoken texts, in the way its voice has elements that imitate spoken language?)

TEXT 1: CULTURE, MEDIA & SPORT COMMITTEE ORAL EVIDENCE: WOMEN & SPORT

Tuesday 10 December 2013 Chair: Mr John Whittingdale

CHAIR: Good morning. This is the third session of the Committee's inquiry into Women and Sport. I would like to welcome our first panel, Kelly Simmons (the Director of the National Game and Women's Football, Football Association), Helen Clayton (former Captain of the England Rugby Team), Alastair Marks (Head of Rugby Growth for the RFU) and Nicky Ponsford (the Head of Performance, Women, Rugby Football Union). I will start by asking you to give us a general summary of the present state. What percentage of players at grassroots are women in each of your sports, how has that changed and what progress are you making in promoting women's sport?

ALASTAIR MARKS: My name is Alastair Marks. I am the Head of Rugby Growth at the RFU and my colleague, Nicky Ponsford, looks after the elite side of the game. We come from a background of significant progress in this area, albeit starting from a very low base, so we thank you very much for the opportunity to come in to talk to you today. Following the integration of the Women's Rugby Football Union last year we now have significant resources in place to support participation at all levels of the game. Women's rugby has seen a steady but rapid increase by around 90% in grassroots participation in the past decade. We look to increase that by an additional two-thirds within the next four years, taking us to around 25,000 players in the overall game. This represents about 7% to 8% of the total rugby-playing population. There is still a way to go in doing that but we now have a strategy in place to focus all of our efforts on driving participation in over 200 focus groups and focus clubs. We have also increased our investment in the elite women's game by over 25% to, now, £5 million in the last year. We are driving considerable cultural change in terms of our leadership, opportunities and position, focusing on creating a pipeline for leadership opportunity in the women's sport, and in our management board we now have four out of our nine members who are female, with considerable work to do in some of the other areas of the game.

TEXT 2: DRAGONS' DEN

PETER:	For me what you have done though is probably for the first time ever in the den. You've made the most convincing argument and presentation based on inaccurate financial forecasts that I think I've ever seen.
POLLY:	Is that a compliment?
THEO:	Nooooo.
PETER:	I don't think the business is sustainable. If I gave you a hundred thousand pounds it would just go down the drain. This is something just to enjoy. Do it yourself. Scale it up. Carry on but this isn't something that an investor is going to give you money at this stage so I'm going to say I'm out.
DEBORAH:	Helen, Polly, I *really* like the product and I think you two are really great but it was really disappointing that the numbers have fallen apart. But there's still something there. You've produced a product... you've got it into Mothercare...
HELEN:	Mmmm...
DEBORAH:	It *is* selling.
HELEN:	(*Nods.*)
DEBORAH:	I'm going to make you an offer.
HELEN:	Great
DEBORAH:	And I'm going to offer you *all* of the money for forty five percent of the business.
POLLY:	Thank you.

TEXT 3: TRANSCRIPT OF A BBC TV NEWS REPORT

Good afternoon. More than 40 people have been killed in a series of bomb attacks in Iraq. Three bombs exploded near an American convoy in Baghdad. Most of the thirty-seven people killed in that attack were children. Scores of people were injured. Two other bomb attacks left seven people dead.

Here a motion urging the early withdrawal of British troops from Iraq has been overwhelmingly defeated at the Labour Party conference. It was rejected by a margin of 85% to 15%.

A British airways jet flying from Berlin to Heathrow was diverted to Schiphol Airport in Amsterdam after what the airline said was a specific threat. All one hundred and eighteen passengers have left the aircraft.

The High Court has heard that a desperately ill premature baby has a quality of life which is both terrible and permanent. Doctors say it would be wrong to resuscitate eleven-month-old Charlotte Wyatt. Her parents want everything done to keep her alive.

The Russian government has approved the Kyoto accord on global warming. It'll go to the country's parliament for final ratification. The treaty needs Russian approval to come into force.

A cross-party group of MPs says public schools should lose their charitable status. The schools which could lose one hundred million pounds in tax relief argue all education is for the greater good and should be supported.

And that's it. I'm going to be back with George with the 6 o'clock news. Now though we join our news teams across the UK. Goodbye for now.

EXTRACT 4: INNOCENT SMOOTHIE PACKAGING

poetry outcast

The mangoes we use are called Alphonso. Not Angus, not Charles, not Cynthia, not Roy. Just Alphonso. We think they're the sweetest tasting mangoes out there which is why we use them in all our recipes. Alphonso also happens to be a cracking name for a parrot, which is interesting because parrot rhymes with carrot and there are lots of those in this smoothie too.

Sadly, we couldn't find a tenuous link for orange because it doesn't rhyme with anything. But rest assured they taste great with carrots and mangoes, even if they ruin every poem they've ever been in.

ALPHONSO

ITALPACK

® = Rhyming

Evaluating Linguistic Approaches to an Unseen Text

This chapter has taken you through many of the key approaches you might take to explore and analyse any non-fiction or spoken text.

This final section gives you the chance to apply what you have learnt to an unseen text. This is something you will be required to do in Component 1 of the **A Level exam**.

1. Read the text on page 64. Talk about your first impressions and thoughts.

2. Think about all of the linguistic approaches you have encountered and decide which of these are most helpful in exploring this text.

LINGUISTIC APPROACHES
• Thinking about context – audience, purpose, genre, time
• Key aspects of language – different levels of analysis
• Conversation analysis
• Rhetoric
• Comparative analysis – finding a foil

3. Drawing on whatever approaches you find most useful, write an analysis of the text and how meanings are constructed in it.

4. Compare your analysis with that of one or two other people in your class. Talk about which linguistic approaches you adopted and which were most fruitful in analysing the construction of meaning in the text.

DON'T BLAME ME FOR BEING POOR AND STUPID: I'M LEFT-HANDED

I think I'm left-handed, but I can't quite remember. I haven't actually hand-written anything since about 2008, when the last smartphone-free human was exiled by society and sent panicking into the wild to carve tweets on a tree. Gradually, as we type more, the issue of choosing 'which hand' to write with will fade. They'll probably release an app in a few years that even gets Siri to wipe your bum too.

One thing I don't miss as I reluctantly become integrated into my keyboard, like some forgotten PC accessory that's grown a beard, is the dip in frequency with which I hear the expression, 'Oh you're left-handed? I hadn't noticed.' An irksome interaction that suggests you're keeping some sort of hand census, and that this vital piece of information had somehow got by one of your pervy informants.

I sometimes wonder if it's similar remarks that caused Jimi Hendrix to set fire to his guitar. 'Ooh, you play left-handed, I hadn't noti- OK I'm sorry!' Keyboards are my camouflage against the manually obsessed.

A fascination with our favoured extremity might be more useful than we previously thought, as a recent study into the effects of left-handedness has made some intriguing findings.

'Left-handed individuals show consistently lower cognitive skills and higher rates of mental and behavioural disabilities,' writes Joshua Goodman in the Journal of Economic Perspectives.

Admittedly, most people would show lower cognitive skills if they spent their first 17 years fixing the smudged nonsense caused by a writing system that involves your hand immediately undoing the hard work of your pen. Children with iPads in schools will never know my frustration at producing an ink-smeared essay that could easily be mistaken for the manifesto of a clumsy squid.

Goodman has further bad news: 'The empirical evidence for greater creativity among the left-handed turns out to be fairly weak.'

So not only are we sinister types probably not very clever, we can't even fall back on the usual trade-offs of being arty and creative either. What next? The left-handed can't tell anecdotes? They're scientifically bad in bed? It turns out the final blow is financial, with lefties receiving '10–12% lower annual earnings than righties', apparently due to their focus on jobs with less emphasis on cognitive skill.

There isn't much consolation for all of this. Some might point to the fact that Barack Obama is left-handed, but I'm not sure that's comforting any more when you consider the fact that he's more likely to have 'emotional and behavioural problems (and) learning disabilities such as dyslexia'. I mean, does he even know what he's signing? Does Obama know he's signing off on drone strikes?

I think shunning ink and sticking to the keyboard might be a good plan. It means I can avoid the 'I hadn't noticed' conversation and ensuing violence, but also I don't want people now saying, 'You're left-handed? Oh dear. You're probably stupid and poor. Want to borrow a fiver?'

Jazz Twemlow, Guardian Comment is Free, 2014

Writing Non-fiction Texts

If you are an AS student, you will have to write a short text of your own in the Component 1 exam. It will always have some connection to the anthology texts you have been asked to write about in the first section of the paper and there will be a choice of task.

How can you prepare yourself for this? By reading and analysing lots of texts in non-fiction and spoken genres and by experimenting with short bits of writing in these genres to develop your confidence in writing in a range of genres and styles, giving you lots of tools and strategies to employ.

If you're doing the full A Level, this will be helpful in developing the skills you need for Component 4 where you write a non-fiction text of your own.

A STARTING-POINT – APPRENTICE YOURSELF TO ANOTHER WRITER

1. Choose one of the texts in the anthology, one of the unseen texts in this chapter or another text that you have chosen for yourself or your teacher has selected for you. It should be a text that you particularly admire for its style.

2. Use a grid like the one below to identify some of the key qualities of the text. Begin by filling in only the first column, with adjectives or short phrases that describe key qualities of the text, e.g. witty, powerful, poetic, clever, simple, understated and so on.

3. Now analyse what linguistic or literary features create those qualities. Fill in the second column of the grid (e.g. understated – no pre- or post-modification of nouns).

4. Finally, choose a completely different subject and use your grid to try writing a paragraph or two in the style of this piece of writing. See how closely you can imitate it.

5. Share your attempt with someone else, asking for advice on what works well and what needs changing.

6. Re-draft it to make it even more like the style of the original.

There's a filled-in example, on page 66, based on Alan Bennett's diary entries in the anthology.

KEY QUALITIES OF THE TEXT – AN OVERVIEW	LINGUISTIC & LITERARY TECHNIQUES THAT CREATE THESE QUALITIES

THE OCR (EMC) ANTHOLOGY

KEY QUALITIES OF THE TEXT – AN OVERVIEW	LINGUISTIC AND LITERARY TECHNIQUES THAT CREATE THESE QUALITIES
Draws the reader into his experiences.	• Use of the present tense. • Goes straight in with actions, what happens rather than description. • Missing verb in 'By train to Cambridge...' takes you straight in.
Scenes strongly evoked visually.	• Much pre-modification of nouns and extended noun phrases e.g. 'a stocky, heavy-shouldered, neatly coiffed woman of around sixty', 'luminous blue and white Victorian tile'.
Lively and engaging voice.	• Informal lexis mixed with more formal lexis, e.g. 'bucketing electric job', 'peps things up', 'gets the audience going'.
Humorous.	• Use of brackets for 'appropriately' drawing attention to the comedy. • The use of 'his mamma' to talk about the Queen – unexpected term of address & perhaps a sense that Prince Charles might use that term (free indirect style?). • Use of joke at the end – final punchline provided by someone else.
Structurally appears to be a set of fairly random thoughts, impressions and ideas, though Bennett's personality and take on life both come through strongly.	• Entries separated by several days, in different locations and on different topics... • ... but each diary entry starts with an 'event' and ends with a thought or observation giving a viewpoint, even if only subtly suggested e.g. 5 Jan, an observation on gender, 8 Jan, his view on a mistaken undervaluing of a painting, an implied idea about the value of theatre.
Reads as if intended not just for himself but for a wider audience – as a literary rather than a personal diary.	• His thoughts (e.g. 'which still seems to me one of the sights of Europe') are often expressed in full sentences, often with subordinate clauses. Not at all in note form. • Literary lexical choices, e.g. 'coiffed' for hairstyle. • Literary syntactic choices, e.g. 'a day of blinding sunshine and bitter cold'. • Use of highly wrought patterning, e.g. alliteration in 'presence...peps up...Prince of Wales...puzzled...press and paparazzi...pursuit' – slightly humorous effect.
Sense of this being a genuine record of a personal set of experiences.	• The jumps from one entry to the next. • The use of the initial only for his companion, to maintain confidentiality.

LANGUAGE AND LITERATURE EMC

Writing a Non-fiction Text or Scripting a Spoken Text of Your Own – Drawing on Your Reading

If you're doing AS Level, these activities are useful preparation for Section B in the AS Component 1 exam.

If you are doing A Level, they will help you develop the skills you need for the introduction to your own creative writing in Component 4.

The anthology texts are from a wide range of genres – letters, speeches, adverts, graphic novels, diaries, scripted TV presentations, newspaper articles and so on.

1. Prepare yourself to write a short piece in any of these genres by identifying texts that you find interesting and engaging or that you admire for their style, either in the anthology or beyond.

2. Try a range of these approaches.

- Draw on the content of one of the anthology texts but use it to write in a different genre or style.

    — e.g. use Grayson Perry's reflections on art in his lecture, to write an introduction to contemporary ideas about art for a BBC children's news programme.

- Draw on the generic conventions and approach of one of the anthology texts but fill the text with your own content – your own experiences, thoughts and ideas.

    — e.g. write a series of three diary entries in the manner of Samuel Pepys or Alan Bennett, written for yourself but in the knowledge that there might be an outside audience as well.

- Write 'against' one of the anthology texts. In other words, try out a completely different way of treating that particular subject matter, either by changing the genre, or making very different use of the generic conventions or by taking a very different line of argument.

    — e.g. write a comment piece, to be published in a newspaper, arguing why the early death of people like Marilyn Monroe creates false icons, glamorised versions of the real person, or write a voiceover script for a children's TV programme on the Stone Age, taking a completely different, more serious humorous approach.

Modelled Writing Using a Non-fiction Text from the Anthology

Here are three openings for non-fiction texts, responding to this sample AS Level examination task based on the Sochi snowboarding final commentary:

Write about an aspect of your daily routine in the style of a sports commentary for TV or radio. Your purpose is to entertain your audience.

1. Talk about what style of commentary each one has chosen, what kinds of conventions and features each one has adopted from sports commentary genres and how successful they are. Decide which you think is most successful and why.

EXAMPLE 1

And so the moment is upon us. This girl, who has become a legend in her time, an icon, a heroine and a role model for young women around the world, is about to take to the bathroom floor and pick up her toothbrush.

She looks unfazed, steely, determined, not even a flicker of nervousness. Just one quick look at herself in the mirror and off she goes. And now she's building up momentum, unscrewing the toothpaste lid, squeezing it out. Perfectly done. Perfect. Not one false move. And here comes the brush up to her lips. Will she... no... yes... she's done it. No problems there. The toothbrush is successfully in her mouth.

EXAMPLE 2

Anne: She looks a bit nervous though doesn't she Glenn? Is she quite in the zone? She's had this kind of trouble before. The mental preparation. Her coach has been working with her on it but she's still not quite got it under control.

Glenn: It's her Achilles' heel. It lets her down. Let's hope for England's sake that this time she's got it sorted. You struggled a bit with the pressure in your time, didn't you Anne? You know how she must be feeling right now.

Anne: Yes. It's not easy, the challenge of keeping focused when you know you've got that toothbrush waiting for you. What she needs to do is forget all the media attention, pretend to herself that it's just an ordinary morning and...

Glenn: She's about to start. What do you think Anne? Can she manage it this time? Or is it going to be another desperate disappointment for all those England fans?

Anne: Fingers crossed. And there she goes... looking good at the start...

EXAMPLE 3

Well she's showing what she's made of. A perfect closed-fist lock grip on the toothpaste tube coupled with a smooth transition. She's squeezing out the toothpaste in one seamless movement. Oh yes, real class! No hesitation at all! That'll be a five from the judges if she carries on like this! And instantly into the mouth with a clean sweep. Oh, look at that technique! A single-handed double-speed horizontal brush stroke, with little short vertical shifts. That's daring. But she's pulling it off.

2. Now have a go at one of these tasks, based on other anthology texts.

- **Captain Scott's diary:** write a diary entry for an outdoor pursuits holiday in the countryside, where something goes wrong and members of the group are put at risk.

- **Julia Gillard's speech to the Australian parliament**: write the beginning of a speech at a school assembly or college forum, where you make a statement about something you feel very strongly about.

- **NSPCC: Hello Can You Help Me**: write the text for a leaflet for a new campaign by NSPCC directed at children, encouraging them to use the Childline service.

- **Emily Post's guide to conversation from *Etiquette***: write a guide for users of Twitter on the art of polite conversation.

EMC

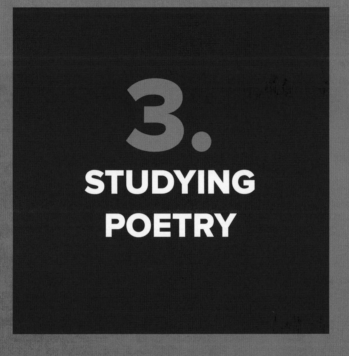

3.
STUDYING
POETRY

3.
STUDYING POETRY

Poetry is part of **AS Level Component 2** and **A Level Component 2**. Whether you are studying AS or A Level, you will study 15 poems by one of the following poets:

- William Blake: *Songs of Innocence and Experience: Shewing the Two Contrary States of the Human Soul* (Oxford Paperbacks, 1970)

- Emily Dickinson: *The Complete Poems* (Faber & Faber, 1976)

- Seamus Heaney: *Opened Ground – Poems 1966-1996* (Faber & Faber, 2002)

- Eavan Boland: *New Collected Poems* (Carcanet, 2005)

- Carol Ann Duffy: *Rapture* (Picador, 2005)

- Jacob Sam-la Rose: *Breaking Silence* (Bloodaxe Books, 2011)

(The editions shown in brackets are those from which the poems on the exam paper will be taken.)

In the AS exam, you will be asked to compare two poems from the text you've studied, both chosen by the examiner. Both poems will be printed on the paper. The AS Level questions ask you to focus on the ways the poet uses language and poetic techniques and to support your answer with reference to relevant contextual factors. For example:

> **Compare the way Duffy uses language and poetic techniques in 'Over' and 'You'. Support your answer with reference to relevant contextual factors.**

In the A Level exam, you will be asked to compare a named poem from the collection, printed on the paper, with a second poem of your own choice, again from the set text. The A Level questions ask you to consider the poet's use of poetic and stylistic techniques and significant literary and other relevant contexts. For example:

> **Explore how Blake presents freedom and control in 'The Garden of Love' and in one or two other poems from your collection. You should consider Blake's use of poetic and stylistic techniques and significant literary or relevant contexts.**

The activities in this chapter will help you develop the skills you need to tackle the AS or A Level exam.

You will carry out some initial exploratory activities into poetry and what makes it special and distinct as a genre, before experimenting with using stylistics as an analytical tool. You will spend time analysing the stylistic and poetic techniques used by your set poet, learning to make judgements about what it is most interesting and significant to discuss and, importantly, connecting your analysis to meaning and impact. You will explore the characteristic and distinctive features of the way your poet uses literary and poetic techniques, and consider relevant literary or other contexts.

If you have not already completed the introductory activity on stylistics approaches on page 18, you might like to do so now.

Introducing Poetry

What Is Poetry?

Below and on page 74 there are 12 attempts to answer the question 'What is poetry?'

1. Read the definitions and share your responses to them. Do any definitions seem particularly useful or perceptive? What do they suggest about the genre of poetry, from the perspective of the writer? What about the reader?

2. How would *you* define poetry? On your own, or in pairs, write your own short definition of poetry, drawing on any of the definitions, if you want to.

> **Poetry is ordinary language raised to the Nth power. Poetry is boned with ideas, nerved and blooded with emotions, all held together by the delicate, tough skin of words.**
>
> **Paul Engle, *New York Times***

> **Form is a straitjacket in the way that a straitjacket was a straitjacket for Houdini.**
>
> **Paul Muldoon**

> **If I feel physically as if the top of my head were taken off, I know that is poetry.**
>
> **Emily Dickinson**

Poetry is like making a joke. If you get one word wrong at the end of a joke, you've lost the whole thing.

W.S. Merwin

Poetry is to prose as dancing is to walking.

Paul Valéry

Poetry is the rhythmical creation of beauty in words.

Edgar Allan Poe

Poetry: the best words in the best order.

Samuel Taylor Coleridge

The poet's pen turns them to shape, and gives to airy nothing a local habitation and a name; such tricks hath strong imagination.

William Shakespeare: *A Midsummer Night's Dream*

Poetry is... speech in which the words come in an order which could not be changed without ruining the verity and power of the whole.

Robert Nye, *Acumen*, 2006

Poetry is not a matter of feelings, it is a matter of language that creates feeling.

Umberto Eco, *The Independent*, 1995

The poet takes language, condenses it, charges it with energy, gives it a bit of oomph – and there's the poem.

Julie O'Callaghan, RTE Radio 1, 1987

Like a piece of ice on a hot stove the poem must ride on its own melting.

Robert Frost

The 'Poetry-ness' of Poetry – Exploring Extracts

Included below and on pages 75-76 are six short extracts from a poem by each of the poets set for this specification.

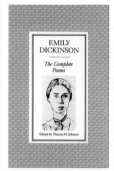

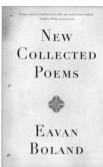
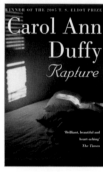

1. What can you learn about poetry as a genre by exploring the different poetic and linguistic choices each poet makes (on page 76)? The notes on the first extract show you the sort of thing you might comment on.

EXTRACT 1

Pity would be no more

If we did not make somebody Poor;

And Mercy no more could be

If all were as happy as we;

COMMENTARY

The first thing you notice in this extract is the way the text is laid out in lines, with the first word of each line capitalised, even when it's not the beginning of a sentence. From extract 1, it seems rhyme might be an important feature of poetry, distinguishing it from other types of writing – it's important enough for the poet to invert the usual syntax in order to stick to the regular rhyme. It's dealing with big ideas – pity, mercy, poverty, happiness. Is that what poetry always does?

STUDYING POETRY

2. Now consider the second extract. What is distinctive or interesting about this extract? What new insights does it give you into poetry as a genre?

EXTRACT 2

Because I could not stop for Death –

He kindly stopped for me –

The Carriage held but just Ourselves –

And Immortality.

---

3. Continue to add the remaining extracts to your discussion, each time asking yourself the question, 'What more can I tell about poetry by introducing this further extract from a different poem?'

EXTRACT 3

I was standing there

at the end of a reading

or a workshop or whatever,

watching people heading

out into the weather,

EXTRACT 4

Uninvited, the thought of you stayed too late in my head,

so I went to bed, dreaming you hard, hard, woke with your name,

like tears, soft, salt, on my lips, the sound of its bright syllables

like a charm, like a spell.

EXTRACT 5

No such thing

as innocent

bystanding.

Her soiled vest,

her little breasts,

her clipped, devast-

ated, scabbed

punk head,

EXTRACT 6

Dear boys on road,

dear girls on bus

top decks, dear hip-hop, dear love letters

pressed deep into vinyl platters, dear Americas

Jamaica and East End –

4. Share what you have discovered as a class, listing the ideas you now have about:

- poetry as a genre

- the different poetic and linguistic choices poets make

- the relationship between these choices and what the
  poem seems to mean.

5. Once you done this, look at the notes below. Is there anything new suggested here?
   If so, add it to your list, if you think it would contribute to your understanding of
   what poetry is.

6. Choose one of the poems from the poet you are studying. Read the poem on your own and
   write a short response, applying what you have discovered about poetry from this activity.

FIRST NOTES TOWARDS A COMMENTARY

Like 1, poem extract 2 also deals with big ideas – life, death, immortality – and it also capitalises in unexpected ways with the surprising idea of stopping for death. Here death is personified. This extract suggests that poetry can be strange, surreal and provocative.

Extract 3 gives a very different angle on poetry. It seems quite un-poem like at first – the tone is conversational and although it is laid out in lines, the sentence punctuation is the same as for prose. The use of rhyme is more conventionally poetic, but even this is less obtrusive than in extract 1, with half-rhymes in 'reading' and 'heading'.

Extracts 1, 2 and 3 are all first person. Is poetry a form particularly suited to the first person?

Poem extract 4 stands out as being intimate and lyrical – again first person. This poem suggests that repetition (in phrases such as 'like a charm, like a spell') and the sound of the words are important features of poetry.

Extract 5 is very striking in terms of the odd things it does with language – it shows that poetry can break all sorts of 'rules' that we expect prose to follow. It has a centred layout, hyphenated text across stanzas, rhyme and half-rhyme at the end of lines and internally (again suggesting sound and rhythm is important in poetry). It launches straight in, with a minor sentence. This poem isn't obviously written in the first person, so maybe a third-person voice is possible.

Reading extract 6 is beginning to seem like repetition is one of the most characteristic features of poetry – it's very noticeable here, as is the emphasis on sound. It's interesting that the same technique (repetition) can be used to such different ends in extracts 4 and 6. The subject matter of extract 6 suggests poetry can be about anything – any place, any subject, any idea.

EMC LANGUAGE AND LITERATURE

STUDYING POETRY

What Makes a Poet's Work Distinctive? First Thoughts

What is it that makes Heaney's poetry different from Duffy's? Or Blake's poetry distinct from Dickinson's?

In part it's the subject matter, the ideas, the themes, and the angle the poet takes on these. But it is also the linguistic and poetic choices he or she makes – the decision to use rhyme or not, to use a formal rhythmic pattern or to recreate the rhythms of the speaking voice, to draw on concrete language rooted in the everyday world or invent words or use language metaphorically, even the decision to capitalise each word at the beginning of a line. Most importantly, it's what use the poet makes of that technique, in combination with other linguistic and poetic choices, in the context of the poem's subject matter and themes, that makes a poet's work distinctive.

- As a class, look briefly at the two poems included here. 'Rapture' is by Carol Ann Duffy, one of the poets set for this specification. The other is not – it's by William Shakespeare. Identify the poetic and linguistic techniques the two poets share, then explore the *different* ways in which these are used to create particular meanings and effect.

CAROL ANN DUFFY: RAPTURE	WILLIAM SHAKESPEARE: SONNET 18
Thought of by you all day, I think of you.	Shall I compare thee to a summer's day?
The birds sing in the shelter of a tree.	Thou art more lovely and more temperate.
Above the prayer of rain, unacred blue,	Rough winds do shake the darling buds of May,
not paradise, goes nowhere endlessly.	And summer's lease hath all too short a date.
How does it happen that our lives can drift	Sometime too hot the eye of heaven shines,
far from ourselves, while we stay trapped in time,	And often is his gold complexion dimmed;
queuing for death? It seems nothing will shift	And every fair from fair sometime declines,
the pattern of our days, alter the rhyme	By chance, or nature's changing course, untrimmed;
we make with loss to assonance with bliss.	But thy eternal summer shall not fade,
Then love comes, like a sudden flight of birds	Nor lose possession of that fair thou ow'st,
from earth to heaven after rain. Your kiss,	Nor shall death brag thou wand'rest in his shade,
recalled, unstrings, like pearls, this chain of words.	When in eternal lines to Time thou grow'st.
Huge skies connect us, joining here to there.	So long as men can breathe, or eyes can see,
Desire and passion on the thinking air.	So long lives this, and this gives life to thee.

The rest of this chapter introduces a range of approaches to help you get to grips with the particular characteristics of the poet you are studying.

Creative Approaches

One of the particular features of the OCR (EMC) Language and Literature specification is its emphasis on the relationship between reading and writing. While this is an explicit focus of the narrative component, the basic idea that writing creatively helps you analyse texts and reading texts helps you write creatively underpins the specification as a whole.

The following short activities all ask you to engage with a text creatively, then reflect on your insights into the ways linguistic and poetic techniques are used to create meaning.

Fragments

Included below are six sets of fragments, each set taken from a single poem by one of the set poets. Both punctuation and capitalisation have been removed and spellings standardised. There are six separate fragments in each set. For this activity, **focus on the fragments by the poet you are studying.**

1. Talk about your expectations of the poem from looking at the fragments. You may want to talk about:

   • the lexical choices

   • the sense of the voice

   • phonology (sounds)

   • figurative language.

2. Try using two or three of the fragments from one poem in lines of poetry of your own. Be playful, experimenting with different ways of using the fragments and reflecting on the effects you achieve each time, as in the example below, based on the Duffy poem 'Over'. You can repeat words and add up to 10 words of your own, if you want.

AN EXAMPLE	
Without spell or prayer **I found you.** **Without prayer or spell,** **I lost you.**	*Used repeated grammatical structures and repeated words rather than rhyme to draw the ideas together. Played around with the word order.*

3. Compare your poem with those of other people in your group.

4. Now read the original poem and discuss the way the words and phrases have been used. Focus your discussion on what the poet's use of the phrases foregrounds.

DUFFY: OVER

- a dark hour out of time
- without spell or prayer
- blazed us
- unlocking all the dark
- piercing the hour
- the garden's sudden scent's

HEANEY: PUNISHMENT

- I can feel the tug
- the frail rigging
- the weighing stone
- the memories of love
- poor scapegoat
- the stones of silence

BOLAND: FROM THE PAINTING 'BACK FROM MARKET' BY CHARDIN

- at all times in her short delay
- what great art removes
- from whose bargaining
- In surging light
- the colours of a country day
- In painted daylight

DICKINSON: ONE NEED NOT BE A CHAMBER

- need not be a chamber to be haunted
- of a midnight meeting
- through an abbey gallop
- in lonesome place
- ourself behind ourself concealed
- bolts the door

BLAKE: THE NURSE'S SONG (INNOCENCE)

- the voices of children
- and every thing else is still
- the dews of night arise
- no no let us play
- till the light fades away
- leaped and shouted and laughed

SAM-LA ROSE: SPEECHLESS III

- wondering when if ever it will be cool
- a black gloved fist in my pocket
- feel like an ink blot on a blank page
- no is inked out
- spit them out like devotions
- rejected its cold dead weight

STUDYING POETRY

Micro-interventions

Playing with the language of a poem, intervening to make small changes to the lexical choices, the grammar or the lineation, can give you both insights into the way poems work in general and highlight the particular decisions a poet made.

The example here uses Eavan Boland's poem 'This Moment' to show you how you can 'play' with a poem and reveals what your creative micro-interventions might alert you to.

MICRO-INTERVENTIONS IN THE LEXIS – AN EXAMPLE

EAVAN BOLAND: THIS MOMENT

A neighbourhood.
At dusk.

Things are getting ready
to happen
out of sight.

Stars and moths.
And rinds slanting around fruit.

But not yet.

One tree is black.
One window is yellow as butter.

A woman leans down to catch a child
who has run into her arms
this moment.

Stars rise.
Moths flutter.
Apples sweeten in the dark.

INTERVENING IN THE LEXIS	REFLECTIONS ON THE INTERVENTIONS
A quiet neighbourhood. At twilight. Things are about to happen out of sight. Stars and moths. And rinds slanting around fruit. But not yet. One tree is silhouetted. One window glows orange. A mother leans down to hold her child who has rushed towards her just now. Stars rise. Moths flutter. Apples ripen in the gloaming.	*Even the smallest changes alter the poem –* *particularly the mood. Swapping 'dusk' for 'twilight',* *a two-syllable word, changes not only the rhythm* *but also the mood.* *'Things are about/to happen' loses the almost* *human connotation of 'Getting ready'. It's* *interesting because it's not only to do with altering* *the simplicity of the poem – in some ways 'glows* *orange' is simpler than the simile 'yellow as butter'.* *What is perhaps most noticeable is that words* *with the same meaning – twilight, dusk, gloaming,* *dark – create different effects in the poem. It's not* *only to do with the connotations but also the sound* *and rhythm of the words ('sk' sounds softer, more* *mysterious than the harder 't' and 'l' sounds).* *Silhouetted rather than 'black' alters both the* *rhythm of the line and the simplicity of the poem.* *The use of 'black' (which for a reader conjures up* *silhouetted anyway) also contrasts with the yellow.* *Sense of jeopardy or risk is lost with the change to* *'lean down to hold'; 'catch' also suggests movement* *of both the child running and the mother's* *action in catching.* *The single syllable ending of 'dark' has greater* *impact, even though the word 'gloaming' might, out* *of context, seem to be more evocative.*

You can try out your creative experiments on a short extract from any of the poems you are studying. The following poems might prove particularly fruitful places to start:

- Duffy: Grief

- Heaney: Fodder

- Boland: An Irish Childhood in England, 1951

- Dickinson: After great Pain

- Blake: Nurse's Song (*Experience*)

- Rose: A Spell for Forgetting a Father

STUDYING POETRY

PLAYING WITH A POEM

Work through the following stages, spending no more than five or six minutes on each intervention.

1. Focus only on changing the **lexis**, for example the use of adjectives and adverbs, words belonging to particular groups, abstract or concrete nouns, monosyllabic or polysyllabic words.

2. Next experiment with the **grammar**, altering one or more of the following: the punctuation, the sentence length or type, verbs (e.g. tense, active or passive), the use of grammatically incomplete sentences (where there is not a finite verb within the 'sentence').

3. As a class, share what you have discovered about the poem you have been playing with. Focus your discussion on your insights into the relationship between the poet's linguistic, grammatical and poetic choices and the meaning and impact.

EXPERIMENTING WITH THE LINE

The American poet and creative writing teacher, John Lennard, highlights the significance of the poetic line, reminding readers that the choice of line break is always worth exploring:

> the handiest distinction between poetry and prose is that poetry uses one unit of words that prose does not: the line. Alternatively poetry uses one form of punctuation which prose doesn't: the line break ... However straightforward or complicated the sense, however long or short the lines, there must be some reasons why the lines are as they are, and the line breaks where they are.

For your final micro-intervention, you are going the experiment with the **layout** of a text, including choices about line breaks.

To do this part of the activity, your teacher will give you one of your set poems written out as a piece of continuous prose, without line breaks.

1. Without looking back at the original text while you are doing the activity, experiment with putting in line and stanza breaks. As you work, be aware of the reasons for your decisions and the impact you're having on the meaning, sound, tone and effect of the poem.

2. Compare your line breaks with other people in the group. Talk about the reasons for your decisions and the different effects you achieved. Did any work well? If so, why do you think this is? What insights do your changes give you into the original text?

Taking a Stylistics Approach to Poetry

Academics who use stylistics to explore texts describe it in the following ways:

Stylistics is the study of language in the service of literary ends.

Leech and Short

To do stylistics is to explore language, and, more specifically, to explore creativity in language use ... it tells us about the rules of language because it often explores texts where those rules are bent, distended or stretched to breaking point.

Paul Simpson

This makes stylistics a very good fit approach for exploring poetry, with its emphasis on pattern-making and pattern-breaking and the non-literal use of words in symbols and metaphors.

The following activities take a broadly stylistics approach to the analysis of poetry. The first activities – 'A Collapsed Poem' and 'Secret Strings' – are very open and exploratory, encouraging you to pay attention to the words the poet chose to use. The activities get progressively more challenging, introducing you to key aspects of stylistics such as parallelism, foregrounding and repetition. There are also sections looking at the techniques of voice, rhyme, metaphor from the perspective of stylistics. This section ends with a sequential approach to analysis which draws in a more systematic way on the methodology of stylistics.

A Collapsed Poem

Collapsing a poem, so that all the words are arranged alphabetically, can be a good way of focusing just on the language of the poem before trying to grapple with the complete text. It highlights repeated words and sounds, foregrounds (or draws attention to) unusual or surprising words, and encourages you to speculate about the relationship between the different words and their possible meaning.

Be warned though that this approach reveals more about some poems than others. Of course, that can be very interesting in itself and may draw your attention to a central aspect of the text (e.g. it is narrative poem, driven by the demands of a story, rather than a lyric poem structured around repeated words and sounds). In cases like this, it is probably best to move on fairly quickly and try a different approach.

1. Before trying this approach on a poem from your set collection, have a look at the example on pages 87-88. Begin by exploring the collapsed poem on page 87, then compare your ideas with the notes on page 88.

The poems suggested here would all be good ones to explore as collapsed poems.

- Duffy: Epiphany

- Heaney: The Haw Lantern

- Boland: The New Pastoral

- Dickinson: A certain Slant of light

- Sam-la Rose: An Undisclosed Fortune

- Blake: The Divine Image

2. Without reading the poem, use the instructions below to 'collapse' it into an alphabetical string of words. (Even better if you can get your teacher to collapse it for you before you see it.)

3. On your own or in pairs, investigate the collapsed poem, drawing out any clusters of words, or patterns or connections, or anything your attention is drawn to because it is repeated or breaks the pattern.

4. Share your observations and your speculative thoughts about their significance.

5. Now read the poem as originally written. Use your observations and speculative ideas as a way into analysing how the poet has used linguistic and poetic effects to create meaning and impact.

HOW TO COLLAPSE A POEM

- Make sure the original text is saved.

- Highlight the text and keep it highlighted throughout.

- Go to the 'Edit' menu.

- Choose 'Replace'.

- Type a space in the top box.

- Type a ^p in the lower box.

- Choose 'Replace all'.

- Choose 'No', the 'Close'.

- Go to the 'Table' menu.

- Choose 'Sort AZ' (or on a Mac, choose 'Sort' and then 'Sort by Field 1').

- Choose 'OK'.

A COLLAPSED POEM – AN EXAMPLE

BLAKE: 'LONDON'				
. x3	cry	hearse	marks	tear
, x7	curse	How	Marriage	Thames
; x1 : x1	does	Howl	meet	the
And	down	I	midnight	The
And	each	I	mind-forg'd	the
And	every	I	most	the
appalls	every	in	Near	the
ban	every	In	new-born	the
black'ning	every	In	of	the
Blasts	every	In	of	thro'
blights	every	in	of	thro'
blood	Every	in	of	voice
But	face	Infant's	Palace	walls
charter'd	fear	Infant's	plagues	wander
charter'd	flow	London	Runs	weakness
Chimney-sweepers	hapless	Man	sigh	where
Church	Harlots	manacles	Soldier's	with
cry	hear	mark	street	woe
cry	hear	Marks	streets	youthful

STUDYING POETRY

FIRST NOTES AND REFLECTIONS ON THE COLLAPSED POEM 'LONDON'

Repetition of 'every' foregrounded.

Use of common nouns – 'Man', 'Infants' – and nouns which highlight the job or role the people have ('Harlots', 'Soldiers' and 'Chimney-sweepers') generalises the point being made.

Sound seems important, in repetition, number of words beginning with same letter or sound (though don't know yet how they will be distributed over the poem) and in near-sounding words ('hear' to 'hearse', for example)

Rhymes – not only words which rhyme fully ('hear' and 'fear', for example) but also eye-rhymes ('hear', 'hearse', 'fear', 'weakness'). How do these words connect up in the poem?

Groups of words with very dark, disturbed, even threatening, connotations, for example:

- *'ruin', 'blights', 'blasts', 'curse', 'plagues', 'marks' (possibly if used as a noun)*
- *sadness or misery in 'cry', 'hapless', 'tear', 'fear', 'woe', 'weakness' (possibly – would rhyme with fear)*
- *darkness in 'midnight', 'black'ning'.*

How do the geographical words (some associated with specific place) fit with these impressions of threat – 'streets', 'walls', 'London', 'Thames'? Why are place names so specific when the names to do with people are very general?

Certain words are foregrounded as being rather different – 'Palace', 'Marriage', 'Church', all somehow associated with or representing institutions. All capitalised – does this mean they are at the beginning of a line? Words identifying (or marking?) people are also capitalised – is that significant?

Use of 'How' is also striking, especially as there are no question marks listed.

WILLIAM BLAKE: LONDON

I wander thro' each charter'd street,
Near where the charter'd Thames does flow.
And mark in every face I meet
Marks of weakness, marks of woe.

In every cry of every Man,
In every Infant's cry of fear,
In every voice, in every ban,
The mind-forg'd manacles I hear:

How the Chimney-sweeper's cry
Every black'ning Church appalls,
And the hapless Soldier's sigh
Runs in blood down Palace walls;

But most thro' midnight streets I hear
How the youthful Harlot's curse
Blasts the new-born Infant's tear
And blights with plagues the Marriage hearse.

LANGUAGE AND LITERATURE

Patterns and Connections, Created and Broken

At an *emagazine* Conference several years ago, the poet Michael Rosen referred to poetry as having 'secret strings' – ways in which words and phrases connect with each other.

The strings that connect words might be to do with:

- sound (alliteration, assonance, rhyme)

- word groups (words from the same lexical or semantic field – words connected by their subject matter or meaning)

- repetitions

- contrasts.

The 'strings' set up echoes and reverberations, working on the reader in relation to each other.

Looking for the connections – the strings – and for the places in a text where the string is suddenly cut, or a new set of connections is created, can be an excellent starting-point for exploring both the way texts work and the underlying ideas.

You could try identifying the secret strings in any of your set poems. The ones suggested here would be a good place to start.

— Duffy: Over

— Heaney: Churning Day

— Boland: Anorexic

— Blake: The Clod and the Pebble

— Dickinson: One need not be a chamber

— Sam-la Rose: Talk This Way

The example on page 90 shows the secret strings one reader identified in 'Magnitude' by Jacob Sam-la Rose, along with some of the questions and tentative insights prompted by doing this.

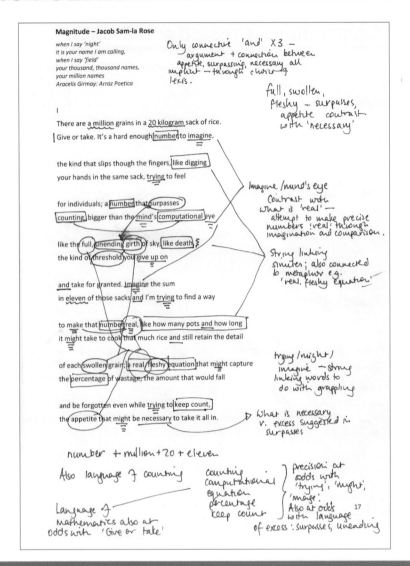

OBSERVING THE SECRET STRINGS – FIRST NOTES AND REFLECTIONS

Very specific language of numbers and mathematics (e.g. 'computation', 'equation', 'percentage') used to explore impossibility of grasping the quantity and the uncountable ('like death', 'unending'). Also set against the absolutely uncountable ('sky', 'death'). Use of language associated with people and possibly greed – 'girth', 'swollen', 'fleshy', 'appetite' to describe not people, but the inanimate and abstract.

These words ('full', 'swollen', 'fleshy') also contrast with 'necessary'.

Specific words contrast with the vast unmanageable ones and the uncountable things like 'death'.

Imagined versus real. The specific versus the vague ('give' or 'take', 'might').

Only connective that is used is 'and', three times, in the second half of the poem. The poet does not explicitly construct an argument in the usual way, through the grammar – yet it does feel like an argument. Through the language choices the reader is forced to make the connection between 'appetite', 'plenty', 'waste', 'want' and what is 'necessary', without the poet ever having to make the point explicitly.

A Tabulated Poem – Focusing on Word Classes

Stylistics involves a close focus on the language of a text, with practitioners engaging in quite a lot of preparatory work before stepping back and evaluating the significance and meaning of their discoveries.

Focusing on the way in which a poet uses words from different classes can give you a different route into exploring how the poem as a whole works, alerting you to distinctive uses of language.

> **Word classes**
>
> • Nouns, main verbs, adjectives and most adverbs can all be described as open class (or content) words.
>
> • Prepositions, conjunctions, determiners and pronouns are all closed class (or function) words.

TABULATING A POEM – AN EXAMPLE

It can be hard to do this sort of focused analysis on the poem itself. For this reason, stylistics readers often tabulate the poem, as in the example on pages 92-93 on Emily Dickinson's poem 'This World is not Conclusion.'

1. On your own or in pairs, look at the tabulated poem and share your immediate response. What leaps out at you? What do you find interesting or puzzling about Dickinson's lexical choices? What questions do they provoke?

2. Compare your ideas with other people in your class or with those summarised in the 'First Observations' box on page 94.

3. Now read and briefly talk about the poem as originally written, drawing on your analysis of the tabulated text.

TABULATING A SET TEXT POEM

1. As a class, choose two or three poems you think it would be interesting to subject to this sort of close analysis and agree which pairs of students will focus on each poem.

2. Working in your pair, tabulate the poem you have been given, as in the example.

3. Make a note of four or five findings – things you have noticed about the use of language. Then look back at the full poem and consider the significance of your findings. (You may, of course, find that in the context of the poem, your findings are not actually that meaningful or convincing.)

4. Present your data collection, findings and analysis on large sheets of paper to display on the wall or to share with the whole class.

	OPEN CLASS				CLOSED CLASS
Line	Nouns	Main verbs	Adverbs	Adjectives	Prepositions, conjunctions, determiners, pronouns
1	World Conclusion	is (not)			This
2	Species	stands	beyond		A
3	Music			Invisible	as
4	Sound			positive	But as
5		beckons baffles			It and it
6	Philosophy	(don't) know			
7	Riddle last (if means Judgement Day)		last (if means 'finally')		And through a at the
8	Sagacity	(must) go			
9	scholars	(To) guess puzzles			it
10	Men	(To) gain (have) borne			it

	OPEN CLASS				CLOSED CLASS
Line	Nouns	Main verbs	Adverbs	Adjectives	Prepositions, conjunctions, determiners, pronouns
12	Crucifixion	shown			And
13	Faith	slips			and
		laughs			and
		rallies			
14		Blushes			if
		see			any
15	twig	Plucks			at
	Evidence				a
					of
16	Vane (is this a noun or variant spelling of 'vain'?)	asks			And
					a
	way				the
17	Gesture			Much	from
	Pulpit				the
18	Hallelujahs	roll		Strong	
19	Narcotics	(cannot) still			the
	Tooth				
20	soul	nibbles			That
					at
					the

STUDYING POETRY

FIRST OBSERVATIONS ON THE WORD CLASSES IN 'THIS WORLD IS NOT CONCLUSION'

Large number of nouns, many of which are capitalised, even though they are common or abstract nouns.

Striking number of 'ands', but very few 'buts' – suggests an accumulation of points, possibly. Repetition of 'It' – what is 'It'? Ambiguity.

Unusual combinations of words from different lexical fields.

Present tense verbs, with diminutive feel to them.

How do these verbs fit with the heavyweight nouns from serious fields and abstract nouns (associated with religion, philosophy, death etc.)?

THIS WORLD IS NOT CONCLUSION

This World is not Conclusion.
A Species stands beyond –
Invisible, as Music –
But positive, as Sound –
It beckons, and it baffles –
Philosophy – don't know –
And through a Riddle, at the last –
Sagacity, must go –
To guess it, puzzles scholars –
To gain it, Men have borne
Contempt of Generations
And Crucifixion, shown –
Faith slips – and laughs, and rallies –
Blushes, if any see –
Plucks at a twig of Evidence –
And asks a Vane, the way –
Much Gesture, from the Pulpit –
Strong Hallelujahs roll –
Narcotics cannot still the Tooth
That nibbles at the soul –

LANGUAGE AND LITERATURE

Foregrounding: Repetition, Parallelism, Deviation

FOREGROUNDING AND STYLISTICS – A FEW KEY POINTS

Readers who use stylistic approaches to analyse a text are particularly interested in **foregrounding**.

Foregrounding, a term drawn from art, simply means to push something into view – into the foreground – to draw attention to it.

Poets can foreground ideas, themes or particular words through a range of poetic techniques, for example rhyme, by creating a pattern and then breaking it, unusual uses of language or metaphor (see page 112).

Three techniques associated with foregrounding particularly interest stylistics critics:

- **Repetition** (e.g. words, sounds, images).

- **Parallelism** – a particular form of repetition in which identical or similar grammatical structures (or repeated lines in a poem) produce a sense of symmetry or balance, for example 'Like father, like son'.

- **Deviation** – anything which is not expected and so comes strongly into view. A deviation can be external (the text 'breaks the rules' of the language in which it is written, or the genre, or the typical style of the particular writer) or internal (a pattern which has been set up in the particular text is broken). A deviation in a text might be at the level of:

  - **discourse** (a deviation from the expected conventions of a text type, for example a novel beginning in the middle of a story)

  - **lexis** (a word used unexpectedly or a newly-coined word, for example)

  - **grammar** (for example, inversion of the expected word order)

  - **graphology** (for example, the layout of a poem, the use of upper and lower case).

The example on the following pages on Carol Ann Duffy's poem 'Betrothal' illustrates how illuminating it can be to pay attention to these aspects of a poem.

1. Read the poem on page 96 and, as a class, share your first thoughts on the use of repetition, parallelism and deviation in the poem. What is foregrounded through these techniques?

2. Read the notes on page 97 and share your thoughts on how a focus on repetition, parallelism and deviation can help you develop an interpretation of a poem.

CAROL ANN DUFFY: BETROTHAL

I will be yours, be yours.
I'll walk on the moors
with my spade.
Make me your bride.

I will be brave, be brave.
I'll dig my own grave
and lie down.
Make me your own.

I will be good, be good.
I'll sleep in my blankets of mud
till you kneel above.
Make me your love.

I'll stay forever, forever.
I'll wade in the river,
wearing my gown of stone.
Make me the one.

I will obey, obey.
I'll float far away,
gargling my vows.
Make me your spouse.

I will say yes, say yes.
I'll sprawl in my dress
on my watery bed.
Make me be wed.

I'll wear your ring, your ring.
I'll dance and I'll sing
in the flames.
Make me your name.

I'll feel desire, desire.
I'll bloom in the fire.
I'll blush like a baby.
Make me your lady.

I'll say I do, I do.
I'll be ash in a jar, for you
to scatter my life.
Make me your wife.

A COMMENTARY ON 'BETROTHAL'

First reading of poem

This seems to me to be a poem expressing something about the desperation of love. I don't find it a comfortable poem to read. The most obvious thing to notice about the style of this poem is the repetition. What is being foregrounded by the poet's use of repetition? Is it lexical only or also grammatical? What about the form? Does Duffy deviate from the repetitive pattern that has been set up – and if so, to what effect?

Descriptive analysis

I first noticed the emphatic lexical repetition of 'I' in line 1 of each stanza.

Then I noticed that the same grammatical structure is repeated as the first line of each stanza: 'I will be'.

The repetition alerted me to the slight internal deviation in 'I will obey', 'I will say'. Use of 'I will' rather than 'I'll' is more emphatic – but might not be meaningful, just a consequence of needing to fit to a rhythm.

But noticing this deviation also highlighted further repetition in the structure of the poem – each stanza follows the same grammatical pattern.

In order to explore this more systematically, I decided to re-present the poem in a table:

I will be yours	I'll walk on the moors	with my spade.	Make me your bride.
I will be brave	I'll dig my own grave	and lie down.	Make me your own.
I will be good	I'll sleep in my blankets of mud	till you kneel above.	Make me your love.
I will obey	I'll wade in the river,	wearing my gown of stone.	Make me the one.
I'll stay forever	I'll float far away,	gargling my vows.	Make me your spouse.
I will say yes	I'll sprawl in my dress	on my watery bed.	Make me be wed.
I'll wear your ring	I'll dance and I'll sing	in the flames.	Make me your name.
I'll feel desire	I'll bloom in the fire.	I'll blush like a baby.	Make me your lady.
I'll say I do	I'll be ash in a jar, for you	to scatter my life.	Make me your wife.

This really highlighted the parallel grammatical structures dominating the poem.

Repeated syntax. Simple declarative in line 1. Middle two lines – future tense. Final line: stark imperative 'Make me'. The use of the imperative usually suggests the speaker is in a position of power, but here it sounds like a plea. It foregrounds the curious (and disturbing) nature of the promise and makes me alert to the possible ellipsis in each stanza. Is the word 'if' implied, as in 'I will do this if you do this'? Is it a bargain?

Deviation from 'Make me your' foregrounds 'Make me be wed' – almost makes it seem as though the state of being wed is more important than the relationship.

Stanza 9 – first time 'for you' – explicit mention of what has been unspoken in the earlier stanzas.

Form: rhyme (which sometimes feels a bit trite) rather at odds with the content. Only dawns on you slowly how sinister the content is because of the easy perfect rhymes. But the deviations are also interesting – 'spade'/'bride' – slant rhyme that feels uncomfortable, alerting me early on to the sinister mood.

STUDYING POETRY

ANALYSING A POEM FOCUSING ON REPETITION, PARALLELISM AND DEVIATION

The following poems all use repetition, parallelism and deviation in ways which are particularly striking and interesting.

    — Duffy: Write

    — Boland: Degas's Laundresses

    — Heaney: Strange Fruit

    — Sam-la Rose: A Spell For Forgetting a Father

    — Dickinson: The Soul selects her own Society —

    — Blake: London

3. Read the poem by your set poet. In pairs, work through each of the following stages, as in the example on 'Betrothal':

- First response to the poem and the way it is written (i.e. what strikes you? Is anything immediately foregrounded?).

- Descriptive analysis – noticing the use of repetition, parallelism and deviation. (Depending on the poem, this might involve you in tabulating the poem or in pulling out particular phrases/lines and presenting them as a list.)

- Interpretative analysis, drawing on what you have noticed about the way repetition, parallelism and deviation are used. Can you use your discoveries to further your analysis?

A Focus on Voice – a Special Form of Foregrounding

1. Read the following quotations about voice in poetry.

> For a poet, the struggle from the beginning is to actually find the confidence and authority of your own voice, not only in terms of historical style but how to get to the point where what you're writing on the page is, metrically and in terms of the tone, the exact voice in which you speak.
>
> **Derek Walcott, BBC Radio Ulster**

> Poetry is closer to speech than prose... Speech involves strategies that are inappropriate to prose but are essential to poetry. Hesitations, repetitions, hints, refrains.
>
> **Germaine Greer, *The Guardian*, 2003**

> Poetry is a dialect of the language we speak.
>
> **Dave Smith, *Local Assays*, 1985**

> Good poets reinvent the language, taking the given of ordinary speech and pushing it beyond itself.
>
> **Jay Parini, *Some Necessary Angels*, 1997**

> Poetry is... speech in which the words come in an order which could not be changed without ruining the verity and power of the whole.
>
> **Robert Nye, *Acumen*, 2006**

As the quotations suggest, voice is a key aspect of any poem. But voice is also a concept that's quite complex, encompassing several different ideas when applied to poetry:

- the use of first person ('I'/'we'), second person ('you') or third person ('he'/'she'/ 'they') – a definition you may be familiar with from your study of narrative texts

- a connection to tone or manner, for example reflective or downbeat

- the creation of a particular voice through particular lexical or grammatical choices

- a connection to the spoken voice, through its roots in oral literature and through its performance – whether by readers reciting the poem out loud or silently 'in the head' or by the poet.

STUDYING POETRY

The creation of the voice can be one of the ways in which the poet draws attention to, or foregrounds, a particular aspect of the poem. Features that might be invisible in prose or drama demand our attention in poetry. For example, if a poet uses a colloquialism or a cliché or idiomatic expression more typical of spoken language, it is foregrounded. It prompts us to ask why it has been included: what contribution is it making to the meaning of the poem? What is its effect on the reader?

The extracts on pages 101-102 are all taken from the poems set for this component.

2. In pairs, explore the extracts focusing on the different ways in which you might talk about voice in this extract, then share your thoughts as a class.

QUESTIONS TO CONSIDER WHEN EXPLORING VOICE IN POETRY

- Whose voice is it? Is it:

  » the persona of the poet, present in the poem as 'I'

  » a more distant poetic voice which does not make its presence felt in the poem

  » the poet as character, for example, the storyteller in a narrative poem or ballad

  » a character explicitly identified, as in a dramatic monologue? More than one character?

- The tone of voice and how this is created through the linguistic and poetic features.

- How close is the voice to the spoken voice? (Does it draw on the lexis or rhythms of the spoken voice, for example? If so, what is the effect of drawing on these features within the formal constraints of a poem?)

- Are there any other voices in the poem (for example, dialogue, quotation from or allusions to other texts, including poems, well-known phrases and so on)?

- In what ways does the poet use the voice to foreground particular aspects of the poem?

BLAKE: THE CHIMNEY SWEEPER

When my mother died I was very young.

And my father sold me while yet my tongue

Could scarcely cry "weep! 'weep!

               'weep!' 'weep!'

So your chimneys I sweep & in soot I sleep.

BLAKE: INTRODUCTION

Hear the voice of the Bard!

Who Present, Past & Future sees,

Whose ears have heard

The Holy Word

That walk'd among the ancient trees,

BOLAND: DEGAS'S LAUNDRESSES

Wait. There behind you.

A man. There behind you.

Whatever you do don't turn.

Why is he watching you?

Whatever you do don't turn.

Whatever you do don't turn.

BOLAND: THE NEW PASTORAL

I am a lost, last inhabitant –

displaced person

in a pastoral chaos.

All day I listen to

the loud distress, the switch and tick of

               new herds.

HEANEY: FUNERAL RITES

Now as news comes in

of each neighbourly murder

we pine for ceremony,

customary rhythms:

the temperate footsteps

of a cortège, winding past

each blinded home.

I would restore

HEANEY: PUNISHMENT

I can see her drowned

body in the bog,

the weighing stone,

the floating rods and boughs.

STUDYING POETRY

DUFFY: WINTERING

All day, slow funerals have ploughed the rain.

We've done again

that trick we have of turning love to pain.

DUFFY: ANSWER

If you were made of air, if you were air,

if you were made of water, if you were water,

if you were made of fire, if you were fire,

if you were made of stone, if you were stone,

or if you were none of these, but really death,

the answer is yes, yes.

SAM-LA ROSE: SONG FOR A SPENT 100W BULB

Too bright to live long,
    too costly, my mother feared
your appetite, guzzling the mains,
    hung from the ceiling, little sun
I rhymed into, close as I could stand,
    imagining the bulbed head of a mic,

SAM-LA ROSE: TALK THIS WAY

Dear boys on road,
                dear girls on bus
top decks, dear hip-hop, dear love letters
pressed deep into vinyl platters, dear Americas,
Jamaica and East End –
                dear Queen's best
cool and clipped as seams pressed sharp
in spite of noon day sun high in a Guyanese sky,

DICKINSON: BECAUSE I COULD NOT STOP FOR DEATH

Because I could not stop for Death –

He kindly stopped for me –

The Carriage held but just Ourselves –

And Immortality.

DICKINSON: GOING TO HEAVEN!

Perhaps you're going too!

Who knows?

If you should get there first

Save just a little space for me

Close to the two I lost –

VOICE IN YOUR SET TEXT

The poets set for this specification span a significant period of time (from the late 18th to the 21st centuries) and a range of traditions, including poetry written for the page, performance poetry and poems which sit somewhere between the two.

The questions in the box on page 100 can all be used to help you explore the way your set poet creates and uses voice. Use these as you work through the following activity.

1. Choose one of the poems in your collection, either at random or because something about it appeals to you.

2. Read the poem out loud, paying attention to the use of sound and particularly the creation of voice.

3. Use the questions in the box to analyse in more detail what type of voice it is, the way it is created and how it contributes to the meaning of the poem.

4. Skim through the rest of the poems in your collection, looking for short quotations where you think the voice is particularly interesting or important, or where it contrasts with the poem you have been focusing on, either because of the way it has been created or because of its function in the poem. Are there any poems where the voice is foregrounded, made a significant part of the meaning, or conversely, where it seems of minimal importance?

5. Is there a consistent voice across the poems you are studying, or do you notice variations? Where there is variation, is it still possible to identify something characteristic or distinctive about the voice?

6. On an A3 sheet of paper, create a representation of voice in the poems you are studying. You could include:

   - annotations, showing your ideas in response to the questions

   - short quotations from your poems, ranging across the collection

   - ideas about voice in the poems – characteristic features, deviations from this, ways in which the voice is foregrounded.

A Focus on Rhyme –
a Special Form of Pattern-making and Breaking

1. As a class, listen to the short texts below being read out loud, then talk about the ways in which they use language and create effects.

Beanz Meanz Heinz

I scream,
You scream
We all scream for ice-cream!

One potato, two potato, three potato, four,
Five potato, six potato, seven potato, more?

Easy-peasy lemon squeezy

An apple a day keeps the doctor away
A Mars a day helps you work, rest and play.

See you later, alligator.
In a while, crocodile.

Clunk click every trip.

Rhyme, a particular form of pattern-making and breaking, of creating connections across a poem, is described here by the poet Ruth Padel.

Rhyme satisfies the ear (...) It satisfies our understanding because it is a way of getting words to greet each other. Poets are conscious of it all the time. Half-rhyme, consonant rhyme, vowel-rhyme; vowels echoing from inside one line and across to another and even across stanzas. And then, of course, there is end-rhyme – which (...) many poets use; always in combination with other sorts of rhyme.

Ruth Padel: The Poem and the Journey

The different types of rhyme referenced here are defined in the box on page 105.

2. Can you identify any of these different rhymes in the short rhymes and advertising slogans opposite?

The extracts on pages 106 and 107 are taken from individual poems by the six set text poets.

3. Look at, and listen to, all six extracts. Talk about how rhyme is used and to what effect, drawing on the rhyming terms and definitions, where you find it helpful, either to identify the rhyme or describe what the poet is doing.

4. Range across the collection of poems you are studying and choose a poem where you think rhyme is being used in an interesting way. Write a short analysis of the poem, focusing on the poet's use of rhyme.

TYPES OF RHYME

End-rhyme

• Rhyme at the end of the line

Internal rhyme

• Rhyme within the line

Masculine rhyme

• Stress on the final syllable of the words (e.g. adv**ice**/ent**ice**)

Feminine rhyme

• Stress on the penultimate syllable of the words (e.g. pi**cky**/tri**cky**)

Half-rhyme (or slant rhyme)

• Matching final consonants but not vowels (e.g. be**nt**/a**nt** or lo**ve**/ha**ve**)

Consonance

• Matching consonants in neighbouring words but, unlike alliteration, not at the start of the words (e.g. sce**nt**ed/hau**nt**s/gra**nt**ing)

Assonance (or vowel rhyme)

• Matching vowel sounds in neighbouring words (e.g. sh**a**ke/h**a**te, w**i**de/s**i**gh)

Eye-rhyme

• Words that look as if they should rhyme but are pronounced differently (e.g. s**aid**/m**aid**, d**ive**/g**ive**)

STUDYING POETRY

EXTRACTS FROM POEMS ACROSS THE COLLECTION

WILLIAM BLAKE: THE HUMAN ABSTRACT

Pity would be no more

If we did not make somebody Poor;

And Mercy no more could be

If all were as happy as we;

And mutual fear brings peace,

Till the selfish loves increase.

Then Cruelty knits a snare

And spreads his baits with care.

EAVAN BOLAND: THE FAMINE ROAD

'It has gone better than we expected, Lord

Trevelyan, sedition, idleness, cured

in one; from parish to parish, field to field,

the wretches work till they are quite worn,

then fester by their work; we march the corn

to the ships in peace; this Tuesday I saw bones

out of my carriage window, your servant Jones.'

SEAMUS HEANEY: MYCENAE OUTLOOK

Some people wept, and not for sorrow – joy

That the king had armed and upped and sailed for Troy,

But inside me like struck sound in a gong

That killing-fest, the life-warp and world-wrong

It brought to pass, still augured and endured.

I'd dream of blood in bright webs in a ford,

Of bodies raining down like tattered meat

On top of me asleep – and me the lookout

The queen's command had posted and forgotten,

The blind spot her farsightedness relied on.

STUDYING POETRY

JACOB SAM-LA ROSE: PLUMMETING

he works it, ear accustomed to the tune

of hard play: left, right, launch-step, discipline like a lump

of lead in his pocket he can melt

into gold. Keeps on until the sky turns plum,

sporting a corona of sweat like a plume

of peacock's feathers, stoking the fire in each lung

CAROL ANN DUFFY: ELEGY

Love loved you best; lit you

with a flame, like talent, under your skin; let you

move through your days and nights, blessed in your flesh,

blood, hair, as though they were lovely garments

you wore to pleasure the air. Who'll guess, if they read

your stone, or press their thumbs to the scars

of your dates, that were I alive, I would lie on the grass

above your bones till I mirrored your pose, your infinite grace?

EMILY DICKINSON: IT WAS NOT DEATH

It was not Death, for I stood up,

And all the Dead, lie down –

It was not Night, for all the Bells

Put out their Tongues, for Noon.

It was not Frost, for on my Flesh

I felt Siroccos – crawl –

Nor Fire – for just my Marble feet

Could keep a Chancel, cool –

A Focus on Rhythm – a Special Form of Repetition & Deviation

1. Read aloud the short extracts below and share your first response to the sound of them, thinking especially about the rhythm (the underlying musical beat).

2. Discuss anything that immediately strikes you about different uses of rhythm in the extracts using adjectives to describe them (e.g. halting, abrupt, languid, jaunty). Don't worry about labelling the rhythms at this stage. Later activities will give you ways of analysing and marking different rhythmic patterns.

WILLIAM BLAKE: THE GARDEN OF LOVE

I went to the Garden of Love,

And saw what I never had seen:

A chapel was built in the midst,

Where I used to play on the green.

And the gates of this Chapel were shut,

And 'Thou shalt not' writ over the door;

EAVAN BOLAND: DEGAS'S LAUNDRESSES

Wait. There behind you.

A man. There behind you.

Whatever you do don't turn.

Why is he watching you?

Whatever you do don't turn.

Whatever you do don't turn.

SEAMUS HEANEY: A KITE FOR MICHAEL AND CHRISTOPHER

Before the kite plunges down into the wood

and this line goes useless

take in your two hands, boys, and feel

the strumming, rooted, long-tailed pull of grief.

You were born fit for it.

Stand here in front of me

and take the strain.

CAROL ANN DUFFY: HOUR

Time slows, for here
we are millionaires, backhanding the night

so nothing dark will end our shining hour,
no jewel hold a candle to the cuckoo spit
hung from the blade of grass at your ear,
no chandelier or spotlight see you better lit

than here. Now. Time hates love, wants love poor,
but love spins gold, gold, gold from straw.

EMILY DICKINSON: THERE'S A CERTAIN SLANT OF LIGHT

There's a certain Slant of light,
Winter Afternoons –
That oppresses, like the Heft
Of Cathedral Tunes –

Heavenly Hurt, it gives us –
We can find no scar,
But internal difference,
Where the Meanings, are –

JACOB SAM-LA ROSE: AFTER LAZERDROME, MCDONALDS, PECKAM RYE

this is the year one of the guys says music is the one thing
that won't ever let him down   that music is his religion

the year we're stopped and searched because we
fit the description   the year jungle music passes
out of fashion   stripped down

to naked beat and bass   and we club together   to dance
alone   in the dark   let the music play us   meat and bone

STUDYING POETRY

IDENTIFYING AND DESCRIBING RHYTHM

Rhythm is one of the clearest forms of pattern-making (and pattern-breaking) in a poem. In English verse rhythm is created through the arrangement or patterning of stressed and unstressed syllables in each line. The four main ways in which the stressed and unstressed syllables can be organised are:

- Anapest: duh-duh-DUH, as in 'but of **course**!'

- Dactyl: DUH-duh-duh, as in '**hon**estly'

- Iamb: duh-DUH, as in 'colla**pse**'

- Trochee: DUH-duh, as in '**pi**zza'.

Each of these rhythmical units is known as a 'foot'.

A line of poetry with three metrical feet in it is known as trimeter. Four feet is a tetrameter, five pentameter and six hexameter.

The rhythm of the poem helps to create the meaning and tone of the poem, for example, serious and certain or mocking and challenging.

1. Here are some of the ways in which a poet could use rhythm to create meaning and impact. Can you think of any others?

- Regular rhythm reflecting the content (e.g. a very regular rhythm in a poem about the certainty of religious faith).

- A rhythmic pattern which seems at odds with the content (e.g. a very regular rhythm in a poem relating anxiety and confusion).

- Deviation from the underlying rhythm to emphasise a particular word (and the idea it conveys).

- Rhythm as a key element of a particular form of poem (e.g. ballad or a sonnet) and the deviation from it.

- The poet uses the rhythm – the use of repeated patterns and deviation from them – to foreground key ideas.

The poet and teacher Mary Oliver comments on the importance of rhythm in her book *The Poetry Handbook*.

2. Read her comments opposite and, as a class, share anything you find striking in what she says about rhythm in poetry.

3. Go back to the extracts and explore whether the poems use variations in the rhythm and to what effect, using the list of ways poets use rhythm above.

LANGUAGE AND LITERATURE

Rhythm underlies everything... Of course when I speak of rhythm I don't mean a rhythm so strict or metronomic that it merely repeats itself exactly. Remember language is a living material, full of shadow and sudden moments of up-leap and endless nuance. Nothing with language, including rhythmic patterns, should be or can be entirely exact and repetitious, nor would we like it if it were... Lines of good poetry are apt to be a little irregular... A prevailing sense of rhythm is necessary, but some variation enhances the very strength of the pattern... Within the poem, irregularities may occur for the sake of variation, they may also occur because of stresses required by the words themselves, for accuracy, for emphasis etc.

Every poem has a basic measure, and a continual counterpoint of differences playing against that measure. Poems that do not offer such variations quickly become boring. The gift of words – their acute and utter wakefulness – is drowned in a rhythm that is too regular, and the poem becomes, instead of musical, a dull and forgettable muttering.

Mary Oliver: The Poetry Handbook

A CREATIVE WRITING EXPERIMENT

1. Have a go at writing a short poem (about four or five lines) on a topic that springs quickly to mind (e.g. what you had for breakfast) with a broadly regular rhythm.

2. Now take the same poem and experiment with deviating significantly from the rhythm, in just one place each time. What effects can you create?

Here is one short example to show you the kind of experiment you might do.

EXAMPLE 1	EXAMPLE 2
Onwards to school I walked, onwards to school, *Up to the class I went, up to the room,* *Onto the seat I sat, up at the front.*	*I walked onwards to school, to school* *I went up to the class, to the room,* *I sat on the seat, up at the front.*

EXPLORING YOUR SET POEMS

1. Browse through the collection you are studying. Choose one poem to explore the way in which the rhythm is used by the poet to create meaning and impact, whether by reflecting or working against the content.

2. Use everything you have learned about rhythm to help you analyse how it works.

A Focus on Metaphor – a Special Form of Deviation

The greatest thing by far is to be a master of metaphor.

Aristotle: *De Poetica*, 322 B.C.

When we resort to metaphor, we contrive to talk about two things at once; two different and disparate subject matters are mingled to rich and unpredictable effect.

Stanford Encylopedia of Philosophy (online)

Figurative language – language used in non-literal ways – is central to poetry. Metaphor, in which one thing is described in terms of another without attention being drawn to the comparison, is particularly important.

Metaphor breaks the rules. It says that one thing is something it is not. It is a form of deviation we all engage in every day, as the examples below suggest.

The students pointed out the weak spot in her argument.

Poor boy – he's lost his way.

This exam will be the death of me.

He broke my heart.

This is a big day for Britain.

She is the light of his life.

This essay is an uphill struggle.

She sliced through his protests.

After the exams, life will be a bed of roses.

I've made leaps and bounds in my understanding of physics since I grasped a few key concepts.

1. In pairs, talk about what is going on in terms of language use in the examples on page 112. Can you identify the metaphor in each case?

You might find it helpful to use the terms **tenor** and **vehicle**. The 'tenor' is the literal term and the 'vehicle' is the figurative term applied to it. The examples below show you these terms in practice:

> **All the world's a stage: world = tenor; stage = vehicle**

> **The road was a ribbon of moonlight: road = tenor; ribbon – vehicle**

We employ metaphors in order to communicate, to get across our meaning to another person. On the whole, the metaphors we use in everyday discourse are conventional or dead metaphors: those which have become a normal part of language so that we're no longer surprised by the implicit point of comparison – and may not even recognise that a metaphor has been used. Writers, and perhaps especially poets, use metaphors creatively, consciously trying to create a particular effect. Once again, the poet is going beyond the simple communication of meaning. For example, a poet might use a metaphor to make the familiar strange, to foreground or draw attention to it. It's a delicate balance – push it too far and rather than providing fresh insights or improving understanding, the reader is left bewildered.

The extracts on page 114 are all taken from the poems set for this specification.

2. In pairs, read the extracts and explore the metaphors. Don't worry about pinning down exactly what is being compared – explore your response, the way in which the metaphor is created (e.g. in the verbs or adjectives or nouns) and speculate about the possible meanings the poet is seeking to create.

3. Share your explorations as a class.

4. Focus now only on the extracts from your set poet. Skim through your collection until you find the two that the extracts are taken from. Read the two poems and choose one to work on. Analyse the metaphor you have been looking at in context, then extend your discussion to look at the way metaphor is used in the poem as a whole. What is foregrounded? How does the metaphor work with the other poetic and linguistic techniques?

5. On your own, range across the poems in your collection and choose one where you think metaphor is being used to create meaning and effect in particularly interesting ways.

6. Prepare either a short oral presentation (four to five minutes) to give to the class or a visual/written presentation to share on the wall.

METAPHOR MINI-QUOTATIONS

FROM SEAMUS HEANEY

- My tongue was a filling estuary,

- The wintry haw is burning out of season,

FROM WILLIAM BLAKE

- O what a multitude they seem'd, these flowers of London town!

- And binding with briars my joys & desires.

FROM EAVAN BOLAND

- They scorch in my self-denials

- your love/Is a closed circuit like your glove

FROM EMILY DICKINSON

- I felt a Funeral, in my Brain,

- This is the Hour of Lead

FROM JACOB SAM-LA ROSE

- We're taught to shape mouths to tame
  voices, taught chorus and harmony

- The light pollution blindfolds every star.

FROM CAROL ANN DUFFY

- The evening sky/worships the ground,

- Your mouth is snow now on my lips, cool, intimate, first kiss

A Stylistics Sequence

FIRST IMPRESSIONS, DESCRIPTIVE ANALYSIS, INTERPRETATION

You have now worked through a number of activities which draw on the practices of stylistics, paying particular attention to what is foregrounded through different forms of repetition and pattern-making, deviation and pattern-breaking.

The sequence outlined on these pages takes you through a stylistics analysis in a more systematic way.

• Work through the different stages to analyse a poem from your set text:

— Duffy: Hour

— Heaney: Anahorish

— Boland: Anorexic

— Dickinson: It was not Death

— Blake: Holy Thursday

— Sam-la Rose: Spell for my Father

STAGE 1: READING THE TEXT AND A FIRST INTERPRETATION

• Begin by reading the poem once or twice and making a note of your first thoughts.

STAGE 2: DATA COLLECTION AND AN INITIAL FOCUS ON WORD CLASSES

• Subject the text to a more objective linguistic analysis, drawing on some of the emphases suggested below.

• Organise your text into a table like the one shown here. Each line of the table represents a sentence (or line) of the text, allowing you to see which of types words feature in (and perhaps dominate) different sections.

	OPEN CLASS				CLOSED CLASS
Line	Nouns	Main Verbs	Adverbs	Adjectives	Prepositions, conjunctions, determiners, pronouns
1.					
2.					

EMC LANGUAGE AND LITERATURE

STAGE 3: A CLOSER LOOK AT OPEN CLASS WORDS

- As you look more closely at the different word classes, make a note of your findings, then reflect on the possible significance of what you have observed. You will need to use the poem as originally written and as organised into the table.

A closer focus on nouns (open class)

• Look again at the nouns listed in your table. Is there anything particularly interesting about them, for instance:

  - any lexical groupings

  - concrete or abstract nouns

  - any unusual words which stand out from the rest

  - particular use of monosyllabic or polysyllabic words?

A closer focus on the verbs (open class)

• Look again at the verbs. Is there anything interesting about them, for example:

  - tense

  - whether the verbs are active or passive

  - the mood of the verb:

    - **declarative** (declares something to be the case)

    - **interrogative** (asks a question)

    - **imperative** (expresses commands, advises, prohibits)

    - **conditional** or **modal** (expresses possibility or necessity, e.g. 'We must go')?

A closer focus on the adjectives and adverbs (open class)

• Look again at the adjectives and adverbs. Is there anything interesting about:

  - the number and type of adverbs and adjectives

  - how the adverbs and adjectives are used?

A focus on the function (or closed class) words

• Is there anything interesting to note about the use of the closed class (or function) words?

LANGUAGE AND LITERATURE EMC

STAGE 4: REPETITION, PARALLELISM, DEVIATIONS

- As you look more closely at the repetition, parallelism and deviation, make a note of your findings, then reflect on the possible significance of what you have observed.

Repetition

- Is there repetition in the text?

- What is foregrounded as a result of this repetition?

Parallelism

- Are there any instances of parallelism in the text?

- If so, what is foregrounded or connected as a result of the parallelism?

Linguistic deviation

- Are there any deviations from the expected use of language?

- What is foregrounded as a result of this deviation?

STAGE 5: USING YOUR INSIGHTS TO DEVELOP AN INTERPRETATION

- After completing a detailed linguistic analysis, step back and consider the insights you have gained into the poem. How could you use these insights to develop your interpretation of the poem, its themes and possible meanings, particularly as foregrounded in the exam question?

SUMMING UP WHAT YOU HAVE LEARNED FROM THIS APPROACH

- As a class, reflect back on this sequence of activities.

- Talk about what difference it has made to your understanding of poetry and how it works.

EMBEDDING THIS APPROACH

- When you work on your set text poems, you will not always want to do such a detailed analysis or follow such a thorough approach. However, having done it once, it should give you some of the tools of analysis that you can apply more generally, allowing you to look out for the way words are used and the effects of repetition, parallelism and deviation.

Using Contexts Effectively

As part of your work on your poetry set text, whether for the AS or the A Level qualification, you are expected to take into account contextual information. The exam questions ask you to consider relevant contextual factors at AS and significant literary or other relevant contexts at A Level.

This can be tricky. The context in which a text was written – the author's life, the social and historical situation – can all be fascinating and can be illuminating of the text, opening up new and exciting interpretative possibilities. But contextual information can also be unhelpful, getting in the way of analysing the poem, having little to do with the poem or the question you've been asked. Knowing something about the historical period in which Blake wrote might help you understand *Songs of Innocence and Experience*; beginning an essay with an account of the times in which Blake lived will not help you write an effective, engaged answer to the question. The key to using context well is in the question – **relevant** and **significant**.

In this quotation from an *emagazine* article, Professor Peter Barry helpfully distinguishes between adjacent (or near) and distant context:

> **If we emphasise context too exclusively then we will soon be doing History rather than English, in all but name. Knowing about the context isn't much use unless it illuminates the poem. So can we suggest any guidelines which will help us to keep some sense of proportion about context?**
>
> **We can do so if we distinguish between 'adjacent context' and 'remote context'. The former is explicit in some way in the text – it's mentioned or alluded to – indeed, we could say that it's the kind of context which is really content. Remote context, on the other hand has no such unambiguous warrant in the text.**

The distant or remote context may be interesting and might help you as you explore the poems. But it is **adjacent context** which is going to be most relevant or significant when you're engaged in making sense of a poem and developing an interpretation. Even then you need to be wary. Ask yourself whether the contextual information helps you answer the particular question on these poems? If so, how could you weave the contextual information into your analysis, without it seeming like a clunky 'add on'?

The examples opposite (one on each of the set poets) show you the sort of reflecting on context you might do.

CAROL ANN DUFFY

For a poem like 'You' in Duffy's collection 'Rapture', the relevant and significant context might be the immediate one of the collection in which this is the first poem, the generic one of the sonnet and the literary context – the long tradition of love poems addressed to the beloved.

WILLIAM BLAKE

For a poem like Blake's 'Garden of Love', the immediate context of the collection 'shewing two sides of the human condition' might be illuminating, as might the knowledge that Blake has used a rhythm often used for hymns but here has used it to criticise the state religion, rather than offer comfort.

SEAMUS HEANEY

To understand 'Churning' you might need a bit of factual contextual information on what 'churning' is – you would not then need to include a lecture on churning in an answer. You could analyse 'Mycennae Lookout' without the contextual information of the Trojan War and the earlier literary versions of this story, but what difference would it make to have this knowledge as a foil for exploring what Heaney has chosen to do with the story?

EMILY DICKINSON

Knowing that Emily Dickinson was steeped in the conventional religious verses of English poets such as Isaac Watts, the Protestant hymnals and the language of the Bible is useful because her poetry both embodies the influence of these religious texts and her distance from them. Slant rhymes, fragmentary and disrupted syntax and the contexts in which she uses religious imagery might suggest a subversive relationship with the orthodox religion of her childhood.

JACOB SAM-LA ROSE

An understanding of the linguistic context of Jacob Sam-la Rose's work might be relevant and significant, as might the fact that these are poems created for performance as well as for the page, as it foregrounds the importance of sound and the poet's use of, and deviation from, the rhythms of the spoken voice.

EAVAN BOLAND

Knowing that Boland is an Irish poet writing during and in the immediate aftermath of the 'Troubles' illuminates the way in which she juxtaposes the political and domestic in her poems, sometimes foregrounding the political, but often alluding to it indirectly and in elliptical ways.

Using Contextual Information to Illuminate any Poem

Contextual information might be:

- the context of the whole work

- the literary or generic context

- the social or historical context

- the context of reception (the reader's or listener's response)

- the biographical context.

The approach outlined here can help you evaluate the significance of contextual information for any poem.

- Read the poem and respond.

- Think about any contextual information you've absorbed from general knowledge or been taught or found out for yourself. For each bit of contextual information, evaluate:

  - what difference it makes to your understanding and analysis of this poem to have this bit of contextual information? For example:

    - Does it alter your understanding of the poem?

    - Does it open up new insights into the poem?

  - how you can use this piece of information to develop your analysis, making it richer and more interesting for your reader.

- Choose the one piece of contextual information that you think is most illuminating of the poem. Practise using this contextual nugget in writing.

You can try out this approach on Eavan Boland's poem 'The Famine Road', below.

AN EXAMPLE – THE FAMINE ROAD BY EAVAN BOLAND

The approach is exemplified here, in relation to Eavan Boland's 'The Famine Road'. Regardless of which poet you are studying, work through the activity in order to develop your ability to use contextual information to sharpen your analysis of a poem.

1. Read the poem on page 121 and the 10 bits of contextual information on page 122. Talk about whether or not the contextual information is useful to you. Try to tease out the difference between contextual information which helps you understand the poem and that which allows you to develop your interpretation further.

2. Give each piece of context a rating from '5' (really significant and illuminating) to '0' (not relevant to, or illuminating of, the poem).

3. Choose the one piece of context you think is most significant of the poem. Write two or three sentences about the poem, using this context to develop your analysis. Remember, you are not trying to teach your reader about the context nor do you need to explain why you are using it.

EAVAN BOLAND: THE FAMINE ROAD

'Idle as trout in light Colonel Jones
these Irish, give them no coins at all; their bones
need toil, their characters no less.' Trevelyan's
seal blooded the deal table. The Relief
Committee deliberated: 'Might it be safe,
Colonel, to give them roads, roads to force
from nowhere, going nowhere of course?'

'one out of every ten and then
another third of those again
women – in a case like yours.'

Sick, directionless they worked; fork, stick
were iron years away; after all could
they not blood their knuckles on rock, suck
April hailstones for water and for food?
Why for that, cunning as housewives, each eyed –
as if at a corner butcher – the other's buttock.

'anything may have caused it, spores
a childhood accident; one sees
day after day these mysteries.'

Dusk: they will work tomorrow without him.
They know it and walk clear; he has become
a typhoid pariah, his blood tainted, although
he shares it with some there. No more than snow
attends its own flakes where they settle
and melt, will they pray by his death rattle.

'You never will, never you know
but take it well woman, grow
your garden, keep house, good-bye.'

'It has gone better than we expected, Lord
Trevelyan, sedition, idleness, cured
in one; from parish to parish, field to field;
the wretches work till they are quite worn,
then fester by their work; we march the corn
to the ships in peace; this Tuesday I saw bones
out of my carriage window, your servant Jones.'

'Barren, never to know the load
of his child in you, what is your body
now if not a famine road?'

STUDYING POETRY

CONTEXTUAL INFORMATION	USEFUL? NOT USEFUL? (E.g. for understanding the poem? For furthering the analysis)
During the 1840s, the starving Irish were forced to construct 'Relief Roads' in return for wages. These roads led nowhere and had no purpose other than to occupy the starving people. They are often known as Famine Roads or Green Roads.	
The immediate cause of the famine was the failure of the potato harvest – a Europe-wide problem. The effect was exacerbated in Ireland by absentee English landlords, political decisions (e.g. not to repeal the Corn Laws) and the dependency of the population on this one crop.	
Charles Trevelyan, who oversaw Irish relief during the Famine, wrote anonymously in the *Edinburgh Review* that the potato famine was an act of God.	
The Book of Ezekiel in the Bible: 'a 3rd part of you shall die of pestilence and be consumed with famine'; 'fathers shall eat their sons in your midst and sons shall eat their fathers'.	
In 1729, Jonathan Swift, an Anglo-Irish clergyman wrote *A Modest Proposal,* a satire in which it was suggested the Irish eat their children.	
Colonel Jones was the Chairman of the Irish Board of Works.	
Throughout her poetry, for example in 'Naoise at 4' and 'Object Lessons' Boland makes links between the domestic experience of a woman and the political situation.	
Eavan Boland has said: 'It's the century of the famine. And I see that as a watershed. A powerful once and for all disruption of any kind of heroic history. The most wrenching part of the story of the Famine is how utterly defenceless people were in the face of a disaster they couldn't control.... Looking at the 19th century was the first time I began to think that writing could add a silence to a work rather than break it. I was interested in turning a light on the silences and erasers that we learn to tolerate in the name of history.'	
Starvation during the famine (known as 'The Great Hunger') in the 1840s led to infertility and a fall in the birth rate.	
Eavan Boland, like other contemporary Irish writers such as Brian Friel, is interested in the idea of geographical mapping and the recording of places. Mapping of the land by the English was an act of colonisation and Boland wants to reclaim territory that has been overlooked or forgotten in this process.	
The chorus – a commentary on the main poem or drama – has a long history stretching back to Greek drama.	

A Close Focus on a Single Poem

In your initial exploratory work on what makes poetry distinctive as a genre, you began to think about the key poetic and linguistic features it might be useful to explore when analysing a poem.

The table below draws together some of these main areas.

KEY POETIC AND LINGUISTIC FEATURES	
• Look on the page	• Syntax and relationship to lineation
• Verse form	• Use of rhyme
• Rhythm	• Structure and development – shifts in thought organisation into lines, stanzas, sentences, groups of words, beginning, ending
• Use of sound/phonology (e.g. alliteration, assonance, consonance, repeated and contrasting sounds)	• Repetition and parallelism
• Voice	• Patterns and pattern-breaking
• Lexis	• Verbs, moods and tenses
• Symbols and images	• Context of poet's use of the genre
• Oppositions	

One of the most significant things you will learn as you progress through your Language and Literature A Level is the importance of evaluating which poetic and linguistic features are most relevant to, or likely to prove most interesting, when exploring the work of a particular poet, or a particular poem. The poetic and linguistic features above are all things it might be interesting to explore in a poem. But which are most important in the poems you are studying?

Making Judgements about What Is Significant

1. As a class, read the poem by Seamus Heaney on page 124 and talk about which of the above features you think it would be most interesting to focus on in your analysis.

2. Compare your choices with those suggested in the box which follows. If you disagree with the choices and reasons given here, take a few minutes to consider why there might be a difference of opinion and whether the different choices are equally valid.

SEAMUS HEANEY: ANAHORISH

My 'place of clear water',
the first hill in the world
where springs washed into
the shiny grass

and darkened cobbles
in the bed of the lane.
Anahorish, soft gradient
of consonant, vowel-meadow,

after-image of lamps
swung through the yards
on winter evenings.
With pails and barrows

those mound-dwellers
go waist-deep in mist
to break the light ice
at wells and dunghills.

NOTES ON THE POETIC AND LINGUISTIC TECHNIQUES IN HEANEY'S 'ANAHORISH'

Phonology: Explicit reference to sound; repetition of 's' and 'w' sounds and open vowels – creating in the poem the 'soft gradient of consonants' and 'vowel-meadow' of 'Anahorish'.

Lexis: Word groups creating physical place, memory (and recreation in writing?) – contrasts in these; neologisms, especially compound words. The compound words contribute to the distinctive lilting rhythm of the poem and contextualise it within a particular cultural history and literary tradition (allusions to Celtic languages).

Syntax and verbs: Parallelism with unusual syntax, with verb delayed; only three finite verbs in whole poem (and ellipsis in the second sentence) – action is not the point, foregrounds an evocation of place, a visual memory, an 'after-image'. Three sentences structure the poem across the four stanzas: place, name, occupants.

Imagery and symbolism: First hill, water/springs washing clean; 'after-image' of the lamps – what is left in the mind's eye; symbolic significance of the place as a whole?

Rhyme: Subtle internal rhyme, setting up patterns of connectedness across the poem, along with repetition of sounds.

*Context of Heaney's work: Poems creating sense of place, movement between physical place, remembered and imagined place, condensed use of language, elliptical. **Cultural/literary context:** Anglo-Saxon poetry – kennings and compound words; the use of 'mound-dwellers' to describe the inhabitants creates a sense of this place as otherworldly, ethereal and belonging to an earlier time.*

A POEM FROM YOUR SET COLLECTION

1. Now choose one of the poems from your set collection, or use the poem suggested below.

   — Blake: The Tyger

   — Boland: Naoise at Four

   — Dickinson: He fumbles at your Soul

   — Duffy: Elegy

   — Heaney: Oysters

   — Sam-la Rose: Turning Darker Still

2. In pairs or small groups, discuss which of the poetic and linguistic features you think it would be most fruitful to focus on in your analysis.

3. If you were now told you could only keep six of those features, which would you choose?

4. Compare your choices as a class, explaining your reasons.

5. Together look at another poem by your poet. Would you make the same choices of poetic and linguistic features? What does this suggest about the work of your poet and of the two poems in particular?

6. Use your discoveries to help you crystallise what you think is distinctive about the ways in which your poet uses poetic and linguistic techniques to create meaning and effect. For example, are certain features most interesting in relation to your poet, as a whole? Are there certain poetic and linguistic techniques which your set poet does not make significant use of?

A Narrow Focus on One Aspect of Language and Style

1. Share out the six features you selected as being particularly interesting or significant.

2. Read, discuss and annotate the poem with your comments on the aspect you have been allocated. Be disciplined! Focus only on your aspect, really challenging yourself to think beyond the obvious.

3. In your pair, look over your annotations and choose one or two to share with the rest of the class.

4. As a class, sum up the insights you have gained into the meaning and impact of the poem through focusing closely on one aspect of the writer's use of language and poetic techniques.

Reading Your Poet Comparatively

The exam question on poetry will ask you to compare poems from your set text.

- **In the AS Level exam**, two poems are selected by the examiner and printed on the paper.
- **In the A Level exam**, one poem is selected by the examiner with one (or two) poems you have studied selected by you. You will be guided in this by the focus of the question.

In each case, the question will ask you to explore the way the poet presents ideas (and/or feelings) about a particular theme (e.g. freedom and control).

Exploring What Makes a Good Text for Comparison

1. Choose one of the poems you have already worked on. This will be your core text.

2. Re-read this poem and in no more than five bullet points sum up what you think is most distinctive about it. You should consider the theme or subject matter and the way the poet's use of poetic and linguistic techniques creates the meaning and impact of the poem.

3. Range across the other set poems in your collection, looking for a poem to compare with your core one. Begin by shortlisting two or three which you think might work well as a comparative text. Explore the possible ways in which your shortlisted poems could be compared with your core text. What would the point of connection be – the reason for comparing the two poems in the first place? The example on page 127 shows the sort of thinking you might engage in to do this, in response to a sample A Level exam question.

4. Share your thinking with another person, exploring the ways in which it might be illuminating to compare your core text with each of your shortlisted poems. Through this process, make your final choice.

5. Record your possible comparative points on Post-it notes so that you can move them around, shifting them to one side if they no longer seem relevant, grouping them together in order to make a really strong point and experimenting with different ways of structuring your comparison.

6. Depending on the time you have available, do one of the following:

   - Write the opening paragraph of the comparison, indicating briefly the reason for your choice of poems, followed by bullet points outlining the development of your comparative argument.

   - Write the comparison, either in your own time or under timed conditions.

7. As a whole group, share your choices of comparative text, how you developed the comparison and how you organised your writing. Use your experiences to reflect on what makes a good pair of texts for comparison.

FINDING A COMPARATIVE TEXT – AN EXAMPLE ON BLAKE'S 'THE GARDEN OF LOVE'

Sample A Level question

Explore how William Blake presents freedom and control in 'The Garden of Love' and make connections with one or two other poems from your collection. You should consider Blake's use of poetic and stylistic techniques and significant literary or other relevant contexts.

> I went to the Garden of Love,
> And saw what I never had seen:
> A Chapel was built in the midst,
> Where I used to play on the green.
>
> And the gates of this Chapel were shut,
> And 'Thou shalt not' writ over the door;
> So I turn'd to the Garden of Love,
> That so many sweet flowers bore,
>
> And I saw it was filled with graves,
> And tomb-stones where flowers should be;
> And Priests in black gowns, were walking their rounds,
> And binding with briars my joys & desires.

Key points on the core text

- *1st person, expressing a set of imagined experiences of freedom and control; deviation in Stanza 2 with single, powerful use of direct speech, 'Thou shalt not'.*

- *Hymn-like form seeming to offer security and certainty – form at odds with the despair at loss of freedom – external deviation.*

- *Contrasts in lexis, e.g. representing restriction v. freedom of thought and action, past v. present, child v. adult.*

- *Rhyme, e.g. full end-rhymes up to end where repression is reinforced by loss of rhyme in lines 2 and 4; internal rhyme 'gowns' and rounds' emphasising this line and the power of the priests.*

- *Wider literary and cultural context e.g. Isaac Watts' hymn forms distorted here to express different view of religion; children's poems with much darker underlying messages; conventional symbols e.g. garden used unconventionally.*

Possible comparative texts

Nurse's Song (Innocence)
Nurse's Song (Experience)
Human Abstract

Reflecting on points of connection

Could connect 'The Garden of Love' to both 'Nurse's Song' ('I') and 'Nurse's Song ('E') through the ideas of gardens, playing, religion, freedom ('Innocence'), control, clamping down ('Experience'). Could explore the use of rhyme in 'Human Abstract' where it is similarly in tension with content.

STUDYING POETRY

Quick Activities to Get You Thinking and Reading Comparatively

GROUPING POEMS

1. Photocopy all the poems you are studying, each on a separate piece of paper or card.

2. Create different pairings or groupings, making a note of both the titles and the reasons for your decisions. If you have a smartphone, you could take a photo to record the pairs/groups.

3. Compare your groupings across the class.

KEY ASPECTS CARDS

You could do this activity on your own or in pairs or groups. If you work in pairs or groups, you could discuss your poem choices and the reasons behind them.

1. Turn this list of key poetic and linguistic techniques into a set of cards. Place these face down on the table.

KEY POETIC AND LINGUISTIC FEATURES		
• Look on the page	• Lexis	• Structure & development
• Verse form	• Symbols & images	• Repetition & parallelism
• Rhythm	• Oppositions	• Patterns and pattern breaking
• Use of sound/phonology	• Syntax & relationship to lineation	• Verbs, moods & tenses
• Voice	• Use of rhyme	• Context of poet's use of the genre

2. Turn over a card and choose two poems from your collection which you think it would be particularly interesting to explore in relation to this aspect.

You could create a similar set of cards on the *themes* you think are of particular interest in relation to your poet, for example freedom, identity, love and so on. In this case, turn over a theme card, consider *how* this theme is explored in your 'core' text (e.g. in the lexis or imagery, or the structural development of the poem), then select another one or two poems which also explore this theme.

PITCHING YOUR COMPARISON

1. Working with a partner, select a core poem. Now each choose a second comparative poem and spend two or three minutes gathering your ideas together on what is particularly effective about your pairing.

2. Take it in turns to 'pitch' your choice of poem to compare with the core one.

3. After the pitch, the person listening could ask questions to push the thinking further.

LANGUAGE AND LITERATURE EMC

What Makes Your Poet Distinctive?

Consolidating Your Thinking

Identifying what makes your poet distinctive is very important.

1. Your task is to select 20 short quotations (no more than three lines each) from the 15 set poems you are studying. Your aim is to represent what you think are the distinctive and characteristic features of your poet's work.

2. Join up with another student or two and compare your selections. Together, work to create a joint set of 20 quotations. Be prepared to defend your selections.

3. Swap mini-quotations with another group. Explore the quotations, grouping them in different ways, and between you pull out between eight and 10 defining features of your poet's work. Be specific about the poetic and linguistic techniques you choose, making a brief comment which highlights the ways in which these are used by the poet and connecting this to meaning. The example below shows you the sort of thing you might do.

EXAMPLE – JACOB SAM-LA ROSE

Voice: first-person conversational voice, created through use of colloquial language, dialect and rhythms which recall spoken voice, set against more a poetic voice in standard English and using extended metaphors.

4. Take it in turns to read out your lists and try to agree the five or six most distinctive features of your poet's work.

5. Share out the set poems between the group. Which of the distinctive features do you think apply to the poem you have been allocated? Pick three or four that seem to you to be most significant or interesting in this poem.

6. Choose one feature that particularly interests you to talk about in more detail and be ready to present your views on it to the rest of the group.

LANGUAGE AND LITERATURE

4.
STUDYING DRAMATIC TEXTS

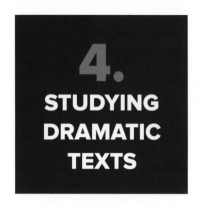

4.

STUDYING DRAMATIC TEXTS

For A Level Component 2 Section B you will study one play, exploring the way the drama works by analysing the playwright's use of dramatic and stylistic techniques. Dramatic texts are not part of the AS course.

The plays set for this component are:

- William Shakespeare: *Othello* (1606; Cambridge School Shakespeare edition, ed Rex Gibson, Jane Coles, Richard Andrews, 2014)

- Oscar Wilde: *The Importance of Being Earnest* (1895; Oxford World's Classics edition, ed Peter Raby, 2008)

- Tennessee Williams: *A Streetcar Named Desire* (1947; Penguin Classics Edition, 2009)

- Brian Friel: *Translations* (1980; Faber & Faber edition, 1981)

- Timberlake Wertenbaker: *Our Country's Good* (1988; Methuen Drama; New Edition, 1995)

- Jez Butterworth: *Jerusalem* (2009; NHB Modern Plays, 2009)

In the exam you will be asked to explore the way the playwright presents an aspect of the drama, such as theme, character or dramatic idea, in an extract printed on the paper and consider its relationship to the rest of the play and the wider dramatic context.

The question you will be asked will look something like this:

> **Explore how Williams presents Blanche and Stella in this extract from** *A Streetcar Named Desire*.
>
> **You should consider the use of dramatic and stylistic techniques in the extract, its significance within the play and any relevant dramatic or other contexts.**

EMC

In this chapter, you will use a range of approaches to develop an understanding of the way your play text works as a piece of drama, on the page and on the stage, for example drawing on:

- stylistics

- linguistics – for example, conversation analysis, pragmatics, lexis and grammar

- the dramatic genre – conventions, dramatic devices and stagecraft

- performance and production contexts, including using theatre reviews.

There is also a section on what you need to do in the exam, with a particular focus on what is meant by context and how you can use it effectively as part of your analysis.

An Introduction to Drama

WHAT IS DRAMA? DEFINITIONS AND ETYMOLOGY

Included here are definitions and the etymology (origins) of some of the key words associated with the literary genre of drama.

- As a class, explore the terms and share any ideas or expectations they prompt in you about the text you are going to be studying – and the ways in which you might go about doing this.

Drama:
A play to be performed – from the Greek 'draein' meaning to do, to act, to perform.

Acting:
Playing a role, performing an action.

Theatre:
From the Greek 'thea' meaning spectacle, 'theon' meaning spectator, theatre being a place to behold.

Playwright:
A dramatist, from 17th century 'play' + 'wright' – a maker, worker or builder of plays.

Reading Drama – on the Page and on the Stage

Any reader of a drama is a producer of the drama for an audience of one. To read is to construct mentally an image of performance.

Walter Nash: Language, Discourse and Literature (ed. Carter & Simpson)

Unlike novels and poetry, plays are written to be performed by actors in front of an audience gathered together in a single place for a short period of time. But plays exist as written texts to be studied as a literary and linguistic construct, as well as a working script.

As a Lang/Lit student, the written text will be the main focus of your study. Considering the play as it might exist in performance is just one approach you might use to develop your analysis of the text.

In an article on the role stylistics can play in analysing drama texts, Mick Short, Professor of Stylistics at the University of Lancaster, said.

Each production of a play would appear to be a play plus an interpretation of it, in that the director and actors have to decide which elements to focus on, emphasize in performance, etc. Note also that some ambiguities which you can see when you read a text may, of necessity, be forced one way or the other by the production.

- Share your response to the points he is making. Do they chime with your ideas? Do they cause you to think differently about the relationship between text, production and critical interpretation?

WHAT IS DRAMA? AN OPEN EXPLORATION

Included here are short extracts from the six texts set for this component. The set texts range from Shakespeare's *Othello*, first performed in 1606 to Jez Butterworth's *Jerusalem* from 2009.

1. Read and discuss the six extracts. You might focus on:

- similarities between the extracts

- differences

- what you notice about the dramatic conventions and features

- ways in which drama might be said to be similar to or different from narrative prose or poetry. For example, a number of the extracts are driven by disagreements (both humorous and serious) between characters on stage and alluded to – perhaps suggesting conflict is at the heart of drama.

2. Choose one of the extracts at random and ask yourself:

   • What can I tell about drama as a literary genre from this extract?

   • What question would it be interesting to ask about drama, based
     on this extract?

3. Choose another extract and do the same, adding to your observations and questions.

4. Continue to do this until you have looked at all the extracts.

5. Share your observations and questions as a class.

WILLIAM SHAKESPEARE: OTHELLO (ACT 1 SCENE 1)

IAGO: Call up her father:
Rouse him, make after him, poison his delight,
Proclaim him in the street, incense her kinsmen,
And though he in a fertile climate dwell,
Plague him with flies: though that his joy be joy,
Yet throw such changes of vexation on't,
As it may lose some colour.

RODERIGO: Here is her father's house; I'll call aloud.

IAGO: Do, with like timorous accent and dire yell,
As when, by night and negligence, the fire
Is spied in populous cities.

RODERIGO: What ho, Brabantio! Signior Brabantio, ho!

IAGO: Awake! What, ho, Brabantio! Thieves, thieves!
Look to your house, your daughter, and your bags!
Thieves, thieves!

(BRABANTIO appears above at a window.)

BRABANTIO: What is the reason of this terrible summons?
What is the matter there?

RODERIGO: Signior, is all your family within?

IAGO: Are your doors locked?

BRABANTIO: Why, wherefore ask you this?

IAGO: Zounds, sir, you're robbed; for shame, put on your gown;
Your heart is burst, you have lost half your soul;
Even now, now, very now, an old black ram
Is tupping your white ewe.

EMC   **LANGUAGE AND LITERATURE**

STUDYING DRAMATIC TEXTS

OSCAR WILDE: THE IMPORTANCE OF BEING EARNEST (ACT 2)

JACK: I wanted to be engaged to Gwendolen, that is all. I love her.

ALGERNON: Well, I simply wanted to be engaged to Cecily. I adore her.

JACK: There is certainly no chance of your marrying Miss Cardew.

ALGERNON: I don't think there is much likelihood, Jack, of you and Miss Fairfax being united.

JACK: Well, that is no business of yours.

ALGERNON: If it was my business, I wouldn't talk about it. (*Begins to eat muffins.*) It is very vulgar to talk about one's business. Only people like stockbrokers do that, and then merely at dinner parties.

JACK: How can you sit there, calmly eating muffins when we are in his horrible trouble, I can't make out. You seem to me to be perfectly heartless.

ALGERNON: Well, I can't eat muffins in an agitated manner. The butter would probably get on my cuffs. One should always eat muffins quite calmly. It is the only way to eat them.

TENNESSEE WILLIAMS: A STREETCAR NAMED DESIRE (SCENE 1)

(*Two men come round the corner, STANLEY KOWALSKI and MITCH. They are about twenty-eight or thirty years old, roughly dressed in blue denim work clothes. STANLEY carries his bowling jacket and a red-stained package from a butcher's.*)

STANLEY: (*to MITCH.*) Well, what did he say?

MITCH: He said he'd give us even money.

STANLEY: Naw! We gotta have odds!

(*They stop at the foot of the steps.*)

STANLEY: (*Bellowing.*) Hey, there! Stella, Baby!

(*Stella comes out on the first-floor landing, a gentle young woman, about twenty-five, and of a background obviously quite different from her husband's.*)

STELLA :   (*Mildly.*) Don't holler at me like that. Hi, Mitch.

STANLEY: Catch!

STELLA: What?

STANLEY: Meat!

(*He heaves the package at her. She cries out in protest but manages to catch it: then she laughs breathlessly. Her husband and his companion have already started back around the corner.*)

EMC

BRIAN FRIEL: TRANSLATIONS (ACT 2 SCENE 1)

YOLLAND: He knows what's happening.

OWEN: What is happening?

YOLLAND: I'm not sure. But I'm concerned about my part in it. It's an eviction of sorts.

OWEN: We're making a six-inch map of the country. Is there something sinister in that?

YOLLAND: Not in...

OWEN: And we're taking place-names that are riddled with confusion and...

YOLLAND: Who's confused? Are the people confused?

OWEN: ... and we're standardising those names as accurately and as sensitively as we can.

YOLLAND: Something is being eroded.

OWEN: Back to the romance again. All right! Fine! Fine! Look where we've got to. (*He drops on his hands and stabs a finger at the map.*) We've come to this crossroads. Come here and look at it, man! Look at it! And we call that crossroads Tobair Vree. And why do we call it Tobair Vree? I'll tell you why. Tobair means a well. But what does Vree mean? It's a corruption of Brian – (*Gaelic pronunciation.*) Brian – an erosion of Tobair Bhriain. Because a hundred-and-fifty years ago there used to be a well there, not at the crossroads, mind you – that would be too simple – but in a field close to the crossroads.

The Arches Theatre Company production of *Translations*
Photo credit: Niall Walker

TIMBERLAKE WERTENBAKER: OUR COUNTRY'S GOOD (ACT 1)

Scene Two

(A lone Aboriginal Australian describes the arrival of the First Convict Fleet in Botany Bay on January 20, 1789.)

THE ABORIGINE: A giant canoe drifts onto the sea, clouds billowing from upright oars. This is a dream which has lost its way. Best to leave it alone.

Photo credit: Robert Workman

Scene Three

Punishment

(Sydney Cove. Governor Arthur Phillip, Judge David Collins, Captain Watkin Tench, Midshipman Harry Bewer. The men are shooting birds.)

PHILLIP: Was it necessary to cross fifteen thousand miles of ocean to erect another Tyburn?

TENCH: I should think it would make the convicts feel at home.

COLLINS: This land is under English law. The court found them guilty and sentenced them accordingly. There: a bald-eyed corella.

PHILLIP: But hanging?

JEZ BUTTERWORTH: JERUSALEM (ACT 1)

WESLEY: Johnny, Listen. Phaedra Cox has gone off again. She ain't been home since Monday night.

JOHNNY: So?

WESLEY: So, I know she comes up here. With the others. Have you seen her?

JOHNNY: You know me, Wesley. I can't tell these rats apart.

WESLEY: It's not funny, Johnny. She's fifteen years old. Troy Whitworth was in the pub. In the saloon bar, asking if anyone had seen her.

JOHNNY: Phaedra Cox ain't my lookout. She's him's. She's Troy Whitworth's. He's her stepdad. Not me.

WESLEY: I just wondered if you seen her, is all. It's just...

JOHNNY: Just what?

A Focus on the Dramatic Genre

Text Transformation

Both drama and narrative prose could be said to share the following purposes:

- to tell a story

- to entertain

- to explore themes or raise ideas

- to construct a fictional world

- to create characters and establish relationships.

So you might ask yourself the following questions.

- What difference does it make to tell a story in the form of a play rather than narrative fiction?

- What is particularly distinctive about the ways in which drama is able to tell a story or explore themes?

- What opportunities does drama open up – and what does it close down?

- How does the dramatist you are studying do this?

Re-writing a short extract as prose, then comparing this with the original text, can highlight some of the key characteristics of drama, as shown in the example from Brian Friel's *Translations* below and on page 140.

TRANSLATIONS – ORIGINAL TEXT

(*Manus holds Sarah's hands in his and he articulates slowly and distinctly into her face.*)

MANUS: We're doing very well. And we're going to try it once more – just once more. Now – relax and breathe in... deep... and out... in... and out...

(*Sarah shakes her head vigorously and stubbornly.*)

Come on Sarah. This is our secret.

(*Again vigorous and stubborn shaking of Sarah's head.*)

Nobody's listening. Nobody hears you.

STUDYING DRAMATIC TEXTS

RE-WRITTEN TEXT

Manus believes Sarah will be taught to speak beautifully, fluently, trippingly – and he will be the one to release her into words. Standing before him – she is a child no more – he takes her hands in his, every cell of his body willing her on. How to encourage her? Surely it can be no more than a belief and an ease. He slows his breathing to match hers. In and out. In and out. 'We're doing very well.' He hears he has said 'we' and falters himself. Will there be offence taken? Stubbornly, fiercely, she shakes her head at his conviction, but her hands too are still, quietly resting in his.

COMMENTARY

Trying to turn the dramatic exchange into prose highlights the economy of the drama and the degree to which the 'reader' (be this director, actor, reader of the script) contributes to the meaning of the text. This is especially clear in the comment on Manus's use of 'we', a word Friel gives him in the script. In the script it could have variously been interpreted as gently supportive or patronising. Although 3rd person, the narrative version favours one perspective, with Manus the focaliser of the action. The narrative version also gives more explicit detail about what Sarah is doing, highlighting the fact that drama is a multimedia genre – we see Sarah throughout Manus's speech so we know how she is reacting. The narrative version quickly becomes descriptive and rather distanced from the characters, unlike the drama.

1. In pairs, range across your drama set text, marking one or two extracts you think it might be interesting to experiment with re-writing as prose.

2. As a class, choose the extract you will all work on.

3. On your own or in pairs, re-write the extract as narrative prose. As you experiment with making the transformation, pay attention to the changes you make and the difference this makes to the meaning and impact of the text.

4. Listen to three or four of the re-written versions, discussing the different ways in which people have chosen to transform the text and what this suggests about their interpretation of the original.

5. Now look again at the original text and compare it with your re-written version. Use the prompts below to focus your discussion of the two texts. What insights do you get into:

   • the possibilities afforded by drama as a genre

   • the way in which your particular playwright uses dramatic techniques to create meaning and impact

   • your interpretation of the text?

From prose to drama

6. As an alternative exercise, choose a short extract from the narrative text you are studying for your A Level and transform it into a piece of drama. You could even experiment with re-writing it in the style of your set play.

Key Dramatic Features

Included here are some key features of literary (and some non-literary) texts.

1. Working in pairs or small groups, select the features you think are particularly significant or relevant to dramatic texts.

2. Compare your selections across the class, identifying the features everyone agrees are relevant to dramatic texts and discussing those where there is some disagreement. For example, you might think that 'telling not showing' is not very relevant to drama texts when you first look at it. However, perhaps after a bit of discussion, you might think about the role of a chorus in some plays, talking directly to the audience. Or you might remember that in some plays there are soliloquies, where a protagonist talks directly to the audience. Are these possible mechanisms for the writer to 'tell' the audience what to think?

3. As you study your set drama text, return to your list, to see if your decisions hold true for your particular text, as well as in general. You might also consider whether any of the rejected features, those more typically found in poetry or narrative fiction, for example, are significant in your play.

KEY FEATURES OF LITERARY (AND SOME NON LITERARY) TEXTS

- Characters and characterisation

- Patterns of imagery and symbolism

- Sound of the language

- Manipulation of time

- Paralinguistic features (body language, facial expressions)

- The look on the page

- Setting the scene

- Ambiguity

- Plot (and perhaps sub-plots)

- Moments of high drama/tension

- Telling, not showing

- Dialogue

- A voice guiding the audience/reader's sympathies

- A physical and visual experience

- An individual experience for the receiver of the text

- A shared experience for the receiver of the text

- Action rather than reflection

- Gaps in the text for the reader/viewer to fill

- Conflict

- Multiple points of view

- Use of revelation

- Direct address to the reader/viewer

- Exists in the reader's imagination

STUDYING DRAMATIC TEXTS

Genre, Audience Expectations and the Playwright

Genre is the term used to refer to different text types (for example, drama, poetry, narrative fiction). It is also used when referring to the different sub-types within each of these.

DRAMATIC SUB-GENRES	
• Tragedy	• Social realist plays
• Comedy of manners	• Kitchen sink drama
• Farce	• Melodrama
• History plays	• Romantic comedy
• Absurdist plays	

The genre or type of play raises certain expectations in the audience, with regard to:

- the storyline or plot

- the characters or character types

- the setting

- the style

- the structural development and outcome.

A romantic comedy, for example, sets up certain expectations in the audience (obstacles to be overcome on the way to marriage and a happy ending).

Like any writer, a playwright can decide to follow the expected patterns and conventions of a genre or to deviate from them (e.g. choose to have a romantic comedy end not with a marriage but a separation). He or she may choose to work broadly within one genre or to draw on (and play with) the conventions from a range of genres.

1. As a class, talk about the genre or genres you think your playwright is drawing on.

2. What generic expectations are set up in the opening scene?

3. In what ways does the play conform to the generic conventions (e.g. structure, outcome)?

4. In what ways does it challenge or subvert them (e.g. character type, setting)?

Applying Stylistics Approaches to Drama Texts

In your introductory work and in the chapter on poetry, you were introduced to the discipline of stylistics. Stylistics focuses on aspects of the text foregrounded through the writer's use of repetition, parallelism and deviation and more generally in pattern-making and breaking. You'll also find some of these same stylistic strategies useful when analysing short extracts from your drama texts.

The following approaches all begin with a close focus on a short extract, before widening out to consider the patterns, repetition and deviation across the play as a whole.

Introductory Activities

PATTERNS – 'SECRET STRINGS'

1. Look back at the secret strings example on pages 89-90 to remind yourself of what this activity involves.

2. Annotate the 'secret strings' in a scene from your drama text, identifying and analysing the impact of connections made and broken, images foregrounded through repetition, parallel grammatical structures. Then broaden out to consider how:

   • the strings extend across the play as a whole

   • other scenes repeat the same patterns and structures.

FOREGROUNDING THROUGH REPETITION AND PARALLELISM

Explore a playwright's use of repetition and parallelism in a single speech or scene.

1. Range across the text looking for examples of the repeated image, word, phrases or grammatical patterns.

2. What is foregrounded through this repetition?

FOREGROUNDING THROUGH DEVIATION

1. Identify the key metaphor in a scene, exploring how this 'deviant' use of language foregrounds key themes or relationships.

2. Or look at how the language in a scene deviates *externally* from the expected uses of language in the world beyond the drama.

3. Or look at how a sudden deviation in style from the established pattern *within* the text foregrounds something new or offers a moment of change.

STUDYING DRAMATIC TEXTS

A Line at a Time

One way of focusing on the patterns in a text is to read a short extract slowly, revealing one line at a time. The following extracts would work well for this activity:

— William Shakespeare: *Othello* Act 1 Scene 3 from 'DUKE OF VENICE: Say it Othello' to 'BRABANTIO: For thy escape would teach me tyranny,/To hang clogs on them. I have done, my lord.'

— Oscar Wilde: *The Importance of Being Earnest* Act 1 Scene 1 from '*Enter LANE*' to 'ALGERNON: ...You are not married to her already, and I don't think you ever will be.'

— Tennessee Williams: *A Streetcar Named Desire* Scene 2 from 'STANLEY: If I didn't know that you was my wife's sister I'd get ideas about you!' to 'BLANCHE: Everyone has something he won't let others touch because of their – intimate nature...'

— Brian Friel: *Translations* Act 1 from 'LANCEY: I'll say what I have to say if I may.' to 'OWEN: ... and the Captain thanks you for listening so attentively to him.'

— Timberlake Wertenbaker: *Our Country's Good* Act 1 Scene 8 from 'The Women Learn their Lines' to 'MARY: Because that's acting.'

— Jez Butterworth: *Jerusalem* Act 1 from 'GINGER: So you're barred from The Cooper's, then.' to 'GINGER: Congratulations. You got the grand slam. To think they said it would never happen.'

1. Read your chosen extract and note down your initial impression.

2. Now cover the extract with a piece of paper. Pull the paper down slowly, to reveal one line at a time. Annotate the text to show:

   • repetition

   • parallelism

   • lexical or image clusters

   • interaction between characters.

3. Take a step back from the detail of your annotation to consider what is foregrounded. Identify one or two aspects which strike you as interesting or significant or which you had not noticed on your first reading. Write up your insights to share with the class.

4. Share your insights, paying attention to the similarities and differences in your reading of the extract.

5. Choose one of your insights (e.g. a repeated image) to explore through the rest of the play. Range across the play, selecting two or three other extracts which 'speak to' your first one in some way.

A Focus on Language – Performance Approaches

The following approaches focus attention on the language of the text and its relationship to performance.

- Use a selection of the approaches on page 146 to help you explore the way the text works. As you try out the different approaches, reflect on:

  - patterns: how these are created and whether they are broken

  - repetition: words, images, grammatical structures

  - anything that is foregrounded, because it deviates from a pattern that has been set up or is an unusual use of language.

These extracts would work well for this activities.

— William Shakespeare: *Othello* Act 2 Scene 3 from 'CASSIO: Welcome, Iago; we must to the watch' to 'CASSIO: I'll do't; but it dislikes me.'

— Oscar Wilde: *The Importance of Being Earnest* Act 3 from 'LADY BRACKNELL: And now as regards Algernon! … Algernon!' to 'LADY BRACKNELL: … who is that young person whose hand my nephew Algernon is now holding in what seems to me a peculiarly unnecessary manner?'

— Tennessee Williams: *A Streetcar Named Desire* Scene 2 from 'STANLEY: So that's the deal, huh?' to 'STANLEY: Open your eyes to this stuff! You think she got them out of a teacher's pay?'

— Brian Friel: *Translations* Act 1 from 'MANUS goes to MAIRE. While he is talking to her.' to 'I couldn't – I can't go in against him.'

— Timberlake Wertenbaker: *Our Country's Good* Act 2 Scene 1 from 'LIZ: And you, Wisehammer, how did you get here?' To 'LIZ: You have to think English… but he's thinking in English, I can tell.'

— Jez Butterworth: *Jerusalem* (2009) Act 3 from 'Enter GINGER in a pith helmet and shades, holding a coconut.' to 'LEE: I don't know. (*Knocks*.)'

EMC LANGUAGE AND LITERATURE

STUDYING DRAMATIC TEXTS

EXPLORING THE GRAMMAR OF THE LANGUAGE – PUNCTUATION, PACE, RHYTHM

- Try reading every sentence of the speech with one breath per sentence. Then read it again, this time pausing for 1 count for a comma, 2 for a semi-colon or a dash, 3 for a colon and 4 for a full stop, an exclamation mark or a question mark.

EXPLORING LINGUISTIC PATTERNING AND COHESION – WORD BEFORE

1. Before reading your line, say a word that jumps out at you from the lines the last person has just said.

   - Reader 1: reads a line out loud.

   - Reader 2: Repeats a word that leaps out at them from the previous line then reads their character's line.

   - Reader 1: Repeats a word from this line, before going on to read the next one. And so on.

2. Together, share anything that strikes you about the words you chose. What do your choices reveal about:

   - the writer's language choices

   - linguistic patterning

   - ideas, themes or tone which seem to be emerging through the language choices?

UNCOVERING THE SUB-TEXT – HOOKING, PRODDING, DEFLECTING

- Consider whether the language suggests your character is trying to draw the other character in, get information out of them or avoid giving them the information they want. As you read the scene again, use a gesture to show your interpretation of the text.

  - Hooking: drawing the other character in.

  - Prodding: trying to get information out of the other character.

  - Deflecting: trying to avoid giving information or reacting to what has been said.

PHONOLOGY – PAYING ATTENTION TO THE SOUNDS OF WORDS

- As you read, emphasise or exaggerate the sounds of the words (e.g. hard/soft sounds, repeated clusters of consonants) and their rhythm. What is the effect of these sounds on meaning? Are there any words that are foregrounded through being very different (e.g. polysyllabic words in a scene or speech dominated by monosyllabic words)?

Linguistic Approaches

Conversation Analysis and Drama

As the quotations below show, plays are created through the dialogue spoken by the characters, their silences and paralinguistic behaviour.

> **Dialogue is the only significant (and signifying) literary means whereby the dramatic text can be imagined and written.**
>
> *Michelene Wandor, playwright*

> **Dialogue is the basic building block of most plays ...**
>
> **It's clear that most statements in the world – and almost all the statements made in plays are infelicitous speech acts ... and their infelicity communicates their meaning. Judgements are made by unauthorised persons, questions are asked to which the speaker knows the answer, people lie, say things they don't mean to say or don't have to say in the first place.**
>
> *David Edgar: How Plays Work*

Conversation analysis which you may already have used to help you to investigate spontaneous conversation can also be usefully applied to dramatic dialogue:

> **Given that plays are mainly conversations between characters on the stage, the most obvious kind of analysis to use will be that developed by linguists to analyse conversational interaction.**
>
> *Lancaster University Stylistics Course*

The box on page 148 gives you a list of the kinds of things involved in conversation analysis.

A warning!

As the dialogue in a play is not spontaneous conversation, your understanding of the 'rules' and conventions of everyday speech (and the ways these are conformed to, manipulated and flouted), will need to be used carefully: your aim in using the tools of conversation analysis is to understand the ways in which the playwright uses language and dramatic techniques to create character, relationships, story and conflict.

STUDYING DRAMATIC TEXTS

CONVERSATION ANALYSIS TOOLS

- Who **initiates** the dialogue? Who responds?

- **Agenda-setting and topic changes:** Who decides what the conversation will be about and who changes the topic?

- **Turn-taking:** Does each person wait till the other has finished or does one person keep interrupting? If the latter, who interrupts? And who is interrupted?

- **Distribution and length of turns:** Who has the most turns? Who has the longest turns?

- **Speech acts:** Who uses speech acts like questioning, commanding, demanding, threatening and complaining? Who uses speech acts like answering, agreeing, acceding, giving in or apologising?

- **Adjacency pairs (a form of parallelism in spoken language):** Are the normal expectations or different expectations followed?

  » Greeting/greeting

  » Question/answer

  » Congratulations/thanks

  » Apology/acceptance

  » Leave-taking/leave-taking

- **Modes of address:** What names do people call each other by?

- **Taboo words:** Who uses them, what provokes their use, how does the other character react?

- Some linguists consider conversation analysis in terms of **politeness** and **co-operation**, using all of the above elements to understand the way conversation works (or breaks down).

  » **Politeness principles:** maintaining or breaking conventions about being polite in conversation (e.g. phrasing criticism positively rather than negatively).

  » **The co-operative principle:** how much each person says, the quality of what they say, how relevant it is and the manner in which it is said.

LANGUAGE AND LITERATURE

DOING CONVERSATION ANALYSIS ON AN EXTRACT FROM YOUR SET TEXT

Try out these tools on any passage from your text – you could start with the extracts suggested here:

— William Shakespeare: *Othello* Act 1 Scene 1 from 'IAGO: Call up her father,/Rouse him: make after him, poison his delight,' to '(*Exit above.*)'

— Oscar Wilde: *The Importance of Being Earnest* Act 1 from 'LADY BRACKNELL: Good afternoon, dear Algernon, I hope you are behaving very well.' to 'GWENDOLEN: ... Mamma has a way of coming back suddenly into a room that I have often had to speak to her about.'

— Tennessee Williams: *A Streetcar Named Desire* Scene 5 from 'BLANCHE: Stella! What have you heard about me?' to 'BLANCHE: ... Just think! If it happens! I can leave here and not be anyone's problem.'

— Brian Friel: *Translations* Act 1 from 'OWEN: Here we are. Captain Lancey – my father.' to 'HUGH: Our pleasure Captain.'

— Timberlake Wertenbaker: *Our Country's Good* Act 1 Scene 10 from MARY: What does indulgent mean?' to the end of the scene.

— Jez Butterworth: *Jerusalem* Act 2 from 'JOHNNY turns. JOHNNY's six-year-old son, MARKY, is stood there. Pause.' to 'DAWN: Unforeseen.'

1. Read the extract and briefly note down your first impression of it (the way the conversation develops, the interactions, relationships). For example:

   • the conversation breaks down

   • there is conflict or something uncomfortable about the dialogue.

2. Using your first response to guide you, choose one or two of the conversation analysis tools on page 148 to look more closely at the way the dialogue works. Does your close analysis support, develop or challenge your first interpretation?

3. Share your discoveries with your group.

A CRAFTED DIALOGUE

A play is *not* a spontaneous conversation. It is a construct, a literary text crafted by a writer.

1. Use your knowledge of stylistics to look again at the extract, this time paying attention to the way in which the playwright uses repetition, parallelism and deviation.

2. Write one or two paragraphs exploring the way the dialogue works in the extract, drawing on both the conversation and stylistics analysis.

Deviations in the Dialogue – Ranging across the Play

Playwrights may choose to alter, or deviate from, the usual pattern of dialogue in order to draw attention to some aspect of the play. (In stylistics, this is known as internal deviation.)

Some possible kinds of internal deviation:

- an extended speech in among the conversational dialogue

- the introduction of verse in a text written in prose

- a move into prose or rhyme in a text written in blank verse

- a shift in register (e.g. from the colloquial to the formal)

- the introduction of another form of discourse (e.g. a poem or song)

- the use of dramatic devices such as the aside or soliloquy (dramatic devices in which the audience accepts the convention that these words are not heard by characters on stage)

- the use of dialect in a play written mainly in standard English.

Internal deviations of this sort depend upon the audience or reader recognising what is the 'norm' for the play.

1. Begin by agreeing a few major features that make up the linguistic 'norm' for your play. Next think what would be deviant language in your text. You could use the features suggested here to help you, or add ones of your own.

EXPLORING DEVIATIONS IN THE DIALOGUE

• Prose	• Extended speech
• Rhyming verse	• Quick repartee
• Blank verse	• Chorus
• Colloquial language	• Public address
• Elevated language	• Standard English
• Dialect	• Private conversation between two or three people
• Direct address to the audience	

---

2. Range across the text, looking for examples of deviation. What is the effect of the deviation? What function does it fulfil within the drama?

3. Share a few of your examples, with your interpretation of the effect of the deviation.

Exploring Character in Drama

The following activities require you to focus on one character from your set drama text. So that a range of characters are covered, agree as a class who will work on which one.

The Role or Function of a Character in a Drama

Included here are some of the different roles or functions a character might fulfil in a drama.

1. Read the list and decide which of these potential aspects of a character's role are most significant in terms of the character you are focusing on.

> ### FUNCTIONS OF CHARACTER
>
> - To play a major or a minor role – the central focus of the drama or a less significant role. (In either case, this might involve fulfilling some of the roles below.)
>
> - To act as a foil or contrast to another character, to bring out their qualities.
>
> - To be representative of a 'type' (e.g. brothers, daughters, wives, lovers).
>
> - To further the plot – playing a key part in the events.
>
> - To create a different kind of dramatic experience (e.g. to create moments of light relief, or provide tragic intensity, or to act as a commentator on the action).
>
> - To develop one or more of the key themes of the play (e.g. loyalty, jealousy, power).
>
> - To carry a mood or tone or be associated with a kind of language (e.g. the poetic, the magical, the crude, the comical).
>
> - Something else particular to an individual play or character.

2. How does the playwright develop the character you are focusing on? Use the prompts on page 152 to help you come up with four or five bullet points.

3. Share your findings in class discussion.

4. Pool your ideas about any significant elements of character development that seem especially important in your text as a whole. For instance, does your playwright use private conversations most of all? Or does your playwright make particular use of stage directions to develop character?

DEVELOPING CHARACTER

- How the character is introduced for the first time.

- What the character says:

  » to himself/herself

  » in private settings

  » in public settings.

- How the character speaks.

- How much or little the character speaks or appears.

- What other characters say about him/her.

- How other characters behave with him/her.

- How the character behaves and what the character does.

- What the character looks like.

- How the stage directions signal the character's behaviour.

- How the character changes during the drama.

- How the character ends up.

- Something else that's particular to your character or drama.

Creating Character in Dialogue – a Focus on Grammar and Lexis

One of the things you have touched on in your exploration of character is the way in which the character speaks – the language the playwright uses to create a particular voice and sense of personality. The following activity will help you sharpen up your analysis of the way the playwright creates character through the dialogue.

Complete the following activities individually. Continue to focus on the character you worked on in the previous activity.

1. Select an extract to analyse, either by flicking through the text, or going back to a passage that has already struck you as interesting.

2. Range across the text for three or four further short passages which allow you to add to your analysis of the character.

Here are some aspects to focus on.

- Words, expressions and particular grammatical structures which the character typically uses (their idiolect). Does the character use language drawn from a particular lexical field, for example?

- The difference between the character's speech and that of other characters. Is the character's language foregrounded by being very different from (internally deviant) from the language of the other characters?

- Occasions when the character deviates from their typical language – an example of the playwright foregrounding what is said or why it is said.

- Shifts across the play, showing changes in a character.

3. Sum up your analysis as series of bullet points to share with the class.

EXAMPLE 1: STANLEY IN SCENE 8 OF A STREETCAR NAMED DESIRE

- *Characterised through use of non-standard grammar e.g. 'I done nothing to no one' and 'ain't I'. This is typical of Stanley's language and foregrounds the difference between him and the sisters Stella and Blanche.*

- *Non-standard spelling of individual words to indicate pronunciation – 'wanta', 'gonna'.*

- *Syntax – short abrupt exclamatory sentences might suggest brutality – here reflecting Stanley's blunt, even brutal, treatment of Blanche.*

- *Similar use of non-standard grammar etc. in Scene 2, but here in conversation with Stella – interrogative, pursuing his suspicions about Blanche and Belle Reve.*

- *Characteristic non-standard grammar.*

- *Scene 7 – interesting – much more extended utterances from Stanley, as he reveals to Stella what he has discovered about Blanche. Almost every sentence is an exclamation, suggesting the insistence with which Stanley tells his story.*

EXAMPLE 2: JOHNNY IN ACT 2 (OPENING) OF JERUSALEM

- *Dialect forms characteristic of Johnny's language throughout e.g. 'Out pops him'.*

- *Minor sentences, use of present tense e.g. 'Loves the lasses.'*

- *Bombastic language reflecting flights of fancy.*

- *Tropes of high rhetoric used bathetically (e.g. 'Friends! Outcasts! Leeches!'), creates Johnny's character.*

- *Extended speech – deviation from typical language of the play.*

Text and Subtext – a Focus on Pragmatics

1. Consider the following interactions. Talk about what's going on, then look at the commentary below:

> **A:**   Can I have a sweet?
>
> **B:**   (*gives A a sweet*)
>
>
> **A:**   I love jelly babies.
>
> **B:**   (*gives A a sweet*)

COMMENTARY

In both cases A communicates the fact she wants one of B's sweets. In both cases B understands this and gives A a sweet. The way A goes about getting the sweet, however, is very different: in the first interaction, the request is direct and straightforward. In the second, B (who has a bag of sweets) understands that A is not simply commenting on her love of jelly babies, but asking for one. The request is indirect, hinted at, implied. B has to use the context, understanding of both social conventions, the way the language works and even perhaps his knowledge of A, in order to interpret what is meant but not said.

In linguistics, the way in which this works is called pragmatics. There are a number of different definitions of pragmatics, but broadly speaking it can be understood as follows:

> The implied meanings, the meaning intended or the way words are understood in context, rather than the words themselves. Here context might include: the setting, what has been said or taken place before, the tone of voice, gesture or other paralinguistic communication, social and cultural conventions such as politeness – or indeed literary conventions.

Pragmatics is key when analysing drama because it is a genre which relies heavily on subtext.

In a novel the author has the facility, should they want it, to offer a gloss on a character's dialogue, to direct the reader's interpretation. In a play, the interpretative gap is much wider: the dialogue is unmediated, leaving the reader to interpret the sub-text. When the play is to be performed, the first readers are the directors and actors who must interpret the subtext, the actor conveying this through his or her performance.

2. Write two or three other short bits of dialogue of your own, such as the one above where the words in the exchange couldn't be fully understood without a broader sense of the contexts in which they are said.

The Subtext – Three Approaches to Exploring Pragmatics

As a class, choose a short extract from your play. Try adding the subtext in one or two of the ways suggested here.

WHY? A PERFORMANCE APPROACH

• Work in pairs. Read up to the end of each sentence, in role. At the end of each sentence, the other person should say 'Why?' and the reader should reply, in role.

The example below on *The Importance of Being Earnest* shows you this in practice.

EXPLORING THE SUB-TEXT THROUGH PERFORMANCE	
ALGERNON: (*languidly.*) I don't know that I am much interested in your family life, Lane.	**Why?** *Why he's a nobody! I'm surprised in fact to learn he has a family. I could have thought he sprang from nowhere to serve me.*
LANE: No, sir; it is not a very interesting subject. I never think of it myself.	**Why?** *I'm a servant – it's not my place to have a family. (And my role in this comedy is as a foil, to add to the humour with a deadpan witticism.)*
ALGERNON: Very natural, I am sure. That will do, Lane, thank you.	

ANNOTATING THE TEXT

• On your own, read and annotate the extract to spell out the sub-text or any points at which you think there is a gap between what is said and what is meant.

RE-WRITING

1. Re-write the scene as a monologue from the perspective of one of the characters, drawing out the implications of what the character actually says. Feel free to use your contextual knowledge of the whole play to interpret the pragmatics of what is said in this scene, but make sure you can justify your interpretation.

2. Return to the text as it is written and, as a class, explore the different ways in which you interpreted the subtext. Work together to unpick the language of the text, what is said, what you understood to be implied and what additional contextual information you used to come to that understanding.

Stage Directions – Genre and Discourse Analysis

So far you have looked at dialogue, a play's primary discourse. Another important aspect of a drama text is the stage directions – the only other means by which a playwright can convey his or her vision of the play.

A warning...

It's worth remembering that the stage directions in *Othello* (as in any text from the early modern period) will have been added by an editor, whereas the directions in *Jerusalem*, for example, are as much the work of Butterworth as is the dialogue. The difference between the two underlines the change in the role and status of the play text – and the role of the playwright.

- Actors in the early modern period would have been expert at reading directions into the dialogue and would also have understood that particular genres required them to act in particular ways.

- The extensive stage directions of more recent playwrights perhaps shows an attempt to exert control over the production and performance of the play, as well as over the text, closing down the opportunities for the director and actors to (mis) interpret.

Exploring Stage Directions

The stage directions on page 157 are taken from Oscar Wilde's *The Importance of Being Earnest* and Tennessee Williams' *A Streetcar Named Desire*.

- Read the two extracts and talk about what you notice. Then compare your ideas with those raised in the notes below.

A Streetcar Named Desire, d. Elia Kazan

EMC

OSCAR WILDE: THE IMPORTANCE OF BEING EARNEST	TENNESSEE WILLIAMS: A STREETCAR NAMED DESIRE
Enter Jack with a hand-bag of black leather in his hand.	She continues to laugh. BLANCHE comes around the corner, carrying a valise. She looks at a slip of paper, then at the building, then again at the slip and again at the building. Her expression is one of shocked disbelief. Her appearance is incongruous to this setting. She is daintily dressed in a white suit with a fluffy bodice, necklace and ear-rings of pearl, white gloves and hat, looking as if she were arriving at a summer tea or cocktail party in the garden district. She is about five years older than STELLA. Her delicate beauty must avoid a strong light. There is something about her uncertain manner, as well as her white clothes, that suggests a moth.
Rushing over to Miss Prism.	
Calmly.	
In a pathetic voice.	
Amazed.	
Embracing her.	
Recoiling in indignant astonishment.	
Tries to embrace again.	
Still more indignant.	
Pointing to Lady Bracknell	
After a pause.	

NOTES

It's striking how different the stage directions are not only in terms of length and detail but also in their content – from practical directions as to the action or stage business or descriptions of the setting, to detailed interpretation of the mood/tone or manner in which the actor should speak the lines, apparently giving fewer opportunities to the actor for individual interpretation.

Stripping out the Stage Directions

The extracts on pages 158-159 from the set plays have all had their stage directions stripped out. For this activity, focus on the play you are studying.

1. Look at the extract without stage directions.

2. Highlight any implicit directions within the dialogue.

3. Consider how you would stage this, adding stage directions to indicate your interpretation.

4. Now compare the stripped back version with the original text in your book. How has your playwright used stage directions? What if anything do they add to the meaning, creation of character, creation of drama and so on? Are any possible interpretations closed down through the inclusion of the stage directions?

EMC LANGUAGE AND LITERATURE

STUDYING DRAMATIC TEXTS

WILLIAM SHAKESPEARE: OTHELLO (ACT 2 SCENE 3)

CASSIO:	Zounds, you rogue, you rascal!
MONTANO:	What's the matter, lieutenant?
CASSIO:	A knave teach me my duty! I'll beat the knave into a twiggen bottle.
RODERIGO:	Beat me!
CASSIO:	Dost thou prate, rogue?
MONTANO:	Nay, good lieutenant, I pray you, sir, hold your hand.
CASSIO:	Let me go, sir, or I'll knock you o'er the mazzard.
MONTANO:	Come, come, you're drunk.

OSCAR WILDE: THE IMPORTANCE OF BEING EARNEST (ACT 3)

MISS PRISM:	I was told you expected me in the vestry dear Canon. I have been waiting for you there for an hour and three-quarters.
LADY BRACKNELL:	Prism! Come here, Prism! Prism! Where is that baby? Twenty-eight years ago, Prism, you left Lord Bracknell's house, Number 104, Upper Grosvenor Square, in charge of a perambulator that contained a baby of the male sex. You never returned. A few weeks later, through the elaborate investigations of the Metropolitan police, the perambulator was discovered at midnight standing by itself in a remote corner of Bayswater. It contained the manuscript of a three-volume novel of more than usually sentimentality. But the baby was not there. Prism! Where is that baby?

TENNESSEE WILLIAMS: A STREETCAR NAMED DESIRE (SCENE 11)

STANLEY:	Did you forget something?
BLANCHE:	Yes! Yes, I forgot something!
STANLEY:	Doc, you better go in.
DOCTOR:	Nurse, bring her out.
MATRON:	Hello, Blanche.
STANLEY:	She says that she forgot something.

BRIAN FRIEL: TRANSLATIONS (ACT 3)

BRIDGET:	The sweet smell! Smell it! It's the sweet smell! Jesus, it's the potato blight!
DOALTY:	It's the army tents burning, Bridget.
BRIDGET:	Is it? Are you sure? Is that what it is? God, I thought we were destroyed altogether. Come on! Come on!
OWEN:	How are you? Are you all right? Don't worry. It will come back to you again. It will. You're upset now. He frightened you. That's all's wrong.
DOALTY:	He'll do it, too.

TIMBERLAKE WERTENBAKER: OUR COUNTRY'S GOOD (ACT 1 SCENE 11)

SIDEWAY:	My handkerchief. Who prigged my handkerchief?
RALPH:	I'm sure it will turn up, Sideway, let's go on.
SIDEWAY:	I can't do my entrance without my handkerchief. I've been practising it all night. If I get my mittens on the rum diver I'll –
RALPH:	Let's assume Worthy has already entered, Sideway. Now, I say: 'What arms-a-cross, Worthy! Methinks you should hold 'em open when a friend's so near. I must expel this melancholy spirit. What are you doing now there Sideway?
SIDEWAY:	I'm being melancholy. I saw Mr Garrick being melancholy once. This is what he did. Hamlet it was. 'O that this too, too solid flesh would melt. O that this too, too solid flesh would melt. O that this too, too –'

JEZ BUTTERWORTH: JERUSALEM (ACT 2)

DAWN:	John –
JOHNNY:	I'm serious. Come over here. Come and stand here. Good. Now. Look in my eyes. Dawn. Look in my eyes. Look at me. What do you see?
DAWN:	Black.
JOHNNY:	Keep looking. Look in my eyes. Deeper. Now I'm going to show you something. Are you ready? Did you see that? Did you see it? Did you see it, Dawn?
DAWN:	Yes.
JOHNNY:	Well, now. There now. What's to worry? Who won Lara Croft?

EMC LANGUAGE AND LITERATURE

Paying Attention to the Stage Directions in Your Text

1. As you explore your text, think about:

- the length of stage directions (is this the same throughout the text?)

- the function of the stage directions, for example:

    — to establish the scene – directions for the creation of a visual or physical world

    — to suggest tone/mood and how this is created

    — to indicate expression, relationships

    — to direct action

    — to do something else (e.g. an interpretation of the speech/ behaviour of the character)

- the relationship between the stage directions and the dialogue.

2. Consider whether:

- the dialogue or stage directions dominate and what effect this has (for example, where a character is silent on stage)

- the stage directions are in tension with dialogue (perhaps indicating a character is unhappy despite the dialogue suggesting they are happy).

Village Theater for The Importance of Being Earnest d. Brian Yorkey
Photo © Jay Koh

LANGUAGE AND LITERATURE

EMC

From Page to Stage – the Text in Performance

One of the advantages of seeing a play in performance is that it foregrounds those aspects of the text which are easily glossed over in reading, for example:

- silent characters

- exits and entrances

- sound effects

- music

- the impact of specific actions (or lack of action)

- what happens off-stage.

(There are, of course, further aspects which are not visible on the page, but these are related more to the decisions of a director rather than the playwright – for example, cast, when to set the play, cuts and so on.)

Although it may not be possible to see the play or to put on your own production, there are some things you can do to help you analyse these vital 'hidden' elements of the text. Try out one or two of the approaches on page 162. As well as giving you insight into the particular act or scene, you should find that they help you become more practised at reading the text as a drama, rather than simply for the 'story'.

Jerusalem Royal Court Theatre, 2011 d. Jan Rickson Photo © Geraint Lewis/Rex Features

STUDYING DRAMATIC TEXTS

DIRECT A SCENE

- Annotate a scene to show how you would direct it, with brief reasons for your decisions.

SILENT CHARACTERS

- Identify two or three scenes in which there are characters on stage who do not speak. If they're not speaking, what are they doing? What function do they play in the drama? If a director decided to cut the character, would anything be lost?

EXITS AND ENTRANCES

- Flick through your play text, focusing only on exits and entrances. Is there anything interesting that you notice about the way the playwright uses these (e.g. to heighten tension, to add pace, to create comedy)?

MUSIC/SOUND EFFECTS

- Choose a scene in which the playwright indicates music or some other sound effect. Now look for where the sound effect/music stops. What difference does it make to the nearby dialogue? To the action?

HIGHLIGHTING ACTIONS – ON STAGE AND OFFSTAGE

- **Onstage**: Identify all the actions taking place in a single scene (indicated in either the stage directions or in the dialogue). What actually happens on stage? Which characters are involved? What are the other characters doing? What causes the action to stop?
- **Offstage**: What is happening offstage? How does the audience know? What impact does this have on what is happening onstage?

Northern Broadsides & West Yorkshire Playhouse, d. Barrie Rutter © Nobby Clark

EMC

Writing about Contexts

In the **A Level exam (Component 2)** you will be asked to explore the playwright's presentation of an aspect of the play in an extract printed on the paper, for example:

Explore how Shakespeare presents power and status in this extract from *Othello*.

All the questions will include the following reminder:

You should consider the use of dramatic and stylistic techniques in the extract, its significance within the play and any relevant dramatic or other contexts.

Context can be tricky: it's very tempting to include a great chunk of fascinating contextual information that you've learned. This is not what's needed. Any contextual knowledge you draw on should be relevant to the specific question and extract and used to further your interpretation of the text. It might be worth thinking about context in two different ways:

1. Contextual information which helps you understand the play.

2. Contextual knowledge which you can use as part of your answer to the question. This includes:

    • the significance of the extract within the play, for example:

      — where does it fit within the play – is it the opening, a turning point, a moment of high drama? Does it foreshadow a key scene or parallel an earlier scene?

      — what role does it fulfil in the play – to relieve tension, reveal character, develop the plot

      — how does it fit into the patterning of the play (images and motifs, lexical groups and so on)?

    • the dramatic context, including:

      — the genre and dramatic tradition (how far does it conform to, draw on, or subvert the conventions of a dramatic genre)

      — productions

      — critical reception.

    • other relevant literary, cultural or historical contexts – to be used only if relevant!

• Choose a short extract from the play you are studying and, using the notes above, annotate it to show how contextual knowledge could be used to further your analysis.

STUDYING DRAMATIC TEXTS

Pulling it all Together

The summary on page 165 pulls together some of the approaches you have been using to analyse drama texts. When it comes to the exam, you should draw on a combination of approaches, paying greater or lesser attention to some aspects depending on the play you are studying, the question you have been asked and the extract set for analysis. What's important is selecting what is most significant and most relevant.

For example, if answering a question on the presentation of social conventions in *The Importance of Being Earnest*, you may find yourself analysing Wilde's use of dramatic techniques, using conversation analysis tools and pragmatics to explore the way the dialogue works as conversation. If you're exploring the presentation of Johnny in *Jerusalem*, you might focus on Butterworth's use of colloquial lexis and syntax to create his voice – and the way he deviates from this at key points, with extended speeches in an elevated style.

CHOOSING AN EXTRACT AT RANDOM

1. Open your text at random and select an extract of about 30 lines. Read the extract a couple of times, then write two or three sentences highlighting what is of particular significance and which aspects and techniques you would select in your discussion.

2. Join up with another person and take it in turns to introduce your extracts, making comments or asking questions to help your partner develop their thinking.

3. Repeat two or three more times.

WORK ON THE SAME EXTRACT

1. As a class, select an extract of the length and type that could be set in an exam.

2. Together, try to write an exam question that you think would work well for this extract. Choose a focus (theme or character or presentation of some other aspect of the drama) that would allow for plenty of interesting points to be raised.

3. Individually, work on the text, deciding on the four or five key points you think you might make in an exam, drawing on the list on page 165.

4. Share your ideas across the class, exploring what you think would be the most interesting and significant points to write about in an exam answer.

EMC

APPROACHES TO ANALYSING DRAMA TEXTS

LITERARY FEATURES AND DRAMATIC TECHNIQUES

• Genres and sub-genres (e.g. comedy of manners, tragedy, realist, farce) and kind of play (e.g. action-packed, play of ideas, physical theatre).

• Form and structure (structural development, division into acts and scenes, development of plot and sub-plot, use of prologues and epilogues).

• Dramatic techniques (e.g. stage directions, exits/entrances, verse/prose, dramatic irony, dialogue, monologue, exposition, chorus, soliloquy and asides, metatheatrical references).

• Performance and production.

• Figurative language and rhetorical techniques such as similes, metaphors, image clusters and motifs.

STYLISTICS

• Foregrounding through:

 » repetition (lexical, structural, figurative)

 » parallelism (grammatical, structural)

 » deviation (internal, external).

LANGUAGE LEVELS

 » Lexis (kinds of lexis e.g. abstract/concrete nouns, lexical patterning – e.g. contrasts, repetition, clusters).

 » Discourse (types of utterance, conversation analysis, register and style of language; naming and terms of address).

 » Grammar (syntax, sentence type, verbs, moods & tenses, parallelism).

 » Pragmatics (implied meanings/subtext, meanings in context).

CONTEXT AND CRITICISM

 » Dramatic context (context of the play – the relationship of the extract to the rest of the play; dramatic tradition; sub-genres of drama).

 » Other relevant contexts (the contexts of writing, performance and reception, including theatre reviews).

LANGUAGE AND LITERATURE

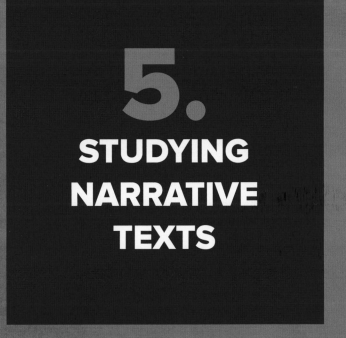

5.
STUDYING
NARRATIVE
TEXTS

5.
STUDYING NARRATIVE TEXTS

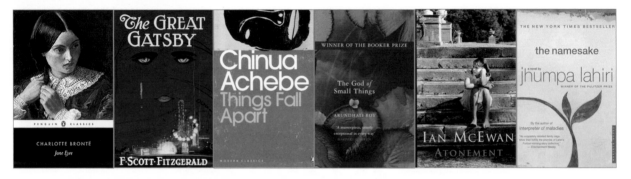

This chapter is about reading, analysing and writing about narrative texts. The novels set for the AS and A Level specifications are:

- Charlotte Brontë: *Jane Eyre* (1847)

- F. Scott Fitzgerald: *The Great Gatsby* (1925)

- Chinua Achebe: *Things Fall Apart* (1958)

- Arundhati Roy: *The God of Small Things* (1997)

- Ian McEwan: *Atonement* (2001)

- Jhumpa Lahiri: *The Namesake* (2003)

At AS level the study of a narrative text is part of Component 2 'The language of literary texts'.

At A level, it is part of Component 3 'Reading as a writer, writing as a reader'.

Both AS and A Level components are about narrative – the way novelists tell stories.

If you're preparing for A Level you'll critically read a novel and write a short narrative text. The second part of A Level Component 3 requires you to write the opening of your own narrative, drawing on what you've learned through studying a novel to (see page 207 for more on this). Practising for this writing task will also give you greater insights into the way your set text works as a narrative.

Students preparing for the AS exam may also find it useful to look at this section and have a go at the short creative writing exercises to learn about the way narratives work from a different angle.

What you will have to do in the exam:

AS students will be given an extract from their narrative text and asked to write about the ways the story is told.

You will be asked to:

- explore the narrative techniques used in the extract

- consider the extract in the context of the novel as a whole and its genre.

This exam is closed text – the extract will be printed on the page but you will need to have a good knowledge of the whole novel so that you can draw in other passages to add depth to your answer.

A Level students will be given a choice of two questions on an aspect of narrative across the text as a whole. The question will look something like this:

How does the writer of your text use settings?

You should range across the text to explore how settings are presented, the role they play in the novel as a whole, and the broader generic context.

This exam is open text, so you'll be able to have a clean copy of the novel with you.

Whichever exam you are preparing for, you will need:

- a good sense of the novel as a whole

- the ability to comment closely on key passages and range around the text

- an understanding of the narrative genre more generally.

Introducing Narrative

From Story to Narrative – an Introduction

- Look at the three short comic strips below. Talk about:
  - what the three versions have in common
  - what is different about each one.

LANGUAGE AND LITERATURE

In the introduction to this chapter, we described the AS and A Level components as being about 'narrative – the way stories are told'. In everyday conversation we may use the terms interchangeably, but in the context of literary study there is an important distinction:

- A story is simply the events in chronological order, i.e. the order in which they took place.

- Narrative is all about the *way* the story is told. It involves everything from decisions about the form (drama, film, novel, poem) and genre (romance, thriller, contemporary manners) to decisions about structure, narrative voice and point of view.

In the graphic texts on page 170, number 1 is the bare story – a representation of the events in the order in which they took place. Numbers 2 and 3 are more fully developed narratives, in which decisions about order and point of view have been made. They each tell the same *story* but in different *ways*.

From Story to Narrative – a Creative Experiment

1. Look at the two photos on page 172.

2. As a class, use one or both photos to come up with a very basic story – that is a series of events told in chronological order, in just five or six points: First..., then... then... then... then... then.

3. On your own, take the class's outline story and turn it into a narrative.

4. As a class, or in small groups, take it in turns to read your narratives aloud, then talk about the different narrative choices you each made.

5. Use the prompts below to focus your discussion if you need to.

- Who tells the story (a narrator, a character, different characters)? From whose point of view are the events seen?

- Structure and the handling of time (e.g. did any of you start at the beginning of the story and tell it in order, or tell it retrospectively or use flashbacks? Did anyone use a frame story or other narrative techniques such as letters or diary entries?).

- The type or genre of story (e.g. did anyone choose to tell the story using the conventions of a particular genre, or draw on, or adapt, the conventions of several genres?).

- The style (e.g. description, narration or dialogue? Chatty and conversational, or more formal? Long, complicated sentences or short simple ones?).

A First Exploration – What Can You Discover?

The extracts below and on pages 174-175 are all taken from the narrative set texts.

1. Read the extracts and, in pairs, list everything you can tell about the way narratives work, based on these extracts. A couple of ideas have been given here to get you started.

> *Some narratives seem to announce what they are – almost like an introduction – while others launch you straight into the action, as though you are familiar with the world already.*
>
> *In some novels, one of the characters takes the part of the storyteller.*

2. As a class, pool your list of features, techniques, uses of language and so on. What do narrative texts share, that makes them recognisably narratives? How do individual novelists make their particular narratives different and distinctive?

3. Talk about the different ways in which the writers have chosen to begin their novels. You could use the prompts below to focus your discussion:

   • the narrator and narrative voice

   • structure (Does it seem to begin at the start of the story? At the end? Does it begin with a frame in which the story is introduced?)

   • the way it is written (style and narrative techniques such as word groups, imagery, sentence type and length, balance of description, narration, dialogue).

CHARLOTTE BRONTË: JANE EYRE

There was no possibility of taking a walk that day. We had been wandering, indeed, in the leafless shrubbery an hour in the morning; but since dinner (Mrs. Reed, when there was no company, dined early) the cold winter wind had brought with it clouds so sombre, and a rain so penetrating, that further out-door exercise was now out of the question.

I was glad of it: I never liked long walks, especially on chilly afternoons: dreadful to me was the coming home in the raw twilight, with nipped fingers and toes, and a heart saddened by the chidings of Bessie, the nurse, and humbled by the consciousness of my physical inferiority to Eliza, John, and Georgiana Reed.

STUDYING NARRATIVE TEXTS

F. SCOTT FITZGERALD: THE GREAT GATSBY

In my younger and more vulnerable years my father gave me some advice that I've been turning over in my mind ever since.

'Whenever you feel like criticizing anyone,' he told me, 'just remember that all the people in this world haven't had the advantages that you've had.'

He didn't say any more, but we've always been unusually communicative in a reserved way, and I understood that he meant a great deal more than that. In consequence, I'm inclined to reserve all judgments, a habit that has opened up many curious natures to me and also made me the victim of not a few veteran bores. The abnormal mind is quick to detect and attach itself to this quality when it appears in a normal person, and so it came about that in college I was unjustly accused of being a politician, because I was privy to the secret griefs of wild, unknown men. Most of the confidences were unsought – frequently I have feigned sleep, preoccupation, or a hostile levity when I realized by some unmistakable sign that an intimate revelation was quivering on the horizon; for the intimate revelations of young men, or at least the terms in which they express them, are usually plagiaristic and marred by obvious suppressions. Reserving judgments is a matter of infinite hope. I am still a little afraid of missing something if I forget that, as my father snobbishly suggested, and I snobbishly repeat, a sense of the fundamental decencies is parcelled out unequally at birth.

CHINUA ACHEBE: THINGS FALL APART

Okonkwo was well known throughout the nine villages and even beyond. His fame rested on solid personal achievements. As a young man of eighteen he had brought honour to his village by throwing Amalinze the Cat. Amalinze was the great wrestler who for seven years was unbeaten, from Umuofia to Mbaino. He was called the Cat because his back would never touch the earth. It was this man that Okonkwo threw in a fight which the old men agreed was one of the fiercest since the founder of their town engaged a spirit of the wild for seven days and seven nights.

The drums beat and the flutes sang and the spectators held their breath. Amalinze was a wily craftsman, but Okonkwo was as slippery as a fish in water. Every nerve and every muscle stood out on their arms, on their backs and their thighs, and one almost heard them stretching to breaking point. In the end Okonkwo threw the Cat. That was many years ago, twenty years or more, and during this time Okonkwo's fame had grown like a bush-fire in the harmattan. He was tall and huge, and his bushy eyebrows and wide nose gave him a very severe look. He breathed heavily, and it was said that, when he slept, his wives and children in their out-houses could hear him breathe. When he walked, his heels hardly touched the ground and he seemed to walk on springs, as if he was going to pounce on somebody. And he did pounce on people quite often. He had a slight stammer and whenever he was angry and could not get his words out quickly enough, he would use his fists. He had no patience with unsuccessful men. He had had no patience with his father.

LANGUAGE AND LITERATURE EMC

ARUNDHATI ROY: THE GOD OF SMALL THINGS

Paradise Pickles & Preserves

May in Ayemenem is a hot, brooding month. The days are long and humid. The river shrinks and black crows gorge on bright mangoes in still, dustgreen trees. Red bananas ripen. Jackfruits burst. Dissolute bluebottles hum vacuously in the fruity air. Then they stun themselves against clear windowpanes and die, fatly baffled in the sun.

The nights are clear but suffused with sloth and sullen expectation.

But by early June the south-west monsoon breaks and there are three months of wind and water with short spells of sharp, glittering sunshine that thrilled children snatch to play with. The countryside turns an immodest green. Boundaries blur as tapioca fences take root and bloom. Brick walls turn mossgreen. Pepper vines snake up electric poles. Wild creepers burst through laterite banks and spill across the flooded roads. Boats ply in the bazaars. And small fish appear in the puddles that fill the PWD potholes on the highways.

IAN MCEWAN: ATONEMENT

The play – for which Briony had designed the posters, programmes and tickets, constructed the sales booth out of a folding screen tipped on its side, and lined the collection box in red crêpe paper – was written by her in a two-day tempest of composition, causing her to miss a breakfast and a lunch. When the preparations were complete, she had nothing to do but contemplate her finished draft and wait for the appearance of her cousins from the distant north. There would be time for only one day of rehearsal before her brother arrived. At some moments chilling, at others desperately sad, the play told a tale of the heart whose message, conveyed in a rhyming prologue, was that love which did not build a foundation on good sense was doomed. The reckless passion of the heroine, Arabella, for a wicked foreign count is punished by ill fortune when she contracts cholera during an impetuous dash toward a seaside town with her intended. Deserted by him and nearly everybody else, bed-bound in a garret, she discovers in herself a sense of humour. Fortune presents her a second chance in the form of an impoverished doctor – in fact, a prince in disguise who has elected to work among the needy. Healed by him, Arabella chooses judiciously this time, and is rewarded by reconciliation with her family and a wedding with the medical prince on 'a windy sunlit day in spring'.

STUDYING NARRATIVE TEXTS

JHUMPA LAHIRI: THE NAMESAKE

1968

On a sticky August evening two weeks before her due date, Ashima Ganguli stands in the kitchen of a Central Square apartment, combining Rice Krispies and Planters peanuts and chopped red onion in a bowl. She adds salt, lemon juice, thin slices of green chili pepper, wishing there were mustard oil to pour into the mix. Ashima has been consuming this concoction throughout her pregnancy, a humble approximation of the snack sold for pennies on Calcutta sidewalks and on railway platforms throughout India, spilling from newspaper cones. Even now that there is barely space inside her, it is the one thing she craves. Tasting from a cupped palm, she frowns; as usual, there's something missing. She stares blankly at the pegboard behind the countertop where her cooking utensils hang, all slightly coated with grease. She wipes sweat from her face with the free end of her sari. Her swollen feet ache against speckled gray linoleum. Her pelvis aches from the baby's weight. She opens a cupboard, the shelves lined with a grimy yellow-and-white-checkered paper she's been meaning to replace, and reaches for another onion, frowning again as she pulls at its crisp magenta skin. A curious warmth floods her abdomen, followed by a tightening so severe she doubles over, gasping without sound, dropping the onion with a thud on the floor.

THINKING ABOUT BEGINNINGS

The narrative extracts you've just read are all taken from the very beginning of the novels.

The novelists Blake Morrison and David Lodge have both written about the importance of getting the beginning right and the different ways in which a writer might choose to open his or her novel.

> Beginnings matter. They always have. Middles have no limits – they can scrunch up or they can sprawl. Endings may be left open, ambiguous, incomplete. But no novel has ever not begun. And if it doesn't begin right, the suspicion is that the rest of it won't be right either.
>
> Blake Morrison: *The Independent* (1999)

> However one defines it, the beginning of a novel is a threshold, separating the real world we inhabit from the world the novelist imagined. It should therefore, as the phrase goes, draw us in.
>
> David Lodge: *The Art of Fiction* (1987)

Some of the ways in which a novel might begin are listed opposite, on page 177.

1. Talk about how each of the novelists set for this component has chosen to begin his or her novel. Use the ideas in the list, adding to or amending them, as you need to.

WAYS TO BEGIN A NOVEL

- A lengthy description of the setting.

- Something shocking or surprising or amusing, intended to unsettle.

- A frame story, setting up the telling of the main story.

- An introduction by the narrator.

- A plunge into the world of the novel, in mid-action or mid-conversation.

- A philosophical reflection, summing up some of the main ideas to be explored.

- A description of the characters.

- A reflection on the story that is about to be told – perhaps hinting at its outcome.

Professor John Mullan suggests that in the opening paragraphs a novel 'must establish its contract with the reader'. He goes on to say:

> The very permissiveness of those rules by which novels are written makes it necessary for a novelist to show a reader, in the beginning, what kind of thing he or she is reading, what he or she has signed up to. (...) we need to be made acquainted with the tenets – the ground rules, as it were – of the fictional world into which we are entering. Our expectations are being shaped before we even read the novel's first sentence. Those introductory elements that usher us into the main narrative are already guiding our habits of interpretation.

2. Look again at the opening paragraphs of the set text novels. What 'contract' do you think is being established with the reader in each case? What are your expectations of the novel?

After reading your set novel, think again about John Mullan's comments. Is he right that the way you read and interpret the whole novel is shaped by its beginning?

READING THE FIRST CHAPTER

3. Go on to read the first chapter of the novel you are studying. How does the rest of the chapter relate to its beginning? You could think about:

- the way the plot is developed

- the use of the narrative voice

- the introduction and development of characters

- the prose style

- the idea of the 'contract with the reader'.

4. Pick out two or three points to share with the rest of the class.

Exploring Key Aspects of Narrative

Use of Genre

As with drama, there are recognised narrative genres which provoke particular expectations in their reader and which the novelist can choose to fulfil or challenge. These genres will be familiar to you both from film and television and from the way bookshops and libraries arrange their stock — romance, crime, horror, thriller and so on are all popular narrative genres.

GENRE AND NARRATIVE PROSE – AN OVERVIEW

Writers draw on the conventions of particular genres:

- to set up expectations in a reader's mind about the type of story this is

- to create a particular fictional world

- to break the rules, undermine, challenge expectations (of plot, structure, character, language)

- to draw attention to events or particular passages or sections of the book.

GENRE CAN BE SEEN IN A NOVEL'S:

• Plot	• Structure	• Language and prose style
• Events/action	• Themes	
• Voice and point of view	• Character types (and behaviours)	

SOME POPULAR NARRATIVE SUB-GENRES ARE:

• Romance	• Thriller	• Adventure
• Mystery	• Family saga	• School
• Horror	• Rites of passage/ coming-of-age	• Detective
• Science fiction		• Fantasy
• Spy	• War	

The typical features and conventions of some popular narrative genres (listed on page 178) are included here.

1. As a class, sort the features and conventions into different genres. (You may decide that some conventions and features are found in two or more different genres.) Do you all agree with the clusters you come up with? If there are differences in the ingredients you include, talk about why this might be and what it suggests about the genre.

FEATURES AND CONVENTIONS OF DIFFERENT NARRATIVE GENRES

- Red herrings and false leads
- Plot-led, clear structure
- Ambiguity about which characters are good and bad
- Everything cleared up at the dénouement
- Back stories used to uncover truths
- Invented worlds
- Focus on a single point of view
- Strange events revealed to have ordinary explanations
- Tells the stories of an extended family
- Focus on emotion
- Often told in the first person
- Focus on the details of everyday life
- Family relationships and conflict
- Discovery of self and others
- Personal challenges to overcome
- Revenge
- Reflects critically on contemporary society
- Obstacles in the way of passion
- A heroine who needs rescuing
- Retrospective narrative
- Sinister settings such as a castle or ruin, with underground passages, labyrinths, dungeons
- Not much focus on the inner life of a hero

- Takes place over several generations
- Character rather than plot-driven
- Clear-cut good and bad characters
- Violent and melancholic heroes
- Use of frame story
- Story focused through the eyes of a detective
- Problems to be overcome – emotional, material, family relationships
- Charts process of growing up and discovery
- The supernatural
- Mysterious characters
- Cursed families or individuals
- Has a hero rather than a heroine
- May use medium of diary/letters to tell story
- Breaking of taboos
- A journey or quest narrative
- Happy ending
- Reflective
- Close focus on hero and heroine
- Clear hero and anti-hero
- Male-dominated
- Gaps in the narrative
- Lots of events and action

STUDYING NARRATIVE TEXTS

A CREATIVE EXPERIMENT

2. Imagine the sentence below is the opening line of a novel.

   It was Christmas Eve.

3. Experiment with re-writing the sentence in two or three different genres (e.g. romance and thriller), so that the genre can easily be recognised. You can write up to three or four sentences for each one.

4. In groups or as a class, take it in turns to read your sentences aloud. Can your listeners guess which genre you are writing in? If so, what is it about your writing that identifies the genre? If not, what didn't quite ring true?

WHAT ABOUT YOUR NOVEL?

5. Does the novel you're studying belong to, or draw on, the conventions of a particular genre or genres? How are these conventions used to tell the story? Explore all the reasons for thinking the writer is using those conventions and all the reasons against. Use the suggestions below to start your discussion.

JANE EYRE	THE GREAT GATSBY
• Gothic novel?	• Rites of passage?
• Rites of passage?	• Social satire?
• Romance?	• Tragedy?
THINGS FALL APART	**THE GOD OF SMALL THINGS**
• Fable?	• Epic?
• Folk tale?	• Postmodern experimental novel?
• Tragedy?	• Postcolonial novel?
ATONEMENT	**THE NAMESAKE**
• Country house?	• Family saga?
• War?	• Rites of passage?
• Historical novel?	• Contemporary realist novel?

LANGUAGE AND LITERATURE

Voice and Point of View

The choice of how to tell the story – which narrative voice to use – is key to the way meaning and effect is created in a narrative text.

The narrator is a creation of the author used to tell the story. The narrator may also:

- comment and judge

- directly address the reader

- be a participant in the story

- be a detached observer

- be 'transparent', appearing to speak with the voice of the author.

On page 182 there is an overview of some of the key choices available to a fiction writer, in terms of voice and point of view.

EXPLORING NARRATIVE VOICE

The short extracts on pages 183-184 are all taken from the novels set for this specification.

1. Read and talk about the narrative voice in each of the six extracts, noting similarities and differences across the extracts. Try to be as precise as possible, paying attention to any shifts in the voice within the extract. Use the information on page 182 to help you.

MICRO-INTERVENTIONS – CHANGING THE VOICE OR POINT OF VIEW

2. Choose one of the first person extracts and re-write a few sentences in the third person. What do you discover about what difference this makes? Now do the same for one of the third-person extracts.

3. Share your discoveries in class discussion.

STUDYING NARRATIVE TEXTS

NARRATIVE VOICE – AN OVERVIEW

FIRST PERSON

First-person narrator

• A narrator who speaks as 'I', often a character who plays a role in the story, although it may not be his or her own story that is being told.

Interior monologue

• First person, as though the narrator is verbalising their thoughts as they occur.

Stream of consciousness

• A narrative style that imitates the qualities of thoughts and feelings, making the reader feel as if they're inside someone's head. The grammar and structure suggest the random and fragmentary nature of thought. In the **first person** it's an extreme version of interior monologue. (See also under Third Person, below.)

Unreliable narrator

• A (first-person) narrator who is perhaps self-deceiving or who cannot be trusted to give a version of events that is to be believed.

Inadequate (or naïve) narrator

• A (first-person) narrator who doesn't seem to understand as much about what's happening as the reader.

THIRD PERSON

Third-person omniscient narrator

• A narrator who is assumed to know everything connected with the story narrated. Refers to the characters as 'he' or 'she'. Often assumed to be the author.

• In a third-person narrative, the action may be seen predominantly from the perspective (or point of view) of a particular character. This character can be described as the **focaliser**.

Free indirect style

• Third-person narration in which a character's thoughts and feelings seem to be directly expressed, freely taking on the views and often the language of that character. Narratives often slide between conventional third-person narration and this style, moving from a more detached voice to one that is more intimately connected to one character or another.

Stream of consciousness

• A narrative style that imitates the qualities of thoughts and feelings, making the reader feel as if they're inside someone's head. The grammar and structure suggest the random and fragmentary nature of thought. In the **third person** it's an extreme version of free indirect style. (See also under First Person, above.)

Intrusive narrator

• A narrator who, telling the story in the third person, intervenes in the narrative with a comment in the first person.

2ND PERSON

• A narrative voice that directly addresses the reader as 'you'. It's rare for a whole text to do this as it's very hard to maintain.

CHARLOTTE BRONTË: JANE EYRE

How full the hedges are of roses! But I have no time to gather any; I want to be at the house. I passed a tall briar, shooting leafy and flowery branches across the path; I see the narrow stile with stone steps; and I see – Mr Rochester sitting there, a book and pencil in his hand: he is writing.

Well, he is not a ghost; yet every never I have is unstrung: for a moment I am beyond my own mastery. What does it mean? I did not think I should tremble in this way when I saw him – or lose my voice or the power of motion in his presence.

F. SCOTT FITZGERALD: THE GREAT GATSBY

The bottle of whisky – a second one – was now in constant demand by all present, excepting Catherine, who 'felt just as good on nothing at all'. Tom rang for the janitor and sent him on for some celebrated sandwiches, which were a complete supper in themselves. I wanted to get out and walk eastward toward the park through the soft twilight, but each time I tried to go I became entangled in some wild, strident argument which pulled me back, as if with ropes, into my chair. Yet high over the city our line of yellow windows must have contributed their share of human secrecy to the casual watcher in the darkening streets, and I saw him too, looking up and wondering. I was within and without, simultaneously enchanted and repelled by the inexhaustible variety of life.

CHINUA ACHEBE: THINGS FALL APART

Okonkwo and his family worked very hard to plant a new farm. But it was like beginning life anew without the vigour and enthusiasm of youth, like learning to become left-handed in old age. Work no longer had for him the pleasure it used to have, and when there was no work to do he sat in silent half-sleep.

His life had been ruled by a great passion – to become one of the lords of the clan. That had been his life-spring. And he had all but achieved it. Then everything had been broken. He had been cast out of his clan like a fish on to a dry, sandy beach, panting. Clearly his personal god or *chi* was not made for great things. A man could not rise above the destiny of his *chi*. The saying of the elders was not true – that if a man said yea his *chi* also affirmed. Here was a man whose *chi* said nay despite his own affirmation.

ARUNDHATI ROY: THE GOD OF SMALL THINGS

He was exasperated because he didn't know what that look meant. He put it somewhere between indifference and despair. He didn't know that in some places, like the country that Rahel came from, various kinds of despair competed for primacy. And that personal despair could never be desperate enough. That something happened when personal turmoil dropped by at the wayside shrine of the vast, violent, circling, driving, ridiculous, insane, unfeasible, public turmoil of a nation. That Big God howled like a hot wind, and demanded obeisance. Then Small God (cosy and contained, private and limited) came away cauterized, laughing numbly at his own temerity. Inured by the confirmation of his own inconsequence, he became resilient and truly indifferent. Nothing mattered much. Nothing much mattered. And the less it mattered, the less it mattered. It was never important enough. Because Worse Things had happened. In the country that she came from, poised forever between the terror of war and the horror of peace, Worse Things kept happening.

IAN MCEWAN: ATONEMENT

Watching him during the first several minutes of his delivery, Cecilia felt a pleasant sinking sensation in her stomach as she contemplated how deliciously self-destructive it would be, almost erotic, to be married to a man so nearly handsome, so hugely rich, so unfathomably stupid. He would fill her with his big-faced children, all of them loud, bone-headed boys with a passion for guns and football and aeroplanes. She watched him in profile as he turned his head towards Leon. A long muscle twitched above the line of his jaw as he spoke. A few thick black hairs curled free of his eyebrow, and from his eyeholes there sprouted the same black growth, comically kinked like pubic hair. He should instruct his barber.

JHUMPA LAHIRI: THE NAMESAKE

At home, his mother is horrified. What type of field trip was this? It was enough that they applied lipsticks to their corpses and buried them in silk-lined boxes. Only in America (a phrase she has begun to resort to these days), only in America are children taken to cemeteries in the name of art. What's next, she demands to know, a trip to the morgue? In Calcutta the burning ghats are the most forbidden of places, she tells Gogol, and though she tries her best not to, though she was here, not there, both times it happened, she sees her parents' bodies consumed by flames. 'Death is not a pastime,' she says, her voice rising unsteadily, 'not a place to make paintings. She refuses to display the rubbings in the kitchen alongside his other creations, his charcoal drawings and his magazine collages, his pencil sketch of a Greek temple copied from an encyclopedia, his pastel image of the public library's façade, awarded first place in a contest sponsored by the library trustees. Never before has she rejected a piece of her son's art. The guilt she feels at Gogol's deflated expression is leavened by common sense. How can she be expected to cook dinner for her family with the names of dead people on the walls?

DESCRIBING NARRATIVE VOICE IN YOUR SET TEXT

Here are some of the ways in which you might describe the narrative voice of a work of fiction.

1. Which one (or ones) would you choose to describe the narrative voice of your set text? Pick up to three statements, adapting them if you need to.

You could use the information in 'Narrative Voice – an Overview' on page 182, if it helps you.

2. For each statement you choose, identify a passage in the novel which illustrates this aspect of the narrative voice.

- First-person retrospective voice telling their own story.

- Single narrative voice throughout.

- A range of first-person narrators.

- Third-person narrator, providing a single omniscient point of view.

- Third-person narrator, privileging different characters' points of view.

- Shifting narrative voice.

- Third-person narrative voice which slips into free indirect style, adopting the language of particular characters.

- Alternative voices integrated into the narrative (e.g. letters, diary entries, stories told by a character).

- First-person narrator telling the story of another character.

STUDYING NARRATIVE TEXTS

CREATING THE VOICE

There is another way in which voice is used in critical discussion of narrative texts: to describe the distinctive *style* of the narrative. The narrative voice might, for example, be detached or intimate, conversational and gossipy or formal and distant, understated and restrained or exuberant and intrusive.

1. Open your set text at random. How would you describe the distinctive features of the voice on the page you have in front of you? Once you've come up with three or four adjectives to describe it, try to work out how the writer has created the voice. Is it through:

   - the lexis

   - the syntax

   - the use of tenses

   - characteristic phrases

   - the use of dialect

   - something else?

2. Take a short extract from your creative writing in response to a photo (on pages 171-172). Experiment with re-creating the narrative voice in the style of your set text.

Alternatively, if you didn't do the response to the photo, write the opening paragraph of another narrative (such as the start of a first-person narrative for young adults). First write the paragraph with one distinctive kind of voice. Then re-write it with some significant changes, to explore what difference these make.

RANGING ACROSS THE TEXT, SELECTING KEY PASSAGES

1. To get a sense of the way the narrative voice is used in your novel, range across the text, identifying passages where you'd have something interesting to say about it. In each case, ask yourself:

   - What is the writer doing with the narrative voice at this point?

   - Why does it seem interesting or different here?

   - How is it being used to tell the story?

2. Present one of your passages to the rest of the class, explaining how you think narrative voice is being used at this point in the text and how it relates to the use of voice in the rest of the novel.

Dialogue in Narrative Texts

> Alice was beginning to get very tired of sitting by her sister on the bank, and of having nothing to do: once or twice she had peeped into the book her sister was reading, but it had no pictures or conversations in it, 'and what is the use of a book,' thought Alice 'without pictures or conversations?'
>
> *Alice in Wonderland*

Your study of the anthology and set play has already introduced you to the ways in which dialogue works in spoken conversation and in the crafted medium of drama. Dialogue is also a key feature of narrative prose – a means by which the story is told, characters created and relationships established. It's also a way for the writer to introduce voices and points of view other than that of the narrative voice.

1. Begin by reading the following short quotations and talking about the ideas they raise.

> The artificiality of the means by which speech is made to seem natural is evident in novelistic dialogue... Fictional conversation is a literary skill rather than a hearing of voices.
>
> *John Mullan: How Novels Work*

> As well as adding variety to a narrative, representing the speech of those who take part in a narrated event, or who are somehow qualified to comment on what takes place, may also contribute importantly to the authenticity and authority of the story, as we appear to be told what happened from 'the horse's mouth.'
>
> *Bronwen Thomas in The Cambridge Companion to Narrative*

2. Read the six extracts on pages 189-190 and talk about what you notice.

3. Choose two extracts which seem to you to deal with dialogue in different ways. Use the 'Dialogue In Narrative Texts – an Overview' box on page 188 to help you look in more detail at how the dialogue is being used. This example shows you the sort of thing you might draw attention to.

EXPLORING DIALOGUE – AN EXAMPLE

Atonement and The Great Gatsby

Both use dialogue to tell the story and to create an atmosphere of social tension. Where Fitzgerald frequently uses descriptive speech tags ('coldly', 'unconvincingly', 'quickly') and links the dialogue to descriptions of the character's behaviour, McEwan lets the dialogue stand alone. There is not even any attribution of the individual utterances, although the dialogue is framed by narrative sections which clearly indicate from whose point of view we are seeing the scene. Although very spare, McEwan's dialogue reveals the awkwardness in the situation – the explanation of the first character, the monosyllabic agreement by the second.

EMC LANGUAGE AND LITERATURE

DIALOGUE IN NARRATIVE TEXTS – AN OVERVIEW

Here are some of the functions dialogue fulfils in a narrative text

- Reveals and develops character.

- Establishes/reveals relationships.

- Moves the plot along.

- Recreates earlier episodes in the life of the character.

- Creates an interpretative gap – between what the character says and what the reader understands.

- Contributes to the creation of the fictional world.

Here are some of things you might want to consider when thinking about the ways in which dialogue is represented in a narrative text:

- Layout on the page and conventions used to mark each new speaker, if any (e.g. dashes, speech marks).

- Attribution of speech to each speaker, using tags such as 'he said' or 'she whimpered' (or lack of speech attribution).

- How much extra information is given in the attribution.

- How much difference there is between the style of the narrative voice and the voices in the dialogue.

- The balance of dialogue to narration.

- The balance between direct speech and reported speech.

- Anything else that strikes you about the use of dialogue in the text.

CHARLOTTE BRONTË: JANE EYRE

'I am willing to amuse you if I can, sir: quite willing; but I cannot introduce a topic, because how do I know what will interest you? Ask me questions, and I will do my best to answer them.'

'Then in the first place, do you agree with me that I have a right to be a little masterful, abrupt; perhaps exacting, sometimes, on the grounds I stated; namely, that I am old enough to be your father, and that I have battled through a varied experience with many men of many nations, and roamed over half the globe, while you have lived quietly with one set of people in one house?'

'Do as you please, sir.'

'That is no answer; or rather it is a very irritating, because a very evasive one; reply clearly.'

'I don't think, sir, you have a right to command me merely because you are older than I, or because you have seen more of the world than I have; your claim of superiority depends on the use you have made of your time and experience.'

'Humph! Promptly spoken. But I won't allow that, seeing that it would never suit my case; as I have made an indifferent, not to say a bad, use of both advantages. Leaving superiority out of the question, then, you must still agree to receive my orders now and then, without being piqued or hurt by the tone of command – will you?'

F. SCOTT FITZGERALD: THE GREAT GATSBY

'Hello, Wilson, old man,' said Tom, slapping him jovially on the shoulder. 'How's business?'

'I can't complain,' answered Wilson unconvincingly. 'When are you going to sell me that car?'

'Next week; I've got my man working on it now.'

'Works pretty slow, don't he?'

'No, he doesn't,' said Tom coldly. 'And if you feel that way about it, maybe I'd better sell it somewhere else after all.'

'I don't mean that,' explained Wilson quickly. 'I just meant –'

His voice faded off and Tom glanced impatiently around the garage.

CHINUA ACHEBE: THINGS FALL APART

'I did not know it was you,' Ekwefi said to the woman who had stood shoulder to shoulder with her since the beginning of the matches.

'I do not blame you,' said the woman. 'I have never seen such a large crowd of people. Is it true that Okonkwo nearly killed you with his gun?'

'It is true indeed, my dear friend. 'I cannot yet find a mouth with which to tell the story.'

'Your *chi* is very much awake, my friend. And how is my daughter, Ezinma?'

'She has been very well for some time now. Perhaps she has come to stay.'

'I think she has. How old is she now?'

'She is about ten years old.'

STUDYING NARRATIVE TEXTS

ARUNDHATI ROY: THE GOD OF SMALL THINGS

Comrade Pillai pushed his spectacles up into his hair in order to read aloud the text. The lenses immediately grew fogged with hairoil.

'*Synthetic Cooking Vinegar,*' he said. 'This is all in caps, I suppose.'

'Prussian Blue,' Chacko said.

'*Prepared from Acetic Acid?*'

'Royal Blue,' Chacko said. 'Like the one we did for green pepper in brine.'

'*Net Contents. Batch No., Mfg date, Expiry Date, Max Rtl Pr. Rs* ... same Royal Blue colour but c. and l.c.?'

Chacko nodded.

'*We hereby certify that the vinegar in this bottle is warranted to be of the nature and quality it purports to be. Ingredients: Water and Acetic Acid.* This will be red colour I suppose.'

Comrade Pillai used 'I suppose' to disguise questions as statements. He hated asking questions unless they were personal ones. Questions signified a vulgar display of ignorance.

IAN MCEWAN: ATONEMENT

He guessed that in a few minutes he would be walking back across the park towards the bungalow.

'It wasn't the version I intended to send.'

'No.'

'I put the wrong one in the envelope.'

'Yes.'

He could gauge nothing by these terse replies and he was still unable to see her expression clearly.

JHUMPA LAHIRI: THE NAMESAKE

'But, sir,' Ashima protests, 'we can't possibly name him ourselves.'

Mr Wilcox, slight, bald, unamused, glances at the couple, both visibly distressed, then glances at the nameless child. 'I see,' he says. 'The reason being?'

'We are waiting for a letter,' Ashoke says, explaining the situation in detail.

'I see,' Mr Wilcox says again. 'That is unfortunate. I'm afraid your only alternative is to have the certificate read 'Baby Boy Ganguli.' You will, of course, be required to amend the permanent record when a name is decided upon.'

Ashima looks at Ashoke expectantly. 'Is that what we should do?'

'I don't recommend it,' Mr Wilcox says. 'You will have to appear before a judge, pay a fee. The red tape is endless.'

'Oh dear,' Ashoke says.

INVESTIGATING THE WAY DIALOGUE IS USED IN YOUR NOVEL

Exploring the dialogue in your text

1. Flick through your set text, looking out for the way in which the writer deals with dialogue – how is it presented? How is dialogue attributed to characters?

2. Choose one passage that seems characteristic of the way in which dialogue is created and represented. Look in more detail at the way the dialogue works in this passage. What is the function of the dialogue in this extract (it may have more than one)?

3. Range across your set text to find two or three further passages with dialogue and consider the different functions it fulfils in each case.

Creative interventions

1. Analyse the way dialogue works in your text by trying one of the following interventions and exploring the difference it makes to the meaning and impact of the passage.

   - Turn direct speech into indirect or reported speech (*'Don't be so sure,' the girl warned him.* becomes *The girl warned him that he should not be so sure.*)

   - Vary the use of speech tags. For instance, remove all speech tags and present the passage as drama; replace speech tags with 'said'; add speech tags wherever they are not used; or replace 'said' with a more specific speech tag (adverb or adverbial phrase).

   - Re-write the dialogue in the narrative voice, using reported speech, free indirect style and so on.

   - Re-write the passage, adding in explanatory sub-text either in the voice of the character or in the narrative voice.

   - Present a passage as drama.

2. Take an extract from a narrative of your own (e.g. written in response to a story outline) and write a section of dialogue in the style of your set text.

3. What is revealed about the original text by making any of these changes?

Can spoken language analysis help you discuss dialogue in novels?

1. Consider whether any of the techniques used to analyse spoken language texts on pages 36 to 41 might also help you explore the representation of speech in narrative texts.

2. Choose a short passage of dialogue from your set text and annotate it, using the conversation analysis tools on page 148. What insights do you get into the way the dialogue works?

3. Try writing a short analysis of the passage, drawing on your conversation analysis but making sure you discuss it as a literary text, not as a real conversation!

STUDYING NARRATIVE TEXTS

Setting

The setting of a novel might seem rather incidental – only important in conjuring up a visual picture for the reader or evoking a particular impression. In most novels, the setting is far more than this: it's not just the place in which the story happens to take place, but one of the ways in which the meaning of the story is created.

One way to test whether or not the setting is significant in your novel is to ask what would happen if you transposed it to another setting.

1. Try this out with your novel now, using a table like the one below to organise your thinking:

SETTING	TRANSPOSED TO	EFFECT

2. If you decide the setting is a significant aspect of the narrative, then think about its function, across the novel as a whole or at specific points. Some of the functions of settings are suggested here:

- as a backdrop to events

- to evoke place and create a sense of realism

- to establish mood/atmosphere

- to signal genre

- to structure the novel

- to act symbolically

- to set up themes

- to create expectations in the reader

- to convey contrasts of character.

The starting-points on each text opposite show you some of the sorts of thing you might begin to think about.

LANGUAGE AND LITERATURE

EXPLORING SETTING – EXAMPLES

Charlotte Brontë: Jane Eyre

- *Structural importance – movement to different places marking shift to new phases of life. Links to rites of passage genre. Foregrounded through journeys between places – moments of transition and the symbolism of doors opening and closing.*

- *Settings associated with particular genres – especially the Gothic, which not only conjure up the atmosphere (and so contribute to the plot) but also create certain expectations in the reader more widely.*

F. Scott Fitzgerald: The Great Gatsby

- *Evocation of place – backdrop to events, detailed and specific descriptions of New York, Valley of Ashes, East and West Egg, for example.*

- *Symbolic significance of the settings, contributing to central themes (wealth, class, appearance and reality).*

Chinua Achebe: Things Fall Apart

- *Essential to whole plot and themes – village life in Nigeria at a time of change.*

- *Structural shifts of Okonkwo's exile and return.*

Arundhati Roy: The God of Small Things

- *Central to the themes of the novel – Indian society and values, the postcolonial context.*

- *Immediacy of the setting in Kerala, e.g. the river, the cinema, the airport.*

- *New York as a foil.*

Ian McEwan: Atonement

- *Settings linked to passage through time – a way of locating the action in time as well as place (pre-War, during the War etc).*

- *Generic expectations to be played with – country house setting.*

- *Structural importance of different sections of the book.*

Jhumpa Lahiri: The Namesake

- *The immigrant experience – movement from India and America and back.*

- *Settings connected to the use of journeys as a structural and symbolic device (scenes set in trains, buses, cars), linking to the idea of change, movement, development.*

- *Contrast in setting on a big scale (India/America) and smaller scale (family houses).*

The Handling of Time

The author's handling of time is one of the ways we distinguish between a story and a narrative. A story is bound by chronological time; a narrative is not. Chronological time and narrative time do not need to run alongside a narrative.

TIME IN NARRATIVE TEXTS – AN OVERVIEW

Some of the things a writer can do to time, include:

- extending it, making a small amount of chronological time take up a lot of narrative time

- compressing it

- reversing it

- leaping over it, missing out days, years, centuries

- moving backwards and forwards across it

- choosing the tense (past, present or a combination of the two)

- using flashbacks

- weaving together two or more time periods

- foreshadowing events with hints of what is to come.

Possible effects of playing with time include:

- drawing attention to relationships between different times

- highlighting particular events

- delaying a resolution

- increasing suspense

- creating a sense of immediacy

- manipulating the reader's response to a character.

---

1. Look back at the narrative beginning you wrote (see pages 171-172) or another piece of narrative writing you have done during the course. How did you handle time?

2. Explore the effects writers can create through manipulating time, by experimenting with a few small changes to your own text.

HOW IS TIME HANDLED IN YOUR NOVEL?

1. In pairs or as a class, share your impressions of how time is handled in your set novel. Is time an important element of the novel (in relation to the plot, keeping the reader in suspense or even thematically)? Share your thoughts.

2. Based on your initial impressions, choose one of the following activities to help you look more closely at the handling of time.

a. Narrative v. chronological order

• Make a list of the main events in your novel.

• Organise them into the order they occur in the narrative and record them in the first column of a table like this one.

NARRATIVE ORDER	CHRONOLOGICAL ORDER

• Now re-organise the events into chronological order.

• What do you discover? If narrative and chronological order coincide, what does this tell you about the novel? If the narrative order is very different from the chronological order, consider why the writer chose to re-order the events. What difference does it make to the meaning?

b. A focus on tense

• Explore the way tense is used by the writer and to what effect by doing the following.

   • Skim through your text and choose four or five choose extracts in which tense or shifts in tense strike you as interesting and annotate them with post-it notes.

   • Write an overview paragraph summing up the way the writer's handling of tenses contributes to the meaning and impact of the novel.

c. Time as a theme

In some novels time has a thematic as well as structural and stylistic function. It might be the relationship between the past and the present that is explored or the awareness of time passing; it might be linked to another theme such as mortality or youth or change; it might even be an explicit concern of the characters.

• Explore the ways in which time could be interpreted as a theme in your set novel.

STUDYING NARRATIVE TEXTS

The Shape and Structure of Stories

> The structure of a narrative is like the framework of girders that holds up a modern high-rise building: you can't see it, but it determines the edifice's shape and character. The effects of a novel's structure, however, are experienced not in space but over time – often quite a long time.
>
> *David Lodge: The Art of Fiction*

The way the writer handles and manipulates time is closely related to the structure or shape of the story. A novel which begins in the present, then moves to an earlier period for the main events of the story, before returning to the present will have a very different shape from the novel which progresses through time chronologically. It will also have a different effect on the reader.

EXPLORING THE SHAPE

The novelist Kurt Vonnegut was very interested in the process of writing and particularly the shape of stories. In a lecture to a group of university students he argued that there are only a limited number of story structures and – with tongue in cheek – proved this by drawing a series of graphs to represent them. For example, one archetypal story structure is that showing how a person of low fortune achieves something great, only to have it taken away from them part way through and have it restored again by the end. This story shape is seen in the fairy tale *Cinderella*.

Some years later Maya Eilam created a series of diagrams, developing these ideas. You can watch Vonnegut's lecture by searching for 'Kurt Vonnegut the shape of stories' on YouTube.

Maya Eilam's story shapes, based on Kurt Vonnegut's lecture

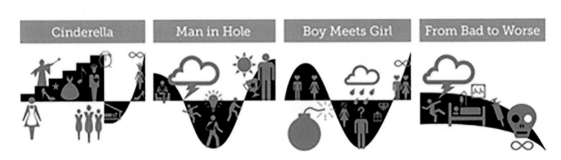

1. In pairs, sketch the shape of your narrative set text. Don't worry about the detail, try to give a broadbrush overview of its shape. Which of the story shapes above would you say is the best fit? Does it deviate from the expected structure in any way? If so, how? Or is the shape of your narrative completely different?

2. Compare your ideas (and shapes) in class discussion.

LOOKING MORE CLOSELY AT THE STRUCTURE

In any narrative, whatever the medium (film, novel, television programme), there are likely to be some recognisable structural elements, as shown here.

KEY STRUCTURAL ELEMENTS

- The set-up
- Disruption
- Complication
- The midpoint
- The turning point/s
- The climax
- The revelation
- The point of no return
- The point of resolution
- The cliffhanger
- The end

1. In pairs, choose a fairly short narrative you know and talk about which of the structural elements you can identify. For example, if you look at *Casualty*, you might decide that each episode follows the same basic structure:

   - the set up

   - the complication

   - the revelation

   - the resolution.

2. What about the story of *Cinderella*? Is there a disruption, for example, and, if so, when in the story does it happen? What about a turning point or resolution?

3. Now try to do the same for your set novel. Draw a horizontal line to represent the novel from first to last page. Identify where the different structural points occur.

4. If asked to write about the structure of your novel, what would be the five or six key points you would want to make? The notes below show you the type of points you might make.

AN EXAMPLE – A FEW KEY POINTS

- *Time compressed in first chapter – overview of early childhood.*
- *Shifts into present tense for central scene which changes everything.*
- *Linked to setting – shifts in place coincide with significant points in structure (disruption, turning point, climax etc).*

5. Use your points to write a broadbrush overview of the structure and its relationship to the meaning and impact of the story.

STUDYING NARRATIVE TEXTS

BROADBRUSH OVERVIEW – THREE EXAMPLES

- *This is a retrospective narrative which uses a frame narrator to introduce and conclude the story.*

- *This is a story told through flashbacks, allowing the reader to piece together the story and made connections between events in the past and the present.*

- *Broadly there is a move through crisis to a resolution with the hope of happiness but lots of little points of crisis along the way.*

Here are some of the key things to consider when exploring the structure of the narrative.

6. Which of these do you think are particularly important to your set novel?

TIME, SHAPE AND STRUCTURE – SUMMING IT UP

- The overall shape and organisation of the narrative (linear, episodic, circular, parallel, embedded).

- The development of the plot.

- The relationship between different sections of the narrative (the opening and the ending, repeated events).

- Chronological versus narrative order.

- The role of genre in shaping the narrative (e.g. the move in a crime novel from unresolved crime to a solution).

- The use of narrative devices such as a frame-story, prologue and epilogue.

- The use of setting/place and change of settings.

- Turning points, moments of climax, revelation and resolution.

- The handling of time (see page 194, above).

- Repeated motifs (such as images or symbols).

WRITING ABOUT STRUCTURE IN THE EXAM

- If you are preparing for the **A Level exam**, range across the novel and select three or four passages which could be used in an essay discussing the structure. With a partner, explain the key points you would make about them in your answer.

- If you are preparing for the **AS exam**, you will need to practise analysing the way the story is told in an extract from the novel (see page 204). Open the text at random. With a partner, discuss how knowing about the structure of the novel as a whole could help you analyse the way the story is told in this particular extract.

Prose Style

What makes a narrative text distinctive? As well as all the other aspects dealt with so far in this book, each writer has their own unique style of writing that makes them recognisable. You can see this in the following short extracts by two American writers, Ernest Hemingway and Henry James.

1. Read the extracts and as a class discuss what makes the two styles distinctive. Use the summary of key aspects of narrative style on page 200, if you need to.

> Her father's life, her sister's, her own, that of her two lost brothers
> – the whole history of their house had the effect of some fine florid,
> voluminous phrase, say even a musical, that dropped first into words,
> into notes, without sense, and then, hanging unfinished, into no words,
> no notes at all. Why should a set of people have been put in motion,
> on such a scale and with such an air of being equipped for a profitable
> journey, only to break down without an accident, to stretch themselves
> in the wayside dust without a reason? The answer to these questions
> was not in Chirk Street, but the questions themselves bristled there, and
> the girl's repeated pause before the mirror and the chimney-place might
> have represented her nearest approach to an escape from them.
>
> *Henry James: The Wings of a Dove (1902)*

> Their room was on the second floor facing the sea. It also faced the
> public garden and the war monument. There were big palms and green
> benches in the public garden. In the good weather there was always an
> artist with his easel.
>
> *Ernest Hemingway: Cat in the Rain (1925)*

2. Now look at this third extract, from the British writer Angela Carter. Talk about which aspects of narrative style make this extract distinctive. Is it the same aspects as you identified for the Hemingway and James extracts?

> As soon as my husband handed me down from the high step of the train,
> I smelled the amniotic salinity of the ocean. It was November; the trees
> stunted by the Atlantic gales, were bare and the lonely halt was deserted
> but for his leather-gaitered chauffeur waiting meekly beside the sleek
> black motor car. It was cold; I drew my furs about me, a wrap of white
> and black, broad stripes of ermine and sable, with a collar from which my
> head rose like the calyx of a wildflower. (I swear to you I had never been
> vain until I met him.)
>
> *Angela Carter: The Bloody Chamber and Other Stories (1979)*

STUDYING NARRATIVE TEXTS

A CLOSE FOCUS ON ASPECTS OF NARRATIVE STYLE

Style is all about the way the writer uses language – everything from the choice of a particular word, to the length of the sentences and the balance between description, dialogue and reflection.

1. As a class, flick through your novel, looking for a passage that strikes you as being typical in terms of style. Annotate this passage with key aspects of the style that seem typical of the novel.

2. Now range across the text for look for another passage where the style seems to you to be different. Make a note of the key ways in which the passage differs and your ideas about the reasons for the difference in style (for example, one passage might be action-packed and the other reflective). Share your passages as a class and talk about how consistent or varied the style is and why.

3. Look at the opening and ending of the novel. Are there significant differences in style? If so, why might that be? If not, why not?

4. Choose one of the aspects of narrative and style you have noticed as particularly characteristic of your writer and pursue it through the text, selecting four or five short extracts which allow you to say something interesting. Sum up your discoveries as bullet points to share with the rest of the class.

KEY ASPECTS OF NARRATIVE STYLE

- Narrative voice.
- Use of repetition, parallels, oppositions, contrasts.
- Use of tenses.
- Tone and register (poetic, conversational, informal, formal etc).
- Sentence types, structure and length.
- Balance of dialogue, plot narration, reflection and description.
- Lexical choices (groups, contrasts, kinds).
- Figurative language, symbols and motifs.
- Use of generic conventions.

A Very Close Focus – Using Stylistics Approaches

Stylistics, paying very close attention to the patterns of repetition and deviation in a text, is often used as a way of exploring poetry texts (see pages 85-117), where the complete text can be analysed. Although it might be possible to apply these approaches to very short short stories, on the whole complete narrative texts are too long.

Even if it's not possible to do a rigorous stylistics analysis of a complete novel, you can still make use of the ideas at the heart of this approach, in looking at short extracts:

- systematic analysis of word classes

- use of pattern-making and pattern-breaking

- foregrounding through repetition

- foregrounding through deviation.

- Select three short paragraphs from different points in the novel. Carry out a stylistic analysis, using the methodology on page 115-117. What do you discover about the style? Can you draw on this analysis to make any more general comments about the style of the novel at different points?

Other Ways of Looking at Style across the Text

PATTERNING – KEYWORDS AND IMAGES

- Investigate the text focusing on just a key word or image, looking for patterns in its use – and points at which the pattern is broken or deviated from. For example, you might notice that one of the characters is always described in terms of the natural world. If the writer then breaks this pattern by using imagery associated with the urban world or money or machinery, it's worth paying attention to that, and asking the question: 'why?'.

SYNTAX

- Focus on the syntax in the opening few paragraphs. Are there repeated structures (parallelism)? What is the effect when this is deviated from? Are the patterns you've noticed repeated throughout the novel?

SECRET STRINGS

- Choose a short passage and look for the 'secret strings' running through it (see pages 89-90). Now consider whether you can follow these strings across the novel.

STUDYING NARRATIVE TEXTS

FOREGROUNDING

- Think of foregrounding through patterning, repetition and deviation on a bigger scale – at the level of the opening and ending of chapters, for example, or in the use of settings.

COMMENTS ON CLOSE READING

- Read the following comments on close reading and talk about how the ideas raised might relate to the requirements of this component.

> **Good close reading should be like looking at a large picture in an art gallery. We don't begin by marching right up to a big canvas to scrutinise a detail – that is not looking at the picture at all. Rather, we stand at a distance first and take in the whole, then move in on something, then stand back again and take in how that and other details relate to each other, and to the whole.**
>
> *Professor Peter Barry*

> **As we read closely, we need to be able to move freely between the 'micro' and the 'macro', the detail and the larger pattern.**
>
> *Professor Ben Knights*

OPEN THE TEXT – PLACING THE EXTRACT IN ITS CONTEXT

1. Working in pairs, open your set text novel at random.

2. Together put the passage you have found in context, using the questions below to prompt you.

   - Where does it occur in the novel?

   - What is its function?

   - What type of passage does it seem to be?

3. Take it in turns briefly to introduce your passages to the class.

EXTRACT IN NUTSHELL

1. Open the book at random.

2. Read the passage, then turn to a partner and sum up in a few sentences what the passage it about.

3. Read it again and this time try to *write* a two or three sentence overview, giving the gist of the passage.

OPEN THE BOOK – 1-MINUTE, 5-MINUTE, 20-MINUTE RESPONSE

Open the book

1-minute: quick snapshot

- What it the extract about?

5-minute: pin it down

- Where it appears in the narrative.

- Overarching shape.

- Its function, for example:

  - a moment of crisis

  - a build-up towards a key event

  - a key event

  - a moment of particular pathos, or tragedy, or hope

  - beginning or ending.

- Select three or four really significant ways in which the story is being told.

20-minute: write it

5-minute: check it:

- Did you:

  - set the chapter/extract in context

  - include a crisp evaluation of what makes the extract distinctive

  - give a sense of the shape and development of the chapter

  - avoid a line-by-line analysis

  - avoid getting sucked into microanalysis

  - explore three or four significant aspects of ways of telling?

The Way the Story is Told – Analysing an Extract (AS)

The **AS Level exam** on the language of literature will ask you to analyse the way the story is told in an extract printed on the page. The question will follow this pattern:

> **Write about the ways in which Arundhati Roy tells the story in this extract.**
>
> **In your answer you should:**
>
> • **explore the narrative techniques used in the extract**
>
> • **consider the extract in the context of the novel as a whole and its genre.**

To do this well, you will need to:

- know the whole text well and be able to place the extract in its context in the novel

- have a good sense of the way the story is told throughout the novel

- analyse the particular passage, focusing on what is really significant and interesting in the way it is told

- marshall your ideas into a coherent written analysis, giving an overview of the passage and moving between 'big picture' comments and detailed analysis.

If you are preparing for the **A Level exam** (see page 205), you will find it very helpful both to get to know your novel and develop the skill of close reading through analysing extracts in the ways suggested here.

Aspects of Narrative – the Novel as a Whole (A Level)

For the A Level exam, you will be asked to discuss an aspect of the narrative, for example, the setting, the voice and so on. You will be asked to range across the novel as a whole and to consider the broader generic context of narrative (and, where relevant, genres such as romance, Gothic, rites of passage).

You will always be given a choice of two questions which will follow this pattern:

How does the writer of your text use settings?

You should range across the text to explore how settings are presented, the role they play in the novel as a whole, and the broader generic context.

Use the suggestions here to help you prepare for the exam.

JUST A MINUTE

1. Prepare a set of aspects of narrative cards, using the list below. (Put each item on a separate card.)

2. Work in twos. Turn over a card. With no advance preparation, try talking for a minute on your narrative text in relation to the topic on the card.

3. When you have each tried it once, pause for a few moments to reflect, prioritise and think of examples to support your ideas. Now do your 'Just a Minute' again.

SOME KEY ASPECTS OF NARRATIVE

- The opening
- The ending
- Suspense/tension
- Repetition
- Character
- Images and symbols
- Structure
- Narrative voice
- Settings
- Generic conventions
- Dialogue
- Time
- Point of view
- Style

STUDYING NARRATIVE TEXTS

SAME IDEA, DIFFERENT TERMINOLOGY

The terms used in the list on page 205 are not the *only* ones that could be used in relation to these key aspects of narrative. A question might ask you to analyse the 'representation of speech' rather than the 'dialogue', for example, or to discuss 'place' rather than 'settings'.

1. In your pairs, come up with as many different ways these aspects could be described in an exam question.

2. Be prepared to think freshly in the exam, if the wording doesn't exactly match the terms you have used in class discussion. You need to recognise that 'place' involves many of the same ideas as 'setting', or that 'narrative perspective' is largely about 'point of view'.

RELATIONSHIP BETWEEN DIFFERENT ASPECTS OF NARRATIVE

It's also worth remembering that some of the aspects overlap. The question will ask you to discuss one aspect of narrative but you may need to range across categories to answer it well.

For example:

- the question asks you to think about setting.

In answering how setting is used in your set text, you might also consider the following.

- The relationship to genre (a castle, a school and a family home are all associated with different genres, for example).

- The structure (is the development of the novel associated with the move to different places? Are there contrasting settings?).

- The creation of mood, atmosphere, tension through setting.

- The symbolic significance of the settings, or the language used to evoke them.

- Exploration of themes raised by choosing a particular setting or shifts in setting.

  EMC

5B.
WRITING AS A READER

Introduction

In **Component 3 of the A Level,** there are two sections, one based on the narrative text that you have studied, the other asking you to write your own brief narrative opening.

This section of the book will help you to prepare for the Section B writing task, bringing together your understandings from work on your narrative text in Section A (and on the nature of narrative techniques), with the requirement to write your own narrative (with a commentary) in Section B. Reading as a writer and writing as a reader should help you become both a better, more reflective reader, and a better, more well-equipped writer.

What is the Section B writing task?

In Section B of the exam, you will be given two sets of bullet points, giving the bare outline of two different stories, with the simple events, listed in chronological order. You will be asked to choose one of these to turn into the opening of a narrative, drawing on everything you have learned in this Component about the way narratives work and the choices available to writers. You will be asked to write a short commentary of approximately 250 words outlining the key narrative and linguistic choices you made in your opening.

The story outlines in the exam might be taken from a range of different types of stories – well-known stories such as legends, realistic stories of everyday life or stories within familiar genres such as thriller, science fiction or crime stories. Each of the two outlines will be different, so you will have a choice of the type of story you'd rather write.

In preparing for the exam, you will want to draw on what you've learned from your study of your set narrative text but you also need to have had plenty of experience of writing different kinds of story openings. The activities that follow offer you some starting-points.

EMC LANGUAGE AND LITERATURE

Re-telling Well-known Stories

One source of ideas for fiction writers is stories that have been told before. Many writers take a basic pre-existing storyline and do something with it – focusing on the themes or characters that particularly interest them, updating it to provide a new perspective, or adapting it for a particular kind of audience, for instance as a young adult novel or children's book. Sometimes novelists choose to write sequels or prequels to famous novels.

Here are some of the kinds of stories that have been successfully adapted:

- Bible stories or tales from other religious faiths

- Greek or Roman myths and legends

- Fairy stories or folk stories

- Updated versions of famous novels from earlier periods

- Prequels or sequels to famous stories or novels.

In preparing for the exam for Component 3 of the A Level, it would be helpful to look at a range of re-tellings, to explore how writers have adapted existing stories. Analysing what they have done will help you to think about ways in which you might turn a story into the opening of a narrative yourself.

Here are some examples of texts you might like to look at:

SOURCE STORY	FICTIONAL RE-WORKING
Little Red Riding Hood	Angela Carter: *The Company of Wolves*
Bluebeard's Castle	Angela Carter: *The Bloody Chamber*
The story of Mary, the mother of Jesus	Colm Toibin: *The Testament of Mary*
The legend of Achilles, from Homer's *Iliad*	David Malouf: *Ransom* Madeleine Miller: *The Song of Achilles*
The story of Odysseus & Penelope	Margaret Atwood: *The Penelopiad*
Jane Austen: *Pride and Prejudice*	Helen Fielding: *Bridget Jones' Diary*
E.M. Forster: *Howards End*	Zadie Smith: *On Beauty*

AN EXAMPLE OF A RE-TOLD STORY: THE TROJAN WARS, FROM HOMER'S ILIAD

These extracts from novels by two different writers take a well-known story from Greek legend, the story of Odysseus and his wife Penelope who is left behind when he goes on his travels to take part in the Greek war against the Trojans.

1. Read the two extracts on pages 210-211.

2. Talk about significant features of the narrative technique and the choices that have been made. Consider differences between the tellings. In each case can you tell anything about the intended audience for the novels, from the way the story is told?

3. Individually, decide whether you prefer one of the tellings, or like both equally for different reasons. Then discuss your preferences.

4. Read this simple telling of another part of the story of the Trojan wars. Try writing your own opening, making decisions about how you are going to tell the story and whether you are going to write for a particular audience – children, young adults, readers of romantic fiction, readers of literary fiction or any other readership.

THE STORY OF THE TROJAN HORSE

- There was a war between Greece and Troy. The Greeks had been besieging the city of Troy for 10 years, without breaking down the resistance of the Trojans.

- The Greeks, led by Odysseus, decided to pretend to sail away.

- They left a big wooden horse behind them, with a select group of soldiers hidden in the horse.

- The Trojans saw the Greeks sailing away and thought they had finally won.

- The Trojan priest Laocoon guessed that this was a trick and warned the Trojans not to bring the horse into Troy.

- The Trojans ignored him and pulled the horse into the city of Troy as a trophy of their victory.

- In the night the Greek soldiers crept out of the horse.

- They opened the gates of Troy so that the rest of the Greek army, who had sailed back overnight, could enter the city.

- The Greek army destroyed the city of Troy, finally and decisively winning the war.

RE-TELLING ONE

ITHAKA – ADELE GERAS

BEFORE THE WAR

Odysseus, his wife Penelope and their baby Telemachus are sitting on a woollen coverlet spread out in the shade of a pomegranate tree. It's early in the morning. The baby, recently fed, is drowsing on his back, his hands flung out above his head, his mouth a little open and his eyes half closed. Penelope is trying hard not to cry. She's blinking to stop the tears from falling. She's turned her head away from her husband.

'Listen to me, Penelope,' he says. 'Look at me. Don't turn away. I have to go. Anyone who calls himself a man has a duty to go.'

'It's not your war. It's not your fight. What's Agamemnon ever done for you? Stay here. Stay with me and Telemachus, I beg of you, Odysseus. Look at your son. How can you bear to leave him?'

Odysseus shakes his head. 'I tried. You saw me trying. I did my best not to go. Didn't I? Didn't I pretend I was mad so as not to have to go?'

'It didn't work, though, did it?'

'Did you want me to run my plough over the body of my son?' Odysseus shakes his head.

'Agamemnon's as cunning as you are. He knew you were only pretending to be crazy. The ruler of Ithaka ploughing his own fields and sowing them with salt!' Penelope's voice breaks as she speaks. 'I saw the look on his face as he picked our baby up and laid him down on the ground, right in the path of your plough. He knew you were putting on a show. Tricking him.'

Telemachus stirs, makes a moaning noise and wakes up. He starts to grizzle and his mother gathers him up into her arms, nuzzling her face into the soft folds of his neck. Odysseus looks at his wife and child and tears stand in his eyes.

RE-TELLING TWO

MARGARET ATWOOD –

THE PENELOPIAD

My Childhood

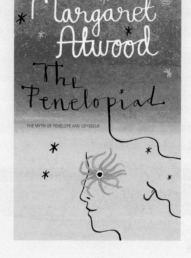

Where shall I begin? There are only two choices: at the beginning or not at the beginning. The real beginning would be the beginning of the world, after which one thing has led to another; but since there are differences of opinion about that, I'll begin with my own birth.

My father was King Icarius of Sparta. My mother was a Naiad. Daughters of Naiads were a dime a dozen in those days; the place was crawling with them. Nevertheless, it never hurts to be of semi-divine birth. Or it never hurts immediately.

When I was quite young my father ordered me to be thrown into the sea. I never knew exactly why, during my lifetime, but now I suspect he'd been told by an oracle that I would weave his shroud. Possibly he thought that if he killed me first, his shroud would never be woven and he would live forever. I can see how the reasoning might have gone. In that case, his wish to drown me came from an understandable desire to protect himself. But he must have misheard, or else the oracle herself misheard – the gods often mumble – because it was not his shroud that was at issue, but my father-in-law's shroud. If that was the prophecy it was a true one, and indeed the weaving of this particular shroud proved a great convenience to me in my life.'

STUDYING NARRATIVE TEXTS

Writing in or around a Genre

Writers often write within particular genres, such as thriller, detective, ghost, horror, science fiction, or romance fiction. Some follow the genre's conventions very closely; others experiment and adapt them, creating something quite different. Some writers use elements of a range of different genres within a single book.

In preparing for Section B of Component 3 of the A Level, you will find it helpful to explore some of the key genres of fiction, by reading some conventional examples that follow the genre closely, and some of the ways in which writers adapt or subvert the genre.

Here are a few examples of texts that have adapted and incorporated elements of a genre:

GENRE	CONVENTIONAL EXAMPLE	NOVEL USING THE GENRE
Fairytale	Cinderella	Charlotte Brontë: *Jane Eyre* (the uncared for orphan child who struggles against harsh treatment by her relatives)
Dystopia	George Orwell: *1984*	Margaret Atwood: *The Handmaid's Tale* (a feminist re-working)
Vampire	Bram Stoker: *Dracula*	Stephanie Meyer: *Twilight* (a contemporary re-working)
Detective	Arthur Conan Doyle: Sherlock Holmes stories Agatha Christie: *The Murder at the Vicarage*	Kate Atkinson: *Case Histories* (literary detective story, more humorous and full of unexpected twists than many and explicitly playing on the idea of coincidence)
Fantasy	*The Hobbit*	Adam Roberts: *The Soddit* (a parody)
Thriller	John le Carré: *The Spy Who Came in from the Cold*	Ian McEwan: *Enduring Love* (elements of the thriller woven into a serious literary novel with quite other themes)

A CONVENTIONAL COUNTRY HOUSE DETECTIVE STORY

The activity that follows will help you develop narrative choices be for the opening of a narrative based on the following storyline.

THE STORY

- Ten people are gathered for a weekend in a country house to celebrate the seventieth birthday of the host, a retired, unmarried Egyptologist who lives on his own with a housekeeper.

- The guests include:

  » a retired doctor and his wife

  » his middle-aged niece and her husband, both of whom are lawyers

  » a young female colleague from the university department where he used to work

  » the local vicar

  » an Egyptian friend from Cairo; his brother and sister, who live close by

  » the housekeeper.

- The guests gather for dinner and talk about strange things that have happened on occasions such as this – crime stories, horror stories and so on.

- One guest tells such a story, frightening the other guests.

- The dinner is served.

- After dinner, one of the guests disappears.

- A search is instigated but he/she cannot be found.

- The police are called.

- Investigations begin and each of the guests is interviewed.

- It seems like an unsolvable puzzle but the detective in charge seems confident that he will get to the bottom of it.

- The detective lays a clever trap and finally one of the guests reveals themselves as responsible for the disappearance. The missing guest is discovered... dead or alive!

STUDYING NARRATIVE TEXTS

1. Talk in pairs or threes about the kinds of choices you might make, using this list of ideas to help you.

   - How might you play with time?

   - What choices are open to you in terms of narrative voice?

   - Would you follow the country house 'whodunnit' genre, or could you play with that and re-invent it? If you follow the generic conventions, what narrative choices would you need to make e.g. they often use flashbacks in embedded narratives, such as letters or diaries.

   - Will you write a parody, writing in a humorous way, or be serious and create genuine fear and suspense, or make it like a puzzle?

   - What options are open to you in terms of narrative style – narration, dialogue, description and so on?

   - Will you do anything 'postmodern', such as a direct address to the reader or using an intrusive narrator, or making metafictional comments along the way?

   - What other kinds of decisions might you make?

2. Try writing two different openings, each of which makes very different choices.

FOLLOW UP – PLAYING WITH OTHER GENRES

1. Choose another genre with which you are familiar. Write an outline story which broadly follows the conventions of that genre in a series of bullet points, like the one on page 213.

2. Then suggest how you could 'play' with this, through the narrative choices you make. Think about what effects might result.

> *For instance, a romance outline might start with a young woman bemoaning her lack of a boyfriend with her best friend and telling her about someone she fancies. The next bullet point might be about a party both are planning to go to. The third might involve her tripping up and spraining her ankle, so that she can't dance. She spends the evening watching her friend dancing with the boy she fancies. And so on...*
>
> *Your playful twisting of the conventions might mean that you start with the twisted ankle.*

3. Alternatively, write a bullet-point story outline in a genre you have been focusing on as a class, for other students to then turn into the opening of a narrative.

Writing Realism

Realist texts aim to create a world that the reader can believe in and characters that seem like real people. Caricature, exaggeration, fantasy and improbability feature in other kinds of narratives – fantasies, satires or social comedies for instance – but they don't tend to figure largely in realist texts. If they are used, it tends to be in relation to minor characters rather than the protagonist or the key figures.

Realist texts try to convey human experience in a way that is true to life and convincing for the reader, but that doesn't mean that they all do so in exactly the same ways.

Included on pages 216-218 are six short examples from the novels that are set as narrative texts for this specification. In each case, there is an attempt to evoke a character in a broadly realistic way.

1. Talk about the different ways in which each of the texts creates character, selecting from this list of possible techniques and adding anything else you notice.

CREATING CHARACTER

- Description of clothing.

- Description of physical attributes.

- What the character says.

- How the character says what he/she says.

- What other characters say about the character, or how they react to him/her.

- The character's actions.

- The narrator's view of the character, giving own feelings about him/her.

- The narrative statement of what the character is like.

- Imagery used to evoke the character (metaphors, similes and so on).

- Recurring words used to describe the character.

- Present tense narration.

CHARLOTTE BRONTË: JANE EYRE

Mrs Reed and I were left alone: some minutes passed in silence: she was sewing, I was watching her. Mrs Reed might be at that time some six or seven and thirty; she was a woman of robust frame, square-shouldered and strong-limbed, not tall, and though stout, not obese: she had a somewhat large face, the under-jaw being much developed and very solid; her brow was low, her chin large and prominent, mouth and nose sufficiently regular; under her light eyebrows glimmered an eye devoid of ruth; her skin was dark and opaque, her hair nearly flaxen; her constitution was sound as a bell – illness never came near

her; she was an exact, clever manager, her household and tenantry were thoroughly under her control; her children, only, at times defied her authority, and laughed it to scorn; she dressed well, and had a presence and port calculated to set off handsome attire.

Sitting on a low stool, a few yard from her arm-chair, I examined her figure; I perused her features.

F. SCOTT FITZGERALD: THE GREAT GATSBY

I looked back at my cousin, who began to ask me questions in her low, thrilling voice. It was the kind of voice that the ear follows up and down, as if each speech is an arrangement of notes that will never be played again. Her face was sad and lovely with bright things in it, bright eyes and a bright passionate mouth, but there was an excitement in her voice that men who cared for her found difficult to forget: a singing compulsion, a whispered 'Listen', a promise that she had done gay, exciting things just a while since and that there were gay, exciting things hovering in the next hour.

I told her how I had stopped off in Chicago for a day on my way East, and how a dozen people had sent their love through me.

'Do they miss me?' she cried ecstatically?

'The whole town is desolate. All the cars have the left rear wheel painted black as a mourning wreath, and there's a persistent wail all night along the north shore.'

'How gorgeous! Let's go back, Tom. Tomorrow!'

CHINUA ACHEBE: THINGS FALL APART

Okonkwo returned from the bush carrying on his left shoulder a large bundle of grasses and leaves, roots and barks of medicinal trees and shrubs. He went into Ekwefi's hut, put down his load and sat down.

'Get me a pot,' he said, 'and leave the child alone.'

Ekwefi went to bring the pot and Okonkwo selected the best from his bundle, in their due proportion, and cut them up. He put them in the pot and Ekwefi poured in some water.

'Is that enough?' she asked when she had poured in about half of the water in the bowl.

'A little more... I said a little. Are you deaf?' Okonkwo roared at her.

She set the pot on the fire and Okonkwo took up his matchet to return to his obi.

ARUNDHATI ROY: THE GOD OF SMALL THINGS

From the way Ammu held her head, Rahel could tell that she was still angry. Rahel looked at her watch. Ten to two. Still no train. She put her chin on the window sill. She could feel the grey gristle of the felt that cushioned the window glass pressing into her chinskin. She took off her sunglasses to get a better look at the dead frog squashed on the road. It was so dead and squashed so flat that it looked more like a frog-shaped stain on the road than a frog. Rahel wondered if Miss Mitten had been squashed into a Miss Mitten-shaped stain by the milk truck that killed her.

IAN MCEWAN: ATONEMENT

All this – the river and flowers, running, which was something she rarely did these days, the fine ribbing of the oak trunks, the high-ceilinged room, the geometry of light, the pulse in her ears subsiding in the stillness – all this pleased her as the familiar was transformed into a delicious strangeness. But she also felt reproved for her homebound boredom. She had returned from Cambridge with a vague notion that her family was owed an uninterrupted stretch of her company. But her father remained in town, and her mother, when she wasn't nurturing her migraines, seemed distant, even unfriendly. Cecilia had carried up trays of tea to her mother's room – as spectacularly squalid as her own – thinking some intimate conversations might develop. However, Emily Tallis wanted to share only tiny frets about the household, or she lay back against the pillows, her expression unreadable in the gloom, emptying her cup in wan silence. Briony was lost to her writing fantasies – what had seemed like a passing fad was now an enveloping obsession. Cecilia had seen them on the stairs that morning, her younger sister leading the cousins, poor things, who had arrived only yesterday, up to the nursery to rehearse the play Briony wanted to put on that evening, when Leon and his friend were expected. There was so little time, and already one of the twins had been detained by Betty in the scullery for some wrongdoing or other. Cecilia was not inclined to help – it was too hot, and whatever she did, the project would end in calamity, with Briony expecting too much, and no one, especially the cousins, able to measure up to her frenetic vision.

JHUMPA LAHIRI: THE NAMESAKE

She lifts up her narrow body and in a single, swift motion arranges the coat beneath her buttocks and legs. It's a face he recognises from campus, someone he's crossed paths with in the corridors of buildings as he walks to and from class. He remembers that freshman year she'd had hair dyed an emphatic shade of cranberry red, cut to her jaw. She's grown it to her shoulders now, and allowed it to resume what appears to be its natural shade, light brown with bits of blond here and there. It is parted just off-center, a bit crooked at the base.

The hair of her eyebrows is darker, lending her otherwise friendly features a serious expression. She wears a pair of nicely faded jeans, brown leather boots with yellow laces and thick rubber soles. A cabled sweater the same flecked gray of her eyes is too large her for, the sleeves coming partway up her hands. A man's billfold bulges prominently from the front pocket of her jeans.

'Hi, I'm Ruth,' she says, recognising him in that same vague way.

WRITING YOUR OWN CHARACTER

In the **A Level Component 3 exam**, you might want to start your narrative by introducing one or more characters.

1. Look at some examples before you start.

Here are four examples of characters being introduced, using the storyline for the country house detective novel outline on page 213.

2. Read each in turn and talk about the techniques of characterisation being used, then discuss which you liked best and why.

EXAMPLE 1

Mrs Elfick was busying herself in the kitchen, assembling the ingredients for the bread and butter pudding and preparing the pheasants and partridge for the game pie. Her apron was covered in flour, her face pink from the heat of the oven, her hair in a state, having made a successful attempt to escape from her white linen cap to the freedom of its natural state – a grey frizzy tangle of curls. When Professor Jamieson poked his head round the door to find out if the preparations for the dinner were going well, she shooed him straight out, with a fierce reminder that the kitchen was her territory. He was most definitely not wanted there.

EXAMPLE 2

Professor Jamieson looked down the list of guests who would be coming to his seventieth birthday party. Among them was his oldest friend, Arthur Wilkinson, the village doctor, alongside his niece, Doris and her husband, Derek, both well-established lawyers in the nearby town. Then there was Arabella Alvarado, a colleague from the Museum who had worked with him on the excavations of the tomb at Luxor, a charming, attractive young woman, barely half his age. He had also invited one or two others whom he felt less close to, the vicar of Durnsfield, Mr Perkins, for instance. He had decided to ask him only at the last minute, purely out of kindness, since the poor man's wife had only just died; he had bumped into him at the village shop whilst buying a bottle of especially nice sherry for the occasion and asked him along. Abubakur Fakhoury, his dear friend and correspondent of nearly sixty years, fortunately happened to have planned a trip to England, and was arriving on the boat from Cairo that very morning. He hoped that he would manage to make his connection and get the fast train down in time for a stroll through the gardens before the other guests arrived.

EXAMPLE 3

We sat in front of the fire, sipping brandies and enjoying watching the flames flickering in the hearth. It had been a splendid dinner and Professor Jamieson had been on good form, telling stories of mummies found in unexpected places, scarabs and other artefacts mysteriously going missing and the singular case of the Egyptologist who'd gone down into a tomb and was never seen again, no trace of his remains ever being found. I was sitting on the edge of the group and a cool draft occasionally swept in from the door behind me. I reached for my tweed jacket and put it on, then turned to ask a question of Lucy Dibble, the Professor's delightful assistant, who had been sitting beside me beside the fire, only to discover that she was no longer there. In my usual rather unconfident way, I havered and hesitated about saying anything. After all, she had probably only gone to find the lavatory. I was a silly fool for feeling nervous, probably just influenced by the Professor's rather strange and disturbing tales of Egypt.

EXAMPLE 4

There was a whole host of people coming to the Professor's party and Chloe looked forward to meeting them, though she thought they sounded like a pretty strange bunch – the kind of people you'd be more likely to find in a corny Agatha Christie novel than a real-life village in Essex. She'd worked with the Prof for a few years now and always told her friends what a great colleague he was. He didn't take himself too seriously and scarcely looked the part of the expert Egyptologist, in his torn jeans, old round necked T-shirts and trainers. He was always full of jokes and quirky little anecdotes from his youth in the 1960s, often about rock heroes he'd encountered, or tales of sad, amorous adventures, told at his own expense. He was a lovely man, really he was, and if he'd been a decade or two younger, she could have even seen herself falling for him. He was certainly more interesting than those young ambitious Egyptologists who only had eyes for a glittering scarab or a well-wrapped mummy.

CHOOSING A CHARACTER AND INTRODUCING THEM IN YOUR OWN NARRATIVE

1. Choose one character from the list below and try writing a description of him/her that might come as their first introduction in a novel. Decide for yourself whether you're going to aim for realism, or instead adopt some of the features of one of the genres explored on pages 212-214.

   You could use ideas for how to convey the character drawn from your reading of the text extracts you've just looked at, and the list of possible techniques on page 215.

   - Someone your narrator meets while backpacking on a summer holiday, or gap year.

   - A badly behaved child who causes mayhem in a public place.

   - A kind, sympathetic teacher.

   - An old person who is frail and in need of support.

   - A detective who doesn't fit the conventional image of the fictional detective.

   - A sinister character, who is going to present a threat in the narrative.

   - The new love interest for your first-person narrator.

2. Share your writing and talk about what worked particularly well.

3. You could go on to write a paragraph about the same character in a very different style – perhaps abandoning purely realistic techniques in favour of something more exaggerated, satirical, humorous or quirky, to explore what difference this makes. For instance, if you've written about a sinister character in a realistic way, how about experimenting with writing them in the style of a horror story or fantasy novel?

EMC LANGUAGE AND LITERATURE

STUDYING NARRATIVE TEXTS

DRAWING ON WHAT YOU'VE LEARNED ABOUT NARRATIVE

Here's a story outline of the kind you might find in Section B of the exam paper for Component 3.

A FIRST WORLD WAR STORY

- A soldier said farewell to his sweetheart in 1915 and boarded a train for France.

- He was taken first to a camp near Arras and then on to the front line.

- He made friends with a soldier who was younger than him, homesick and finding it very hard to cope. He looked after him.

- He wrote letters home, telling his sweetheart about the young man.

- The men were asked to go out, over the trenches, to bring back some guns and ammunition from bodies of soldiers who had been killed.

- On this expedition, the young man was injured.

- The soldier risked his own life to drag his young friend back to the safety of the trenches.

- When they got back, the young man was taken to a makeshift hospital behind the lines.

- Later someone came to tell the soldier that his young friend had died.

---

1. Experiment with narrative technique by reminding yourself of a few key features of your set text novel and trying to draw on any that specially appeal to you, in writing an opening to this narrative.

For example, if you've been studying *Jane Eyre*, you might want to try out a first-person retrospective narrative voice and maybe include a strong motif of doors opening and closing to mark the closing of one period of the soldier's life (at home with his sweetheart) and the opening of another (the experience of war). Of if you've been studying *The God of Small Things*, perhaps you could choose to start with a very vivid, lush and inventively described evocation of place – maybe starting the narrative with the soldier arriving at the camp in Arras, or in the trenches.

A warning!

Do note, though, that in the exam, you will *not* be expected to imitate features of your set text, by parodying the text and its narrative features, or writing a pastiche of it. This is just an exercise in helping you to try out narrative techniques, drawing on what you've learned from studying one novel in depth.

WRITING A COMMENTARY

The commentary is a short, explanatory piece of writing to accompany your narrative and the examiners will use it to help them understand what you were aiming for and give them a sense of whether you were drawing on knowledge about narrative technique and language in your own writing, in other words, writing as a reader. Your commentary should:

- draw attention to some of the key features of narrative technique and language that you have chosen

- engage the reader by letting them into your thinking and your reasons for making the choices that you did.

Here are a few openings of commentaries that take different approaches, to give you some ideas of alternative ways in which you might begin to talk about your own choices. There is no single, correct way of doing it. The most important thing is to reveal your thinking in an interesting way.

- To practise writing a commentary, go back to one of the openings you have written. Try writing a short 250-word commentary on it, explaining your choices, drawing on any of the approaches taken in the examples below.

EXAMPLE 1

'One of the most important elements in my narrative was the way I chose to play with time. I decided to start the story at the end when...'

EXAMPLE 2

'Whodunnits often follow a very conventional structure. I wanted to subvert this, so I chose to start by revealing the murderer and work back, to show how she was trapped...'

EXAMPLE 3

'Starting with a bit of dialogue allowed me to leap straight into the story and arouse the reader's interest. Setting the scene comes later with...'

EXAMPLE 4

'I chose a first-person narrator, a character who would go on to witness the main events and come to know the main protagonist, rather than being the central character herself.'

EXAMPLE 5

'I spent a lot of my opening setting the scene, with a long descriptive passage, because the place is so important to the narrative. I used lots of minor sentences, just with noun phrases and no verbs, to paint the picture rapidly and in a strikingly direct way.'

LANGUAGE AND LITERATURE EMC

6.
THE NON-EXAMINED COMPONENT

6.
THE NON-EXAMINED COMPONENT

An Introduction to the Component

A Level Component 4 offers you a chance to draw on everything you've studied for your A Level, using your knowledge and skills to write two pieces of independent writing.

Task 1 – Analytical and Comparative Writing

The task is to write an analytical comparative essay on an aspect of the two texts, in 1500-2000 words. You are required to choose one non-fiction text from a list of set texts and pair it with another text of your own choice. The only other requirement is that at least one of the two texts must have been published post-2000.

— Solomon Northrop: *Twelve Years a Slave* (1853)

— George Orwell: *Down and Out in Paris and London* (1933)

— Truman Capote: *In Cold Blood* (1966)

— Bill Bryson: *The Lost Continent* (1989)

— Jenny Diski: *Skating to Antarctica* (1997)

— Anna Funder: *Stasiland: Stories from Behind the Berlin Wall* (2001)

— Alexander Masters: *Stuart A Life Backward* (2005)

— Xinran: *What the Chinese Don't Eat* (2006)

— Jeannette Winterson: *Why Be Happy When You Could be Normal?* (2012)

— Allie Brosh: *Hyperbole and a Half* (2013)

— Anon: *I am The Secret Footballer* (2013)

— Stephen Grosz: *The Examined Life: How we Lose and Find Ourselves* (2013)

EMC

The second free choice text could also be taken from the list, or it could be any other text that you choose, from any genre of poetry, fiction, non-fiction or drama, so long as it has been published in book form at some point in its life.

Task 2 – a piece of original non-fiction writing, with a short introduction

The original writing should be 1000-1200 words, including a short introduction of approximately 150 words, outlining some key elements that you would like to draw the reader/examiner's attention to.

You can write in any non-fiction genre. It's a chance to draw on what you've learned through your reading of non-fiction texts throughout the course, including preparation for Component 1.

Analytical and Comparative Writing

Similarity and Difference – a Way of Thinking about Texts

Comparison is a key element in the analysis of texts. It is integral to our way of thinking about them. We consider texts in terms of what they *aren't*, as much as what they are and we make sense of them by categorising them in relation to other texts.

Genre, for instance, is all about similarity and difference – grouping texts into categories like poetry, drama, fiction or non-fiction or into sub-categories like travel writing, journalism, memoir or biography involves thinking about how they relate to other texts and why they are in one category rather than another. In making decisions about categories, we think about how a text is like other texts in that genre, or how it differs from other genres. And within a genre, we group texts by how similar they are to other texts in the genre (following closely its conventions) or how different (breaking the rules or overlapping with other genres). So thinking about similarity and difference is central to the act of literary and linguistic textual analysis.

Why make individual choices rather than a whole class doing the same thing?

This is an opportunity for you to do a piece of independent research, on something that you've chosen for yourself. You should feel committed to the choice. It will also be very good preparation for future study or work, where you have to take control of a project, or piece of writing and organise your thinking for yourself. At university, for instance, most subjects and courses require students to write dissertations on a choice of topic or title, where they have only a small amount of support from a tutor.

Here's what the specification says about this:

> The non-examined assessment should provide opportunities for learners' independent choice and specialisation. It is not advisable for any two learners to do the same task on the same two texts.

What will your analytical and comparative writing be focused on?

The focus of your analytical and comparative writing will depend very much on the texts you've selected and the angle you choose. A tight focus on a significant aspect of the texts works much better than a very broad, loose topic.

- Look at these topics and discuss whether you think each one is tightly enough focused, too tightly focused or well judged, and explore the reasons why.

- Comparing the use of the first-person voice in two travel books.

- Comparing women and the way they are presented in a memoir by one writer and a novel by a different novelist.

- Comparing the way in which two non-fiction texts play with time, using flashback, memory, frame narratives and other non-chronological devices.

- Comparing sentence structure and variety in two texts notable for the use of sentences.

- Comparing satirical techniques in two satirical texts.

- Comparing a book of blogs about football with a memoir about football.

- Comparing the way the game itself is described, in a book of blogs and a memoir about football.

- Comparing two memoirs about growing up.

- Comparing the use of dialogue in two memoirs about growing up.

How to Choose Your Text from the Set Text List

The openings of all the set texts, along with a brief description of the text, are included on pages 230 to 241.

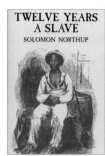 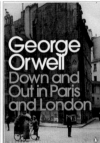    

  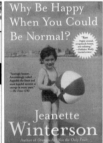   

Your teacher may have selected a handful of texts for your class to choose between, or may give you completely free choice from the list. Either way, you'll need to decide on which one to read in full, to make it the focus for your essay.

A word of advice!

You should start this process of reading and choosing early on, well before you need to actually write your essay.

1. Read all the openings you are going to choose between and individually pick the two or three that you would be most interested in reading in full.

2. Now join up with some other students and share your choices, discussing your reasons and hearing why others have chosen the same or different texts from you. In your discussion talk about the following issues:

   • Which texts did you find immediately engaging and want to continue reading? Why?

   • Which texts could you imagine having plenty to say about in an essay (e.g. in relation to their genre, or the interesting way they're written, or their use of voice or point of view, or anything else?)

   • In what ways do your choices relate to the genre of the text and/or your previous reading experiences and preferences?

TWELVE YEARS A SLAVE (1853)

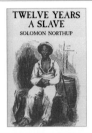

This book was first published in 1853 and is a first-person account of a man who lived as a freeman in the northern states of America, was kidnapped, taken to the Deep South and sold into slavery, spending twelve years in captivity before finally being rescued. In 2013 a film of the book was released, winning three Oscars and the Golden Globe for Best Motion Picture. The director, Steve McQueen, was quoted as saying that he thought the book should be set for all students to study in the National Curriculum.

Having been born a freeman, and for more than thirty years enjoyed the blessings of liberty in a free State – and having at the end of that time been kidnapped and sold into slavery, where I remained, until happily rescued in the month of January, 1853, after a bondage of twelve years – it has been suggested that an account of my life and fortunes would not be uninteresting to the public.

Since my return to liberty, I have not failed to perceive the increasing interest throughout the northern states, in regard to the subject of slavery. Works of fiction, professing to portray its features in their more pleasing as well as more repugnant aspects, have been circulated to an extent unprecedented, and, as I understand, have created a fruitful topic of comment and discussion.

 I can speak of slavery only so far as it came under my own observation – only so far as I have known and experienced it in my own person. My object is, to give a candid and truthful statement of facts: to repeat the story of my life, without exaggeration, leaving it for others to determine, whether even the pages of fiction present a picture of more cruel wrong or a severer bondage.

As far back as I have been able to ascertain, my ancestors on the paternal side were slaves in Rhode Island. They belonged to a family by the name of Northup, one of whom, removing to the State of New York, settled at Hoosic, in Rensselaer county. He brought with him Mintus Northup, my father. On the death of this gentleman, which must have occurred some fifty years ago, my father became free, having been emancipated by a direction in his will.

Henry B. Northup, Esq., of Sandy Hill, a distinguished counselor at law, and the man to whom, under Providence, I am indebted for my present liberty, and my return to the society of my wife and children, is a relative of the family in which my forefathers were thus held to service, and from which they took the name I bear. To this fact may be attributed the persevering interest he has taken in my behalf.

Sometime after my father's liberation, he removed to the town of Minerva, Essex county, N.Y., where I was born, in the month of July, 1808.

DOWN AND OUT IN PARIS AND LONDON (1933)

This memoir, first published in 1933 by George Orwell, the writer of 'Nineteen Eighty-Four', is an account of a period of his life in Paris and of his return to London. In both cities, he shared his life with the poor and destitute, working in Parisian restaurants and living as a homeless person in London. This book is one of his best known works of non-fiction, giving a vivid picture of life for the have-nots in society. The style of documentary writing that he adopts has become a model for many more books about life in contemporary Britain.

THE rue du Coq d'Or, Paris, seven in the morning. A succession of furious, choking yells from the street. Madame Monce, who kept the little hotel opposite mine, had come out on to the pavement to address a lodger on the third floor. Her bare feet were stuck into sabots and her grey hair was streaming down.

Madame Monce: 'Salope*! Salope! How many times have I told you not to squash bugs on the wallpaper? Do you think you've bought the hotel, eh? Why can't you throw them out of the window like everyone else? 'Putain**! Salope!'

The woman on the third floor: 'Vache***!'

Thereupon a whole variegated chorus of yells, as windows were flung open on every side and half the street joined in the quarrel. They shut up abruptly ten minutes later, when a squadron of cavalry rode past and people stopped shouting to look at them.

I sketch this scene, just to convey something of the spirit of the Rue du Coq d'Or. Not that quarrels were the only thing that happened there – but still, we seldom got through the morning without at least one outburst of this description. Quarrels, and the desolate cries of street hawkers, and the shouts of children chasing orange-peel over the cobbles, and at night loud singing and the sour reek of the refuse-carts, made up the atmosphere of the street.

It was a very narrow street – a ravine of tall, leprous houses, lurching towards one another in queer attitudes, as though they had all been frozen in the act of collapse. All the houses were hotels and packed to the tiles with lodgers, mostly Poles, Arabs and Italians. At the foot of the hotels were tiny bistros, where you could be drunk for the equivalent of a shilling. On Saturday nights about a third of the male population of the quarter was drunk. There was fighting over women, and the Arab navvies who lived in the cheapest hotels used to conduct mysterious feuds, and fight them out with chairs and occasionally revolvers.

* Salope: slut ** Putain: whore *** Vache: cow

IN COLD BLOOD (1966)

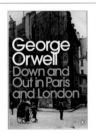

Truman Capote's book, first published in 1966, is a prose reconstruction of the murder in 1959 of four members of a farming family, the Clutters, living in the small town of Holcomb, Kansas. Capote conducted interviews with the two accused, the investigators and members of the local community, using them to write a non-fiction account of the events leading up to the conviction and execution of the two men. Though sub-titled 'A true account of a multiple murder and its consequences', 'In Cold Blood' draws heavily on the techniques of a fiction writer and is seen as a pioneering work of 'new journalism', a genre of non-fiction that blurs the boundaries between fact and fiction.

The village of Holcomb stands on the high wheat plains of western Kansas, a lonesome area that other Kansans call 'out there'. Some seventy miles east of the Colorado border, the countryside, with its hard blue skies and desert-clear air, has an atmosphere that is rather more Far West than Middle West. The local accent is barbed with a prairie twang, a ranch-hand nasalness, and the men, many of them, wear narrow frontier trousers, Stetsons, and high-heeled boots with pointed toes. The land is flat, and the views are awesomely extensive; horses, herds of cattle, a white cluster of grain elevators rising as gracefully as Greek temples are visible long before a traveller reaches them.

Holcomb, too, can be seen from great distances. Not that there is much to see – simply an aimless congregation of buildings divided in the center by the main-line tracks of the Santa Fe Railroad, a haphazard hamlet bounded on the south by a brown stretch of the Arkansas (pronounced 'Ar-kan-sas') River, on the north by a highway, Route 50, and on the east and west by prairie lands and wheat fields. After rain, or when snowfalls thaw, the streets, unnamed, unshaded, unpaved, turn from the thickest dust into the direst mud. At one end of the town stands a stark old stucco-structure, the roof of which supports an electric sign – DANCE – but the dancing has ceased and the advertisement has been dark for several years. Near by is another building with an irrelevant sign, this one in flaking gold on a dirty window – HOLCOMB BANK. The bank failed in 1933, and its former counting-rooms have been converted into apartments. It is one of the town's two 'apartment houses', the second being a ramshackle mansion known, because a good part of the local school's faculty lives there, as the Teacherage. But the majority of Holcomb's homes are one-story frame affairs, with front porches.

Down by the depot, the postmistress, a gaunt woman who wears a rawhide jacket and denims and cowboy boots, presides over a falling-apart post office. The depot itself, with its peeling sulphur-coloured paint, is equally melancholy; the Chief, the Super-Chief, the El Capitan go by every day, but these celebrated expresses never pause there. No passenger trains do – only an occasional freight.

LANGUAGE AND LITERATURE

THE LOST CONTINENT – TRAVELS IN SMALL-TOWN AMERICA (1989)

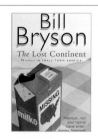

This is the first of many travel books by Bill Bryson. He was born in Iowa, in the USA and lived in England between 1977 and 1995. He returned to the United States to do a road trip of almost 14,000 miles, in search of the America of his youth and found a continent that was 'lost', both in the sense of being a culture that had lost its way and also lost to him because he could no longer recognise it as the land that he had grown up in and felt part of. The book is characterised by a humorous, light-hearted style, for which Bryson has become famous.

I come from Des Moines. Somebody had to.

When you come from Des Moines you either accept the fact without question and settle down with a local girl named Bobbi and get a job at the Firestone factory and live there for ever and ever, or you spend your adolescence moaning at length about what a dump it is and how you can't wait to get out, and then you settle down with a local girl named Bobbi and get a job at the Firestone factory and live there for ever and ever.

Hardly anyone ever leaves. This is because Des Moines is the most powerful hypnotic known to man. Outside town there is a big sign that says WELCOME TO DES MOINES. THIS IS WHAT DEATH IS LIKE. There isn't really. I just made that up. But the place does get a grip on you. People who have nothing to do with Des Moines drive in off the interstate, looking for gas or hamburgers, and stay for ever. There's a New Jersey couple up the street from my parents' house whom you see wandering around from time to time looking faintly puzzled but strangely serene. Everybody in Des Moines is strangely serene.

The only person I ever knew in Des Moines who wasn't serene was Mr Piper. Mr Piper was my parents' neighbour, a leering cherry-faced idiot who was forever getting drunk and crashing his car into telephone poles. Everywhere you went you encountered telephone poles and road signs leaning dangerously in testimony to Mr Piper's driving habits. He distributed them all over the west side of town, rather in the way dogs mark trees. Mr Piper was the nearest possible human equivalent to Fred Flintstone, but less charming. He was a Shriner and a Republican – a Nixon Republican – and he appeared to feel he had a mission in life to spread offence. His favourite pastime, apart from getting drunk and crashing his car, was to get drunk and insult the neighbours, particularly us because we were Democrats, though he was prepared to insult Republicans when we weren't available.

SKATING TO ANTARCTICA (1997)

> *Jenny Diski's award-winning book first published in 1997, is both memoir and travelogue, describing the writer's journey to Antarctica, interwined with another kind of journey, to discover herself and come to an understanding of her strange and horrific childhood and adolescence. It has been described by the 'Mail on Sunday' as 'astonishing, harrowing, very funny' and by the 'Observer' as 'the most unusual and beautiful of memoirs'.*

I am not entirely content with the degree of whiteness in my life. My bedroom is white: white walls, icy mirrors, white sheets and pillowcases, white slatted blinds. It's the best I could do. Some lack of courage – I wouldn't want to be thought extreme – has prevented me from having a white bedstead and side-tables. They are wood, and they annoy me a little. Opposite my bed, in the very small room, a wall of mirrored cupboards reflects the whiteness back at itself, making it twice the size it thought it was. Some time ago, I had a builder in to make another room. He wanted to know what I was going to do with the walls. White, I told him, like the walls throughout the flat. 'I suppose it stops arguments about what wallpaper to have,' he said unenthusiastically. It was the only good reason he could think of for having white walls.

In the morning, if I arrange myself carefully when I wake, I can open my eyes to nothing but whiteness. The soft white of the sheet, the darker white shadows in the folds of the duvet. A brasher white with scored lines at the point where the walls meet the ceiling or turn the corner: ninety-degree angles in shades of white. A repetition of white when I raise my eyes slightly to the mirror opposite. Morning moments of indescribable satisfaction. Eventually, I'll have to let colours in to my day, but for a while I can wallow in a seemingly boundless expanse of white.

If I trace it back, that wish for whiteout began with the idea of being an inmate in a psychiatric hospital. Not during my first stay in a mental hospital, in Hove, when I was fourteen, but later, aged twenty and twenty-one, in London's Maudesley psychiatric unit, hospital became my preferred environment.

STASILAND (2001)

Anna Funder's award-winning book, first published in 2001, tells the stories of a range of people who lived in East Germany before the fall of the Berlin Wall in 1989. She recounts the terrible experiences of those who suffered at the hands of the Stasi, the secret police, as well as giving the view of some of the Stasi men themselves. Her account shows the physical and emotional scarring of those who have lived under a brutal and oppressive regime.

Berlin, Winter 1996

I am hungover and steer myself like a car through the crowds at Alexanderplatz station. Several times I miscalculate my width, scraping into a bin, and an advertising bollard. Tomorrow bruises will develop on my skin, like a picture from a negative.

A man turns from the wall, smiling and zipping up his fly. He is missing shoelaces and some teeth; his face and his shoes are as loose as each other. Another man in overalls, with a broom the size of a tennis-court sweeper, pushes disinfectant pellets along the platform. He makes arcs of green powder and cigarette butts and urine. A morning drunk walks on the ground like it might not hold him.

I'm catching the underground to Ostbahnhof to board the regional line down to Leipzig, a couple of hours from here. I sit on a green bench. I look at green tiles, breathe green air. Suddenly I don't feel too good. I need to get to the surface quickly and make my way back up the stairs. At ground level Alexanderplatz is a monstrous expanse of grey concrete designed to make people feel small. It works.

It's snowing outside. I move through the slush to where I know there are toilets. Like the train lines, these too are cut into the ground, but no-one thought to connect them to the station they serve. As I go down the steps, the sick smell of antiseptic is overpowering.

A large woman in a purple apron and loud makeup stands at the bottom. She is leaning on a glass-paned counter guarding her stash of condoms and tissues and tampons. This is clearly a woman unafraid of the detritus of life. She has shiny smooth skin and many soft chins. She must be sixty-five.

'Good morning,' I say.

NON-EXAMINED COMPONENT

STUART: A LIFE BACKWARDS (2005)

This is a biography of a homeless young man, Stuart Shorter, told by the writer Alexander Masters. It won the Guardian First Book Award in 2005. It tells the story of Stuart in a very unusual way, going 'backwards' from his adult self towards his childhood and using much of the dialogue between Stuart and the writer, so giving an extraordinarily fresh and engaging view of the subject.

Stuart does not like the manuscript.

Through the pale Tesco stripes of his supermarket bag I can see the wedge of my papers. Two years' worth of interviews and literary effort.

'What's the matter with it?'

'It's bollocks boring.'

He fumbles in the lumpy bulges of his pockets, looking for roll-up papers, then drops into my armchair and pushes his face forward, surveying the drab collection of twigs and dead summertime experiments on my balcony. One arm remains, as it landed, squeezed in beside his thigh. Outside, it is getting dark; the trees in the garden have started to grow in size and lose their untended shapes.

'I don't mean to be rude. I know you put a lot of work in,' Stuart offers.

Put briefly, his objection is this: I drone on.

He wants jokes, yarns, humour. He doesn't admire 'academic quotes' and background research. 'Nah, Alexander, you gotta start again. You gotta do better than this.'

He's after a bestseller, 'like what Tom Clancy writes.'

'But you are not an assassin trying to frazzle the president with anthrax bombs,' I point out. You are an ex-homeless, ex-junkie psychopath, I do not add.

Stuart phrases it another way, then: 'Something what people will read.'

WHAT THE CHINESE DON'T EAT (2006)

This is a collection of weekly columns written by Xinran for the 'Guardian' and published as a book in 2006. It reveals many fascinating aspects of Chinese culture and social behaviour, in relation to modern British society. She deals with everything from food and Christmas shopping, to young people's respect for traditions, art and whether handwriting still matters in a world of computers.

22nd June 2003

Chinese whispers: When radio presenter Xinran got a letter asking her to help free a kidnapped 12-year-old child bride, she realised how little was known about the lives of real women in her country. So she resolved to tell their stories in her book The Good Women of China

Early one spring morning in 1989, I rode my Flying Pigeon bicycle through the streets of Nanjing dreaming about my son PanPan. The green shoots on the trees, the clouds of frosty breath enveloping the other cyclists, the women's silk scarves billowing in the spring wind, everything merged with thoughts of my son. I was bringing him up on my own, without the help of a man, and it was not easy caring for him as a working mother. Whatever journey I went on, though, long or short, even the quick ride to work, he accompanied me in spirit and gave me courage.

'Hey, big-shot presenter, watch where you're going,' shouted a colleague as I wobbled into the compound of the radio and TV station where I worked.

My office was on the 16th floor of the forbidding, 21-storey modern building. I preferred to climb the stairs rather than risk the unreliable lift, which broke down frequently. When I arrived at my desk, amidst the large pile of letters, one immediately caught my attention: the envelope had been made from the cover of a book and there was a chicken feather glued to it. According to Chinese tradition, a chicken feather is an urgent distress signal.

The letter was from a young boy, and had been sent from a village about 150 miles from Nanjing.

WHY BE HAPPY WHEN YOU COULD BE NORMAL? (2012)

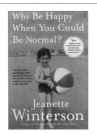

Jeanette Winterson's first award-winning novel, 'Oranges are Not the Only Fruit' was published in 1985 and told the story of a young girl who was adopted and brought up by a Pentecostal mother and raised to be a missionary. However things didn't work out quite as her mother had planned! The novel was based very heavily on Winterson's own life experiences. 27 years later, Winterson returned to the same material, this time writing a non-fictional memoir about her childhood experiences.

The Wrong Crib

WHEN MY MOTHER WAS ANGRY with me, which was often, she said, 'The Devil led us to the wrong crib.'

The image of Satan taking time off from the Cold War and McCarthyism to visit Manchester in 1960 – purpose of visit: to deceive Mrs Winterson – has a flamboyant theatricality to it. She was a flamboyant depressive; a woman who kept a revolver in the duster drawer, and the bullets in a tin of Pledge. A woman who stayed up all night baking cakes to avoid sleeping in the same bed as my father. A woman with a prolapse, a thyroid condition, an enlarged heart, an ulcerated leg that never healed, and two sets of false teeth – matt for everyday, and a pearlised set for 'best'.

I do not know why she didn't/couldn't have children. I know that she adopted me because she wanted a friend (she had none), and because I was like a flare sent out into the world – a way of saying that she was here – a kind of X Marks the Spot.

She hated being a nobody, and like all children, adopted or not, I have had to live out some of her unlived life. We do that for our parents – we don't really have any choice.

LANGUAGE AND LITERATURE

HYBERBOLE AND A HALF (2013)

Allie Brosh's blog 'Hyperbole and a Half' has gained a huge, cult following, for its quirky stories about her childhood, her dog, her everyday life experiences and her struggles with depression. This book version of the blog, published in 2013, including some of the original blogposts and some new writing, is an unusual combination of pictures and words recounting 'stories about things that happened to me' and 'stories about things that happened to other people because of me' and 'stories about dogs'.

It seems like there should be some sort of introduction to this.

Here is a re-creation of a drawing I did when I was five:

It's a guy with one normal arm and one absurdly fucking squiggly arm. If you look really closely, you can see the normal arm under the squiggly one. What you can't see is that in the original, the squiggly arm continues for the entire length of a roll of butcher paper. It started on one end and then just kept going until I ran out of paper.

I remember drawing it and thinking, *This is insane... I can't even believe how long this guy's arm is.* If I had not run out of paper, who knows what would have happened.

In its entirety, the arm takes up more paper than this book. Theoretically, I could have cut the roll of butcher paper into squares, stapled them together, and created *Squiggly Arm Book*.

I didn't, though.

I considered that possibility, but, in the end, I decided I couldn't realistically expect to get away with it.

I AM THE SECRET FOOTBALLER (2013)

The Guardian newspaper had a column called 'Secret Footballer', from 2011 to November 2014, giving an insider's view of the Premier League, the life of the professional footballer and all those involved in the game, from managers and players, to agents and WAGS. The true identity of the Secret Footballer has been much discussed but, at the time of publication, is still not confirmed. The text set for this component is a book version, giving a commentary on different aspects of the game.

When I started playing football for a living, I vowed that I would never turn out like the embittered older professionals that my new club seemed to have made a point of collecting. Far from offering any advice or guidance, they took every opportunity to rub my face in a mistake or faux pas. In those days I had no idea that footballers started training at 10am and finished at midday. I remember hanging around in the changing room after my first session waiting to be told that I could go home. Nobody sits you down with a 'how to' guidebook and fills you in on football etiquette. You're either what managers refer to as 'streetwise', or you're too naïve for your own good. In my case, I was as raw as my football.

I still think that I am incredibly lucky never to have gone through the youth system, for two reasons. Firstly, I have always had huge problems with anyone in authority, especially if that authority is abused for the purpose of making the rulemaker feel more important than they actually are. Secondly, I much prefer to play what has become known as 'street football'. You can spot a manufactured footballer a mile off but the players who are naturally gifted and are almost uncoachable always offer the most excitement. For example, Lionel Messi and Wayne Rooney do not need to be coached: they play like they did in the street as 10-year olds. Granted, they may need integrating into a style of play or formation but on the whole they are playing off the cuff. I am no Messi or Rooney – let's make that absolutely clear – but for the best part of my career I played as if I had nothing to lose.

THE EXAMINED LIFE: HOW WE LOSE AND FIND OURSELVES (2013)

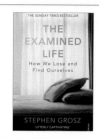

Stephen Grosz has worked for twenty-five years as a psychoanalyst. This book, published in 2013, is a collection of stories of the lives of the people he has worked with, tales from his day-to-day practice, recounting the process of talking and listening to them and how this helps them understand more about themselves and make sense of their lives. Grosz says it's a book about 'helping people to change'. Reviewers have commented on how simple and moving the book is and how well Grosz uses storytelling as a way of revealing deeper truths.

Beginnings

I want to tell you a story about a patient who shocked me.

When I was first starting out as a psychoanalyst, I rented a small consulting room in Hampstead, on a wide leafy street called Fitzjohns Avenue. It was near a number of well-known psychoanalytic clinics and a few minutes walk from the Freud Museum. At the south end of Fitzjohns Avenue, there is a large bronze statue of Freud.

My consulting room was quiet and spare. There was a desk just large enough for writing up notes and preparing my monthly bills, but no bookshelves or files – the room wasn't for reading or research. As in most consulting rooms, the couch wasn't a couch, but a firm single bed with a dark fitted cover. At the head of the bed was a goose-down cushion, and on top of that a white linen napkin that I changed between patients. The psychoanalyst who rented the room to me had hung one piece of African folk art on the walls many years before. She still used the room in the mornings and I used it in the afternoons. For that reason it was impersonal, ascetic even.

I was working part-time at the Portman Clinic, a forensic outpatient service. In general, patients referred to the Portman had broken the law; some had committed violent or sexual crimes. I saw patients of all ages and I wrote quite a few court reports. At the same time, I was building up my private practice. My plan was to reserve my mornings for clinic work; in the afternoons I hoped to see private patients who had less extreme or pressing problems.

As it turned out, my first private patients were fairly demanding too. Looking back, I see many reasons why these first cases were difficult. Partly, there was my own inexperience. I think it takes time – it took me time – to realise just how very different people are from each other. And it probably didn't help that I'd received a number of referrals from senior psychiatrists and psychoanalysts trying to help me get started. Doctors often refer patients to junior analysts that they don't want to see themselves or can't place anywhere else. And so I was struggling with: Miss A., a twenty-year-old undergraduate.

How to Choose a Second Text and What Makes a Good Pairing

One way to think about which texts might make good comparative texts is to consider how you might compare something quite different, like animals, or TV programmes or food, evaluating which pairings would allow you to make interesting and convincing points.

Here's an example of a food comparison:

- Spag bol and trainers

- Spag bol and lamb biryani

- Spag bol and fruit salad

- Spag bol and tiramisu

- Spag bol and ravioli

- Talk about which of these would give you the most interesting points of comparison and why, if you had to write an extended essay on them, then read the commentary below.

COMMENTARY

Spag bol and trainers – one's a food, one's an item of clothing. Not much to compare beyond that.

There's more to say about spag bol and lamb biryani because they're both savoury dishes involving meat, sauces and so on, with strong elements of difference in terms of the cultures from which they originate.

Comparing with desserts is tricky, though the common Italian origin of tiramisu offers some point of contact.

However, spag bol and ravioli provides much fuller material for detailed comparison because of their major shared features and more subtle differences:

Both are Italian meals; both involve tomato sauce; both are savoury and appear in the same slot on menus, either 'pasta dishes' or 'main courses'; both involve pasta.

In terms of differences, though, spag bol has long strings of pasta, whereas ravioli are parcels. Ravioli have either meat or other fillings, such as cheese, ricotta, or pumpkin, with tomato sauce poured over, whereas spag bol has no filling, just a meat and tomato sauce. Spag bol is often eaten with a fork and spoon, whereas ravioli is usually eaten with a knife and fork. Spag bol is messy to eat; ravioli are easier not to get all over your chin and clothing. Ravioli of different kinds are sold as a 'speciality' or 'fine' food in supermarkets, with all kinds of unusual fillings whereas spag bol, as its shortened name suggests, is seen as a more basic, down-market kind of pasta dish.

If you apply what you've discovered to choosing texts for comparison, you'll see that it's good to choose texts that have some really major element or elements in common. This allows you to explore some significant similarities, before considering what makes each of them special and different.

Here are some different potential elements of similarity in texts:

> • **Same genre** e.g. two non-fiction texts.
>
> • **Same sub-genre** e.g. two examples of travel writing.
>
> • **Same subject but different genre** e.g. two books about struggling with a difficult childhood, one a memoir, the other a collection of poetry.
>
> • **Same purpose and tone** e.g. two pieces of satirical writing, one humorous non-fiction, the other a novel.
>
> • **Same theme** e.g. madness, ageing, betrayal, childhood, repression.
>
> • **Same writer, mining similar territory differently, or mining different territory in similar ways.** e.g. a novel and a memoir by Jeanette Winterson.

Your two texts should have something major in common, that allows you to say plenty about points of similarity before going on to explore the more subtle differences.

Suggestions for Text Combinations for Each of the Set Texts

TWELVE YEARS A SLAVE (1853)	
A pre-2000 text, so the partner text must be published in the 21st century.	
NOVELS	• *A Mercy* – Toni Morrison • *Property* – Valerie Martin • *47* – Walter Mosley • *The Long Song* – Andrea Levy • *Transatlantic* – Colum McCann
DRAMA	• *Caroline, Or Change* – Tony Kushner
POETRY	• *Bloodlines* – Fred D'Aguiar

NON-EXAMINED COMPONENT

DOWN AND OUT IN PARIS AND LONDON (1933)

A pre-2000 text, so the partner text must be published in the 21st century.

NON–FICTION	• *Stuart: A Life Backwards* – Alexander Masters
	• *Hard Work: Life in Low-pay Britain* – Polly Toynbee
	• *No Fixed Abode* – Charlie Carroll
	• *Behind the Beautiful Forevers: Life, Death, and Hope in a Mumbai Undercity* – Katherine Boo
	• *The Lady in the Van* – Alan Bennett
	• *Chavs: The Demonisation of the Working Class* – Owen Jones
	• *London: The Biography* – Peter Ackroyd

IN COLD BLOOD (1966)

A pre-2000 text, so the partner text must be published in the 21st century.

NON-FICTION	• *Columbine* – Dave Cullen
	• *Into the Wild* – Jon Krakauer
	• *Gomorrah* – Roberto Saviano
	• *The Suspicions of Mr Whicher* – Kate Summerscale
	• *Orange is the New Black: My Time in a Women's Prison* – Piper Kerman
	• *Zeitoun* – Dave Eggers
NOVELS	• *A Place of Execution* – Val McDermid
	• *Galveston* – Nic Pizzolatto
	• *The Siege* – Helen Dunmore
	• *Blackwater Rising* – Attica Locke
	• *A Crime in the Neighbourhood* – Suzanne Berne
	• *An Officer and a Spy* – Robert Harris
	• *Arthur and George* – Julian Barnes
	• *Dancer: A Novel* – Colum McCann
	• *The Emigrants* – W.G. Sebald
	• *What Is the What?* – Dave Eggers

THE LOST CONTINENT (1989)

A pre-2000 text, so the partner text must be published in the 21st century.

NON-FICTION	
	• *The Life and Times of the Thunderbolt Kid* – Bill Bryson
	• *One Summer: America, 1927* – Bill Bryson
	• *At Home: A Short History of Private Life* – Bill Bryson
	• *Stephen Fry in America* – Stephen Fry
	• *America Unchained* – Dave Gorman
	• *Long Way Round: Chasing Shadows Across the World* – Ewan McGregor and Charley Boorman
	• *Pole to Pole* – Michael Palin
	• *The Old Ways: A Journey on Foot* – Robert Macfarlane
NOVELS	• *Digging to America* – Anne Tyler
	• *Americanah* – Chimamanda Ngozi Adichie
	• *The Corrections* – Jonathan Franzen
	• *Freedom* – Jonathan Franzen
	• *Transatlantic* – Colum McCann
	• *Let the Great World Spin* – Colum McCann
SHORT STORIES	• *Olive Kitteridge* – Elizabeth Strout
	• *Tenth of December* – George Saunders
OBSERVATIONAL COMEDY	• *Let's Explore Diabetes with Owls* – David Sedaris
	• *How I Escaped my Certain Fate* – Stewart Lee

NON-EXAMINED COMPONENT

SKATING TO ANTARCTICA (1997)	
A pre-2000 text, so the partner text must be published in the 21st century.	
NON-FICTION	• *The Magnetic North – Travels in the Arctic* – Sara Wheeler • *The Wild Places* – Robert Mcfarlane • *Stranger on a Train* – Jenny Diski • *Walking Home* – Simon Armitage • *Why Be Happy When You Could be Normal?* – Jeanette Winterson • *The Music Room* – William Fiennes • *Don't Let's Go to the Dogs Tonight: An African Childhood* – Alexandra Fuller • *The Life and Times of the Thunderbolt Kid* – Bill Bryson • *Hyberbole and a Half* – Allie Brosh • *The Examined Life* – Stephen Grosz
POETRY	• Kathleen Jamie poetry

STASILAND (2001)	
A post-2000 text, so the partner text can be pre- or post-2000.	
NOVELS	• *All that I Am* – Anna Funder • *Alone in Berlin* – Hans Fallada • *Goodbye to Berlin* – Christopher Isherwood • *Berlin Tales* – Ed. Helen Constantine • *The Wall Jumper* – Peter Schneider • *The Spy Who Came In From The Cold* – John le Carré • *The Innocent* – Ian McEwan • *1984* – George Orwell • *We* – Yevgeny Zamyatin • *Fahrenheit 451* – Ray Bradbury • *The Handmaid's Tale* – Margaret Atwood • *The Trial* – Franz Kafka
NON-FICTION	• *The File* – Timothy Garton Ash • *The Wall: The People's Story* – Christopher Hilton

EMC

STUART: A LIFE BACKWARDS (2005)

A post-2000 text, so the partner text can be pre- or post-2000.

NON-FICTION	• *Hard Work: Life in Low-pay Britain* – Polly Toynbee
	• *No Fixed Abode* – Charlie Carroll
	• *Behind the Beautiful Forevers: Life, Death, and Hope in a Mumbai Undercity* – Katherine Boo
	• *The Lady in the Van* – Alan Bennett
	• *The Missing* – Andrew O'Hagan
	• *Chavs: The Demonisation of the Working Class* – Owen Jones
	• *Simon: The Genius in My Basement* – Alexander Masters
	• *Philomena: The True Story of a Mother* – Martin Sixsmith
	• *Flaubert's Parrot* – Julian Barnes
	• *What is the What?* – Dave Eggers
NOVEL	• *The Emigrants* – W. G. Sebald
DRAMA/ SCREENPLAY	• *Cathy Come Home* – Jeremy Sandford
	• *London Road* – Alecky Blythe

WHAT THE CHINESE DON'T EAT (2006)

A post-2000 text, so the partner text can be pre- or post-2000.

NOVELS & SHORT STORIES	• *Wild Swans: Three Daughters of China* – Jung Chang
	• *The Joy Luck Club* – Amy Tang
	• *Falling Leaves: The True Story of an Unwanted Chinese Daughter* – Adeline Yen Mah
	• *The Woman Warrior* – Maxine Hong Kingston (short stories)
NON-FICTION	• *Battle Hymn of the Tiger Mother* – Amy Chua
	• *A Year in Tibet* – Sun Shuyun
	• *My Family and Other Disasters* – Lucy Mangan
	• *The Guardian Columns 1998-2000* – Julie Birchill
	• *The Hell of it All* – Charlie Brooker
	• *America* – Alistair Cooke

WHY BE HAPPY WHEN YOU COULD BE NORMAL? (2012)

A post-2000 text, so the partner text can be pre- or post-2000.

NON-FICTION	• *The Examined Life* – Stephen Grosz
	• *Skating to Antarctica* – Jenny Diski
	• *Father and Son* – Edmund Gosse
	• *Giving up the Ghost* – Hilary Mantel
	• *Don't Let's Go to the Dogs Tonight: An African Childhood* – Alexandra Fuller
	• *Once in a House on Fire* – Andrew Ashworth
	• *Bad Blood* – Lorna Sage
	• *I Know Why the Caged Bird Sings* – Maya Angelou
	• *A Boy's Own Story* – Edmund White
	• *This Boy* – Alan Johnson
NOVELS	• *Oranges Are Not the Only Fruit* – Jeanette Winterson
	• *Bodies of Light* – Sarah Moss

HYPERBOLE AND A HALF (2013)

A post-2000 text, so the partner text can be pre- or post-2000.

POETRY	• *Look, Clare, Look!* – Claire Pollard
	• Sylvia Plath poetry
FICTION	• *The Secret Diary of Adrian Mole Aged 13¾* – Sue Townsend
	• *The Catcher in the Rye* – J.D. Salinger
NON-FICTION	• *Moranthology* – Caitlin Moran
	• *Back Story* – David Mitchell
	• *The Hell of it All* – Charlie Brooker
	• *The Examined Life* – Stephen Grosz
	• *Skating to Antarctica* – Jenny Diski
	• *Reasons to Stay Alive* – Matt Haig
BOOKS OF BLOGS	• *A Girl Called Jack: 100 Delicious Budget Recipes* – Jack Monroe
	• *I am the Secret Footballer* – Anon
	• *Baghdad Burning: Girl Blog from Iraq* – Riverbend

I AM THE SECRET FOOTBALLER (2013)

A post-2000 text, so the partner text can be pre- or post-2000.

NON-FICTION	• *Invincible: Inside Arsenal's Unbeaten 2003-2004 Season* – Amy Lawrence
	• *Fever Pitch* – Nick Hornby
	• *A Season with Verona* – Tim Parks
	• *Futebol: The Brazilian Way of Life* – Alex Bellos
	• *Manchester United Ruined My Life* – Colin Schindler
	• *I Think Therefore I Play* – Andrea Pirlo
	• *My Father and Other Working Class Football Heroes* – Gary Imlach
BOOKS OF BLOGS	• *Moranthology* – Caitlin Moran
	• *Football Clichés* – Adam Hurrey (angleofpostandbar.blogspot.co.uk)
NOVELS	• *The Damned United* – David Peace

THE EXAMINED LIFE (2013)

A post-2000 text, so the partner text can be pre- or post-2000.

NON-FICTION	• *Skating to Antarctica* – Jenny Diski
	• *Hyperbole and a Half* – Ali Brosh
	• *Why Be Happy When You Could be Normal?* – Jeanette Winterson
	• *Instead of a Letter* – Diana Athill
	• *Nothing to be Frightened Of* – Julian Barnes
	• *Reasons to Stay Alive* – Matt Haig
	• *Sunbathing in the Rain* – Gwyneth Lewis
NOVELS	• *Essays on Love* – Alain de Botton
	• *Stoner* – John Williams
	• *The Bell Jar* – Sylvia Plath
	• *All in the Mind* – Alistair Campbell
	• *One Flew Over The Cuckoo's Nest* – Ken Kesey
	• *Mr Chartwell* – Rebecca Hunt
	• *The Shock of the Fall* – Nathan Filer
	• *The Trick Is to Keep Breathing* – Janice Galloway
	• *Bodies of Light* – Sarah Moss
POETRY	• Sylvia Plath, Emily Dickinson, Gwyneth Lewis, Michael Symonns Roberts, Alice Walker

Confirming Your Choice

Once you've started reading your second choice, it's worth confirming whether you think there'll be plenty of scope for a comparative piece. After you've read three or four chapters, try doing the following tasks.

FREE WRITING

1. Do free writing for twenty minutes in class, simply writing down absolutely everything that strikes you as interesting about the two texts in relation to each other, without worrying about style or organisation – a form of brainstorming.

2. At the end of the twenty minutes, think about how much there was to say. Did the ideas come easily? If so, it suggests that there won't be a shortage of ideas to draw on for a comparative piece. If not, you might want to talk to your teacher, to get some ideas about possible angles, or reconsider whether your choice of text is a good one. The example below shows you the sort of thing you might do.

FOR EXAMPLE: IN COLD BLOOD AND ZEITOUN

Both hover on the border between fact and fiction, using fictional techniques to write about real events and people. 'ICB' is about a real-life murder and 'Zeitoun' is about a real man (hero?) during Hurricane Katrina. There's a crime element to both and in both cases the protagonists end up in jail (though their 'crimes' are very different and presented differently.) Both writers are 'investigating' and reporting in some way – talking to witnesses, family, friends and so on – but they both use techniques of storytelling closer to fiction, such as using lots of dialogue, long descriptions of scenes, suspense. Both seem to be able to give the thoughts and feelings of the main characters. It's interesting to think about how sympathetic the books are to the main protagonists and how far that is conveyed in the writing. Also, to think about what difference it makes to know about the events after 'Zeitoun' was published, where Zeitoun and Kathy were divorced and Zeitoun was charged and found not guilty of murder. Does that change your reading of the book? Should it?

Is there more of a sensationalist element to 'In Cold Blood'? The way narrative techniques are used to provoke a reaction in the reader build up a sense of suspense and create shock. Is 'Zeitoun' more measured in tone?

Both end up being commentaries, in some way, on American life and society, perhaps with Dave Eggers having a stronger, underlying political thread (about police abuses of power, anti-islamic sentiments and discrimination, how individuals can be destroyed by the police and judicial system).

JUST A MINUTE WITH OTHER STUDENTS ON YOUR TWO TEXTS

1. Try doing 'Just a Minute' with another student, where you spend a minute explaining interesting points of connection between your two texts. After the minute is up, allow them to question you to see if they can prompt you to come up with more similarities and differences.

2. After this process, decide whether you think there's plenty to say about your two texts.

A TITLE FOR YOUR COMPARATIVE PIECE

1. Look back at the comments on pages 227-228 about a tight focus for comparative writing.

2. Write a few possible titles for your comparative piece. Show them to other students to get advice and comments about which they think might work best. In the light of their feedback, refine your title.

3. Show your title to your teacher to ask for advice about the title. Refine it again, on the basis of your teacher's comments before you start writing.

AN EXAMPLE

- *A comparison between 'In Cold Blood' and 'Zeitoun' – too broad*
- *A comparison between the accused in 'ICB' and 'Zeitoun' in Eggers' book – too focused on character, not enough on charaterisation or presentation of character?*
- *The different ways in which 'ICB' and 'Zeitoun' present the theme of guilt and innocence – good focus but needs to be careful to have a linguistic as well as literary approach.*
- *A comparison between the evocation of places in 'ICB' and 'Zeitoun' – more closely focused on the way in which the texts are written and the impact created by the choices made. Could work well.*
- *The way Capote and Eggers present the backstory of their main protagonists, using a combination of fiction and non-fiction techniques. Could work well. Fiction and non-fiction techniques in general could be huge, so limiting it to the back stories might tighten the focus and allow for detailed exploration as well as an overview.*

Original Non-fiction Writing

This task gives you the chance to write a piece of non-fiction in any genre or style. You will be assessed on how well you write, in your chosen genre but that doesn't mean slavishly following the conventions. You might want to adapt or subvert the conventions for your own purposes, much as you might for the narrative writing for A Level Component 3.

You may have already done some creative activities on the non-fiction anthology and exercises to prepare you for AS non-fiction writing. Think back to these so that you can draw on what you learned for your own non-fiction writing for the non-examined unit.

Deciding What to Write – Writing as a Reader

Reading as a writer, writing as a reader are key ideas in this A Level. Drawing on what you have learned as a *reader* of non-fiction will help you to write better yourself.

1. To start the process of deciding what to write, remind yourself of all the non-fiction texts you have read during the course and think about which you particularly enjoyed or learned a lot from and why.

2. Do a brainstorm of all the different possible angles that they suggest to you for writing a piece of non-fiction of your own, like the one on page 250.

3. Share your ideas with other people in your class and/or with your teacher, exploring the ideas you've been thinking about and getting feedback or suggestions from each other.

Here are a few ideas for non-fiction tasks that would work well. The list just offers examples – other ideas could work equally well.

• A blog	• An interview
• A script for a speech	• A piece of travel writing for a newspaper, or travel book
• An extract from a memoir	
• A feature for a newspaper colour supplement	• A piece of reportage about an event you witnessed or took part in
• A series of diary entries, for publication in a book	• A chapter in a book of popular science/archaeology/history/geography/politics
• A piece of biographical writing (for a newspaper, magazine or part of a book)	

FOR EXAMPLE: BRAINSTORM FOR POLITICAL WRITING

MY 'A MODEST PROPOSAL' READING

Anthology of Non-fiction and Spoken Texts (set text for Component 1)
- Jonathan Swift's brilliant satire.
- Obama's speech – Craig Brown – humour but not much of a political message – parody, with a particular focus on the style of speech-making and the patterns of language, rather than the content.
- Julia Gillard – arguing strongly, without humour – impassioned, angry – unscripted or semi-scripted?

My comparative analytical piece for Section A of the Non-Examined Unit: 'Down and Out in Paris and London' – strong political messages coming out of 1st person account – reportage AND 'Stuart: A Life Backwards' – addressing serious issues of homelessness and exclusion – biographical – some humour – real sense of people's lives – quirky style.

'I am the Secret Footballer' – just dipped into, in choosing comparative texts. More interested in content than style of writing.

Own reading: 'Private Eye' – short, satirical, humorous pieces.

IDEAS FOR MY NON-FICTION WRITING

EITHER: A satirical piece – a blog? Or for 'Private Eye'? 'Guardian' Comment is Free website? Speech at a football fan club meeting? – on the scandal of football club finances (footballers' wages, football agents, ownership, low wages for club staff etc).

OR: A satirical piece for a blog, on the language of politicians, focusing on the speeches of the leaders of the main political parties at their party conferences.

Two notes of caution!

- Be aware that what you choose should allow you to do high quality writing of a substantial length (1000-1200 words) in that genre. So, think about whether a particular genre will allow for this. For instance, a sports report on a single football match might be too short and rather limited in scope, whereas an opinion piece on the state of the game, or on the troubles faced by a particular club, might give more opportunities for really thoughtful, well-tuned writing.

- This is non-fiction, rather than fiction. So it's best to root what you write in real experiences or knowledge, rather than imagined experience. So, for example, a pretend interview with Lady Gaga wouldn't be acceptable because you're inventing the content, whereas if you've *really* interviewed someone, your carefully crafted write-up for a magazine could be an excellent piece of independent writing. Equally, a remembered event, written as memoir, with all the narrative licence that memoir writers take, would be acceptable, whereas a fictional account of something that didn't happen at all, would not be acceptable.

WHAT MAKES A GOOD PIECE OF NON-FICTION WRITING

One key to writing a good piece of non-fiction is being clear about what you're trying to do. You need to think hard about the following.

- Your purposes in writing.

- Your intended audience.

- What use (or adaptation) you're making of a particular genre.

- Your use of form and language, to develop your ideas effectively for your purposes and audience.

THE 150-WORD INTRODUCTION

Your 150-word introduction will give you the chance to point out some of the key elements in your writing and signal what you were trying to achieve. In itself it should be an interesting read, well-written and thoughtful, rather than 'going through the motions'. In other words, like your non-fiction piece, it should be a well-crafted piece of writing.

On page 254 are three example introductions. Each takes a slightly different approach. Each is likely to be equally acceptable.

1. Read the introductions. Talk about what you notice about how each person introduces their writing. What kinds of things do they say? What do they choose to focus on? Which do you find most interesting and engaging and why? Which do you think provides the best introduction to the writing?

NON-EXAMINED COMPONENT

COMMENTARY 1

I loved reading 'Skating to Antarctica' for my comparative task and decided to write a short memoir of my own, based on a particular time in my childhood that was specially difficult, when my younger brother was very ill. My piece is written in diary form, giving a snapshot of what life was like at the time by taking six different moments and writing about them as if they'd just happened. The diary form makes it very immediate, without any retrospective comment but the final entry tries to bring out the significance of the events by reflecting back, from a more distanced perspective, a few months later. I hoped that writing it as a diary would allow me to create a strong personal voice, recreating myself as I was then. I used a distinctive, idiosyncratic, disjointed style of language to give a glimpse of what was going on in my head at the time.

COMMENTARY 2

I've listened to many years' worth of talks in assemblies and have been struck by the difference between the best and the worst. What makes a talk really engaging? Things that really work for me are a sense that it's been thought through and carefully structured, the use of humour, an unusual angle or approach that grabs your attention, or a feeling that the speaker really means what they say. Watching some TED talks, these qualities were also noticeable. I decided to write a speech for a sixth form assembly on something that I feel strongly about and tried to find an unusual angle, write with humour but also create a sense that what I say matters. That's why, hopefully, you'll find a rather surprising start, an unusual string of metaphors to explain my ideas and an ending that pulls it all together more emotionally than you might have expected at the beginning.

COMMENTARY 3

Blogging is a new genre, a new form of writing. At least, it can be, but all too often blogs are just articles posted up on the web, following just the same conventions as print journalism. From time to time, however, you come across a blogger who really uses the medium in fresh and imaginative ways, showing how a blog can do something very different from a newspaper or magazine article. Inspired by these kinds of bloggers, I've tried to do something innovative of my own. My blog tries to break down the boundaries – between print and image, speaking and writing, reader and writer. It uses language in new ways but hopefully isn't so experimental that it confuses the reader/observer. It's meant to be enjoyable rather than giving the reader a headache, making them hurry back to their print magazine in the hope of a more comfortable experience!

7. Index of Key Terms

INDEX OF KEY TERMS & SUGGESTED READING

8. Suggested Reading

EMC: *Doing Close Reading*

EMC: *Studying Narrative*

Geoffrey Leech & Mick Short: *Style in Fiction: A Linguistic Introduction to English Fictional Prose*

Mick Short: *Exploring the Language of Poems, Plays and Prose*

Marina Lambrou and Peter Stockwell: *Contemporary Stylistics*

Lesley Jeffries and Daniel McIntyre: *Stylistics*

Paul Simpson: Stylistics: *A Resource Book for Students*